BEYOND
THE QUICK FIX

BEYOND THE QUICK FIX

MANAGING FIVE TRACKS TO ORGANIZATIONAL SUCCESS

RALPH H. KILMANN

BEARD BOOKS

Copyright © 1984 by: Jossey-Bass Inc., Publishers
433 California Street
San Francisco, California 94104
&
Jossey-Bass Limited
22 Banner Street
London, EC1Y 8QE

Copyright transferred to Ralph H. Kilmann as of December 4, 1998.

Reprinted 2004 by Beard Books, Washington, D.C.

Library of Congress Cataloging-in-Publication Data

Kilmann, Ralph H.
    Beyond the quick: managing five tracks to organizational
success / [Ralph H. Kilmann].
        p. cm.
    Originally published: 1st ed. San Francisco: Jossey-Bass, 1984.
    Includes bibliographical references and index.
    ISBN 1-58798-218-8
        1. Management. 2. Organization. 3. Organizational effectiveness. I. Title.

HD31.K467 2003
658--dc22

2003065374

Preface

Freedom to determine one's destiny is a recurring struggle for mankind. It is no less important to any modern-day organization. Members want to contribute to a worthwhile cause. Often, however, the organization holds them back. Members are caught in a bureaucratic grip, one that prevents them from fully contributing their talents and efforts to the organization's mission. For them to get free of this grip, all barriers to success must be transformed into channels for success. Channels facilitate high performance; barriers keep the membership in a deadlock.

Every few years, a new approach is offered for unleashing the full potential of organized efforts. But this is like the search for the Holy Grail: Each new approach looks for the one single answer. For example, in the 1940s, human relations training was considered the key to organizational success. In the 1950s, management by objectives was heralded as the new solution to performance problems. "In the 1960s, decentralization was the vogue in management. In the 1970s, corporate strategy became the buzzword. Now, corporate culture is the magic phrase that management consultants are breathing into the ears of American executives" (Salmans, 1983, p. D1).

It is a shame that managers will have to learn the hard way—one more time—that a brand-new culture cannot solve their performance problems either. Eventually, managers will drop the culture fad and move on to the next promised remedy, and the cycle will continue. All too often, the baby is thrown out with the bath water. Single approaches are discarded because they have not been given a fair test. Essentially, it is not the single approach of culture, strategy, or restructuring that is inherently ineffective. Rather, each is ineffective only if it is applied by itself—as a quick fix.

It is time to stop perpetuating the myth of simplicity. The system of organization invented by mankind generates complex problems that cannot be solved by simple solutions. The only alternative is to develop a truly integrated approach—a complete program for managing today's organization. Complete programs, however, are often preached but seldom practiced.

This book provides a complete program for creating and maintaining organizational success. By *complete* I mean a program that integrates a wide variety of approaches—ranging from those that recognize the intrapsychic conflicts of individuals to those that act on the system-wide properties of organizations. By *success* I mean achieving both high performance and high morale over an extended period of time—an outcome that is only possible by managing *all* controllable variables in the organization. The complete program consists of five tracks: (1) the culture track, (2) the management skills track, (3) the team-building track, (4) the strategy-structure track, and (5) the reward system track. If any of these tracks is implemented without the others, any effort at improving performance and morale will be severely hampered. Any benefits derived in the short term may soon disappear. Lasting success can be achieved only by managing the full set of five tracks on a continuing basis.

The five tracks—in contrast to a quick fix—are integrated in a carefully designed sequence of action; one by one, each track sets the stage for the next track. The culture track enhances trust, openness, and adaptiveness among members, the

necessary conditions to proceed with any other improvement
effort. The management skills track augments ways of coping
with complex problems and hidden assumptions. Without an
adaptive culture, each manager will keep his assumptions to
himself. The team-building track helps members identify and
solve their most complex business problems. Without the skills
to cope with complexity and without an adaptive culture, members cannot and will not share their expertise and information
with others. The strategy-structure track aligns all the organization's structures and resources with the strategic directions of
the firm. If the prior tracks have not been handled properly,
this very difficult problem will be addressed through politics
and vested interests, not through an open exchange of ideas
and a sincere commitment to achieve organizational success.
The reward system track completes the whole change program
by paying for performance. If the earlier tracks have not been
managed as intended, it will be impossible to measure performance objectively and members will not believe that rewards
are linked to performance; they will not be motivated to excel.

　　To illustrate the integrated nature of the five tracks, consider the following scenario: If I could investigate only one aspect of an organization in order to predict its long-term success,
I would choose the reward system. In essence, if members feel
that (1) the reward system is fair, (2) they are rewarded for high
performance, and (3) the performance appraisal system regularly provides them with specific and useful information so that
they know where they stand and can improve their performance, then, in all likelihood, all tracks have been managed
properly. The reward system could not motivate members to
high performance if all the other barriers to organizational success had not been removed by the preceding four tracks. Thus,
a well-functioning, performance-based reward system generally
signifies that the organization is ready for whatever problems
and opportunities will come its way.

　　This book is written for managers, consultants, and researchers, although each group would be expected to study this
material differently.

　　Managers need to see how an orchestrated approach to

organizational success can be undertaken. Managers and all members are frustrated by the many barriers to success. In some cases, they feel helpless, inept, and out of control. The older the organization and the more single approaches for managing problems have been utilized, the more members are caught in a web of outdated cultures, ineffective management skills, poorly functioning work groups, bureaucratic red tape, and a reward system that ignores performance. Alternatively, even organizations that are considered successful today may become unsuccessful tomorrow. The circumstances surrounding success can change radically without prior notice. In a fast-paced world, barriers can return overnight. All managers, therefore, must learn to identify barriers as they arise and then transform these barriers into channels for success.

Consultants need to update their skills in defining and solving organizational problems. They should not blindly and foolishly perpetuate the simple solutions that may have worked well in the past. They would not be serving their clients or their profession very well. However, I have found that most consultants apply their single "pet" approaches just as managers do. But this specialization just will not work in today's complex world. Thus, consultants must expand their range of skills and methods once they accept responsibility for implementing complete programs instead of quick fixes.

Researchers need to see how a wide variety of theories and methods can be synthesized, regardless of the reductionistic habit of the social sciences. Perhaps this book will motivate researchers to develop other integrated programs for managing real-world problems. Certainly, practitioners need such relevant programs much more than they need rigorous solutions to theoretically interesting questions. At the least, research should no longer downplay clinical methods for developing and testing theory (where intuition is more important than replication) or in-depth case studies of multiple change efforts (where the relative impact of each single approach cannot be distinguished). Just because these qualitative methodologies do not satisfy the traditional criteria of rigorous research—simplicity, perfection, and certainty—does not mean that social scientists cannot contribute to understanding messy problems. On the contrary, complexity, imperfection, and uncertainty may be the most important qualities to examine in order to explain the inner workings of *real* organizations.

The material in this book was developed during my twelve years of research at the University of Pittsburgh. The five tracks first emerged one by one before I recognized the true power of an integrated package. Companies such as Gulf, Xerox, General Electric, United States Steel, General Foods, and Westinghouse contributed to the development of my theories and methods. Such organizations as the public school systems of Pittsburgh and Houston, the Presbyterian-University Hospital of Pittsburgh, the U.S. Bureau of the Census, and the Office of the President helped me generalize my theories and methods to the nonprofit sector. The bibliography includes my research publications that led to the five tracks. I chose this form of documentation rather than giving extensive citations to my own work.

Much of the material in this book is being studied by other researchers in the organizational sciences. However, rather than give sentence-by-sentence citations just to add support to my propositions, I cite in the text only those works that directly pertain to a specific point. Since this material is being discussed in the popular press, I have included numerous illustrations from companies such as Merrill Lynch, General Telephone and Electronics, Texas Instruments, Honeywell, American Telephone and Telegraph, General Motors, Commodore, and Digital Equipment Corporation.

The traditional use of the pronoun *he* has not been superseded by a convenient, generally accepted pronoun that means either *he* or *she*. Therefore, I will continue to use all forms of the masculine gender to signify male and female persons equally.

Overview of Contents

The book is organized into nine chapters. Chapters One through Three provide the necessary introduction to the five tracks.

Chapter One, "Principles for Organizational Success," summarizes six key distinctions for the practice of management: (1) world as a complex hologram versus world as a simple machine, (2) complex versus simple problems, (3) multiple versus single tracks, (4) participative versus top-down approaches for managing tracks, (5) what managers can do with consultants versus without consultants, and (6) books to study versus books to skim. As we shall see, the first item in each of these six distinctions represents what is necessary for success today, while the second item represents what was acceptable for yesterday.

Chapter Two, "Theory Behind the Five Tracks," outlines the full range of individual and organizational barriers to success. These include the tangible (strategy, structure, and reward systems) and the intangible (cultures, assumptions, and psyches). Some of these barriers are uncontrollable, but members can monitor and adjust to them. Other barriers have "leverage points," and thus members can control them via the five tracks.

Chapter Three, "Practice Behind the Five Tracks," describes how managers and consultants can join together to create and maintain organizational success. The process of planned change includes initiating the program, diagnosing the problems, scheduling the tracks, implementing the tracks, and evaluating the results. The story of the Synthetic Fuels Division (SFD) of Westinghouse Electric Corporation is told to illustrate how the five tracks can be managed as a completely integrated program.

Chapters Four through Eight detail the particular methods that make up the five tracks. They are presented in the order in which they need to be practiced. However, each of these chapters summarizes only those methods that are best suited for managing complex problems and that have largely been ignored until recently. The other methods that can be sorted into the five tracks are not only well documented in the management literature but are most suited for addressing simple problems.

Chapter Four presents "The Culture Track." This track explores the unwritten, unstated "norms" that guide each member's behavior: Don't disagree with your boss; don't make waves; treat women as second-class citizens; don't share information with other groups; do as little as is necessary to get by. Often, work groups pressure each member to follow such dysfunctional norms out of habit. The culture track first exposes the old culture and then, if necessary, creates a new culture. Without an up-to-date, *adaptive* culture, it is most difficult to engage in any other improvement effort. Controlling culture, rather than being controlled by it, gives the membership enough freedom to proceed with the next track.

Chapter Five presents "The Management Skills Track." This track outlines the new set of skills managers need for handling today's complex problems. This chapter offers a systematic method for uncovering the underlying assumptions that drive all decisions into action. If these assumptions have remained unstated and therefore untested, managers may have continually made the wrong decisions. Managers may have assumed: No new competitors will enter the industry; the economy will steadily improve; the government will continue to restrict foreign imports; the consumer will buy whatever the firm produces; employees will continue to accept the same working conditions. In short, all previous decisions may have been based more on fantasy and habit than on reality and choice. Outdated assumptions may have steered the organization into adopting the wrong strategy, structures, and reward systems as well. However, given a new culture that encourages trust and openness, members now will be able to analyze their previously unstated assumptions before any critical decisions are made. No longer will the membership be held back by its own faulty assumptions.

Chapter Six presents "The Team-Building Track." This track infuses the new cultural norms and the new management skills into every work unit. Included in this track is a method for controlling the organization's "troublemakers," those individuals who continually restrict cooperative efforts by their self-serving, disruptive behavior. As the troublemakers are put in check, and as each work group approaches its business problems with its new culture and skills, high-performance teams gradually replace the old-fashioned cliques. The best possible decisions and actions result as work groups gain greater control over their culture, expertise, and assumptions.

Chapter Seven presents "The Strategy-Structure Track." This track attempts to fine tune all the formally documented systems in the organization. Strategy first sets the firm's directions; then structure ensures that the right objectives, tasks, and people are synchronized into action—for each work unit and each job in the organization. This alignment cannot proceed if cultures, management skills, and team efforts are not ready. However, if the earlier tracks have been implemented as intended, the necessary culture, expertise, and assumptions will come forth to address the strategy-structure problem. In this way, the members remove a two-sided barrier to success: bureaucratic red tape that moves the organization in the wrong direction. In its place is a structure aligned with the firm's strategy.

Chapter Eight presents "The Reward System Track." This track completes the program by making sure that members are rewarded for performing the right tasks with the right objectives in mind. However, it will become clear that implementing this last track is futile if all the other tracks have not been managed properly. Without a supportive culture, members will not believe that rewards are tied to performance. Instead, they will believe that it is useless to work hard and do well. Similarly, if managers do not have the skills to conduct performance appraisal, for example, any well-intentioned reward system will be thwarted. Furthermore, if the strategy and structures are not designed properly, the reward system cannot measure performance objectively. Alternatively, the short-term benefits derived from the other four tracks will not be sustained if the membership is not ultimately rewarded for high performance. Thus, the reward system is the last major barrier to be transformed into a channel for success, the "bottom line" for the membership.

Chapter Nine concludes the book with "Commitment to Organizational Success." I present a challenge to all top managers. Essentially, if executives do not take responsibility for change—moving their companies from a simple machine to a complex hologram via the five tracks—their organizations will not maintain whatever success has been achieved. Their organizations will continue to live in the past, hoping for a return to simplicity, perfection, and certainty. This never-never land is gone. Complexity must be fought with a completely integrated program: It is the only way to organizational success.

Acknowledgments

Many individuals have been very supportive of my efforts. To show my appreciation, I would like to give them special acknowledgment.

At the University of Pittsburgh, Dean H. J. Zoffer has provided a most creative setting for my professional career. Repeatedly, he has removed the typical organizational barriers so that my work could flourish. I also appreciate the genuine interest he has shown in my personal and professional development, independent of his university position. Everyone should have such an inspiring and caring leader.

Ian Mitroff has been a continual source of ideas, energy, and friendship. Our joint adventures transcend any of my singly authored works. His influence is always felt. Other social scientists who have affected my development in significant ways are Chris Argyris, Warren Bennis, West Churchman, Ed Lawler, Ken Mackenzie, Tom Saaty, Herb Simon, Bob Tannenbaum, and Jerry Zaltman. Similarly, I have learned much from a number of practitioners who have continued to encourage the relevance of my work. I am especially indebted to Vince Barabba, Peter Mathias, and Roy Serpa.

Some of my most challenging mentors have been students who cared enough to learn from and become involved in my projects: Dick Herden, Bob Keim, Marjorie Lyles, Walt McGhee, Joe Seltzer, and Dave Wood—members of the old MAPS Group. Betty Ann Velthouse and Teresa Joyce have given me many critiques and suggestions, always in just the right manner. Mary Jane Saxton is the one student who has had the greatest impact on me in the past several years and who worked with me on some of the projects that led to this book. Her creative mind and zest for learning, her ideals about doing something worthwhile, and her commitment to excellence have affected my research and development greatly. Thank you, Mary Jane.

One organization stands out for the special role it played in the five tracks to organizational success: The Synthetic Fuels Division (SFD) of Westinghouse Electric Corporation. This organization demonstrated how barriers can be overcome when individuals join together, recognize their problems, open their minds and hearts to change, and care about one another. Bill Peace, the general manager, and Tom Kelley, the personnel manager, set the tone and provided the leadership to see this project through. However, I also must express my appreciation to the 217 division members who contributed their efforts to making the SFD story a success.

I would also like to thank my extra exceptional senior secretary, Kathy Robbins, for her help in preparing the final manuscript and for her sincere interest in my work. Jossey-Bass people provided very useful comments, especially Steve Piersanti. Dick Mason, as consulting editor, provided many suggestions for revision as well. However, I take full responsibility for the final product.

My family understands and appreciates my commitment to these efforts and remains a constant source of encouragement and idea testing: My parents and brother are always there. My daughter, Catherine Mary, was very helpful in supporting this work and in preparing the typewritten materials. My son, Christopher Martin, was content to watch Daddy on his PC.

Pittsburgh, Pennsylvania   Ralph H. Kilmann
July 1984

Contents

Beyond the Quick Fix

Managing Five Tracks to Organizational Success

CHAPTER ONE

❧❧❧

Principles
for Organizational
Success

> American management, especially in the two dec-
> ades after World War II, was universally admired for its
> striking effective performance. But times change. An ap-
> proach shaped and refined during stable decades may be ill
> suited to a world characterized by rapid and unpredictable
> change, scarce energy, global competition for markets, and
> a constant need for innovation. This is the world of the
> 1980s and, probably, the rest of this century.
>
> The time is long overdue for earnest, objective self-
> analysis. What exactly have American managers been doing
> wrong? What are the critical weaknesses in the ways that
> they have managed the technological performance of their
> companies? What is the matter with the long-unquestioned
> assumptions on which they have based their managerial
> policies and practices?
>
> —Hayes and Abernathy, 1980, p. 68

Creating and then maintaining organizational success is a different kind of problem from that of only a few decades ago. The
world has grown increasingly complex—resulting from the

1

greater interdependence among world economies. At the same
time, the world has become increasingly dynamic—resulting
from the information explosion and worldwide communications. This "dynamic complexity" means that organizations
cannot remain stable for very long. Rather, constant change on
the outside requires constant change on the inside. Success is
largely determined by how well the organization adjusts all its
tangible and intangible properties to keep itself on track with its
surroundings.

The older and larger the firm, the more difficulty it has in
changing. Essentially, the organization becomes rigidified. Just
as hardening of the arteries sets in with age for individuals, hardening of the documents (and assumptions and culture) comes
with age and size for organizations. Making matters worse, if the
organization has been successful in the past, its managers may
fall into the trap of "erroneous extrapolation." This occurs
when managers make the false assumption that what worked in
the last decade will also work in the next decade. Here, the
managers draw a straight line from the past into the future.
With dynamic complexity being the new rule, however, the line
is dotted at best, and it twists and turns as well. In some cases,
the very thing that brought the organization success will bring
about its sudden downfall.

Because of this tendency for erroneous extrapolation,
one must note with great caution the recent clamor for discovering the key attributes of excellence in American corporations.
The best-seller by Peters and Waterman (1982) carries with it
potential danger in that many companies may choose to adopt
the attributes of the touted ones. This danger stems from the
criteria Peters and Waterman used to designate companies as
"excellent." Essentially, a company was considered excellent if
it was in the top half of its industry on at least four out of six
performance measures averaged over the past two decades
(1961 to 1980). As already noted, what worked in the last decade will not automatically lead to success in the future. While a
few principles of management may be universally applicable to
all organizations for all time, dynamic complexity forces us to
question precisely those principles that produced success in the

past. Each of Peters and Waterman's eight principles for running a successful business is based on assumptions that already may be outdated. As a result, what one learns about excellent companies may be more an interesting lesson in history than a valuable prescription for success.

A *Business Week* report, "Merrill Lynch's Big Dilemma" (1984, pp. 60-62), examines quite poignantly the danger of success breeding failure:

Merrill's stock is down to $32 from a 1983 high of $57, and Wall Street is wondering if, as one former Merrill manager asserts, "the bull is out of control."

At the very least, the company is in traumatic transition. As deregulation melds together the once-distinct financial service industries, Merrill Lynch faces increasingly direct competition from Sears Roebuck, American Express, Citicorp, and other formidable companies outside the securities industry. In recent years, Merrill has proved itself the equal of anyone in innovating financial products and services. But in the way it delivers them to consumers, in its compensation methods, and in its culture, Merrill Lynch remains quintessentially a brokerage house. . . . Some observers wonder whether Merrill's senior executives—most of whom have spent their entire careers with the company—are equal to the task of adapting to rapid, sweeping change. "The guys who rise to the top there are those that can get along and are not all that dynamic," says one former company executive. "They're not equipped to deal with the big picture."

But if Merrill is to thrive in the fully deregulated world ahead, its top executives and outside observers agree, it must transform itself from the mightiest sales machine Wall Street has ever seen to a true marketing company—one principally and intimately attuned to its customers' needs.

The critical focus on self-analysis—to see how today's organizations need to be fundamentally different from yesterday's, regardless of their past or present success—must extend to the deepest reaches of the corporation rather than remain in lofty strategic corridors.

American businessmen are groping toward an understanding not just that strategy by itself isn't enough, but why it isn't enough, and what else they're going to have to apply themselves to in order to approach the nirvana held out to them by strategy's early proponents. As Walter M. Miller, head of planning at Becton Dickinson, puts it, "What we're moving toward is an integrated theory of management, one that assigns strategy its proper place and identifies the other factors you have to manage to make strategy work" [Kiechel, 1982, p. 39].

While companies are struggling with the challenge to reexamine their strategies and "the other factors," consulting firms are caught in the same time warp. If consultants do not recognize and adapt to the new dynamic complexity of the world, they and their solutions for corporate problems will be left behind. In the end, consultants have to take their own advice ("The Future Catches Up with a Strategic Planner," 1983, p. 62):

Four years ago, Bruce D. Henderson, founder and chairman of Boston Consulting Group [BCG] Inc., and, many argue, the architect of modern corporate strategic planning, wrote: "Success in the past always becomes enshrined in the present by overvaluation of the policies and attitudes which accompanied that success."
Ironically, critics contend, it is now BCG and other "strategy boutiques" that are wedded to "overvalued" policies that brought wild success in the past two decades. A growing number of companies now recognize that a brilliant strategy does not always guarantee bottom-line success.
Moreover, growing numbers of chief executives—and consultants—realize that the successful implementation of a strategy depends on having the right resources, organization, compensation program, and culture. "We are trying to approach [customers] with an awareness of the need to look at management processes as an interrelated system rather than as fragmented pieces," says Walter I. Jacobs, a partner at Hay Management Consultants.

The temptation for both managers and consultants is to gravitate toward the single approach that offers the promise of organizational success. In today's world, however, single approaches are the fragmented pieces, not the interrelated systems. The quick fix is the Band-Aid applied directly to the symptom of the problem. If, for example, managers complain about a lack of direction, top executives (with or without the aid of consultants) then institute a strategic planning system. No effort is made to find out how all the other properties of the organization may be contributing to the problem; nor is there any concern that the problem, whatever it turns out to be, cannot be solved without altering cultures, structures, reward systems, and management skills. Boyle (1983, p. 22) aptly describes the "Band-Aid" style being used by managers in most organizations:

> This reactive style responds to each problem in the organization as if it were an isolated phenomenon. Instead of preventing fires, it's always fighting fires. Because it favors the quick fix over the long-term solution, it may not be fixing the right thing at all. Because there isn't any process in place that allows the organization to anticipate the need for change before a crisis breaks, it is always one step behind the times.

Kiechel (1982, p. 36) refers to "the flight of the sea gull" as a metaphor for the incessant use of the quick fix by consultants:

> It was, according to the industry joke, the sea gull model of consulting. You flew out from Boston, made a couple of circles around the client's head, dropped a strategy on him, and flew back.

Moving beyond the quick fix of strategy or any other Band-Aid treatment requires an integrated approach—for all types of organizations, including consulting firms. As we shall see, the quick fix, if it ever was appropriate and successful, was so for yesterday's world. For today's dynamic complexity, a completely integrated program for managers and consultants is mandatory for long-term success.

In this book, integration comes in the form of five tracks: (1) the culture track, (2) the management skills track, (3) the team-building track, (4) the strategy-structure track, and (5) the reward system track. Each track is a series of specific action steps conducted by managers and consultants in a borative manner. Each track directly addresses only of an organization. What, then, distinguishes the program of five tracks from all the quick fixes? Any one track does not have much meaning—nor is it likely to have a lasting, positive effect on the organization—unless all five tracks are implemented in their entirety. There is no shortcut to success.

Furthermore, the five tracks must be conducted in sequence—(1) through (5)—to ensure integration. The first track develops a culture to foster trust, openness, and commitment, the qualities needed to proceed with all other change efforts. During the second track, all managers learn new skills for solving complex problems, especially the methods for uncovering and then updating assumptions; without a supportive culture, managers would keep their assumptions under lock and key. The third track enables each work group to make use of the new culture and of updated assumptions for solving important business problems; gradually, former cliques and nominal groups become effective teams. The fourth track guides these effective teams to address two of the most important yet most close-to-home problems an organization can face: its own strategy and structures. Once the organization and all its members are moving in the right direction, the fifth track designs a reward system to sustain high performance and morale into the future. Naturally, the five tracks must be examined periodically to evaluate whether they need to be conducted again. Any external changes in the organization's setting may require corresponding internal changes, and the cycle of managing the five tracks continues.

The Six Principles

Six key principles highlight why an integrated program is so necessary for organizational success and why any quick fix inevitably will lead to failure. The six principles are (1) world as a complex hologram versus world as a simple machine, (2) complex versus simple problems, (3) multiple versus single tracks, (4) participative versus top-down approaches to managing tracks, (5) what managers can do with consultants versus without consultants, and (6) books to study versus books to skim. Just as the five tracks are integrated into a particular sequence of action, these principles are synthesized into a deliberate line of thought.

Specifically, the first principle recognizes the new holographic image of the world—adding the third dimension of unconscious forces to the traditional at-the-surface perspectives. The second principle suggests why complex problems emerge from this new world view. The third principle suggests why multiple tracks are essential to solve complex problems. The fourth principle outlines why only a participative approach can hope to capture all the expertise and information needed to implement multiple tracks effectively. The fifth principle emphasizes how management may need to utilize internal or external consultants in order to conduct the very sensitive portions of any tracks. The sixth principle argues that integrated approaches cannot be learned by a quick reading—they must be studied.

In essence, the six principles describe important contrasts between what may have worked in the past and what is needed now. If these principles are not fully appreciated and understood, organizations will not even recognize the full range of barriers to success. More importantly, without *acting* on these principles, organizations will not be able to transform each barrier—via the five tracks—into a channel for success. Barriers will continue to hold the organization back, whereas channels will provide the freedom to move forward. Whether the organization is plagued with barriers or blessed with channels is very much top management's choice. These issues will appear again and again as the theory and practice behind the five tracks, as well as the five tracks themselves, are presented.

Principle 1: World as a Complex Hologram
Versus World as a Simple Machine

The reason for an integrated program of five tracks is lodged in the new kind of world in which we live. Three types of world view can be distinguished: the world as a simple machine, the world as an open system, and the world as a complex hologram (Mitroff and Kilmann, 1984a).

The first world view, a simple machine, argues for single efforts at change, much like replacing one defective part in some mechanical apparatus: The one defective part can be replaced without affecting any other part. This single approach works only for fixing a physical, nonliving system. The quick fix cannot hope to heal a human being, much less a living, breathing organization.

The second world view, the open system, argues for a more integrated approach, in which several parts must be balanced simultaneously in order to manage the whole organization. Here, a dynamic equilibrium exists between an organization and its changing environment. The organization consists of systems, such as strategies, structures, and rewards. The environment contains its own systems, too, such as the government, suppliers, competitors, and consumers. This world view, however, remains at the surface level, where things can be easily observed and measured. The open system represents two-dimensional thinking—much like studying the world with a flat map.

The third world view, the complex hologram, argues for adding depth to the open system—analogous to forming a three-dimensional image by reflecting beams of light at different angles. Here, the complex hologram probes below the surface to examine unconscious psyches (the deepest reaches of the mind), tacit assumptions (unquestioned beliefs behind all decisions and actions), and hidden cultures (shared but unwritten rules for each member's behavior). An example of penetrating the depths is shown by examining the organization's "troublemakers"—individuals whose disruptive behavior interferes with the performance and morale of other members. Only by seeing how unresolved childhood struggles lead to such dysfunctional antics can the troublemakers finally be understood and managed. Similarly, only by surfacing hidden assumptions and unwritten rules can managers and consultants gain sufficient control over additional barriers to success.

Essentially, the complex hologram represents a completely integrated view of all living systems, whether individuals, groups, organizations, or societies—the eternal sphere. In fact, these various levels of analysis become meaningless; we cannot understand one without the others. An individual's behavior can be understood only within the context of its setting and of the historical development of that individual's deepest motives. At the same time, the functioning of organizations cannot be separated from the psychic struggles of its members. Only with a simple machine view of the world can one pretend that individuals and organizations are two discrete, tangible parts.

I believe the simple machine view of the world is already outdated. It had its heyday in the industrial revolution back in the eighteenth and nineteenth centuries. Yet, looking at the way contemporary organizations are designed and managed would lead one to conclude that the simple machine conception is still alive and well. Managers continue to search for the timeless fantasy of simplicity, absolute perfection, and complete certainty. In contrast, a hologram provides a more penetrating and realistic analysis of contemporary organizations. The hologram represents the most compelling approach when complexity, imperfection, and uncertainty are the norm—a three dimensional view of life beyond the five senses.

Writing in a recent issue of *Esquire*, Rose (1983, p. 84) expresses the challenge of moving away from the simple machine model to a richer integration and synthesis:

American engineers are taught the value of analysis, of pulling apart, but not of synthesis, of putting together. American students are taught to appreciate mathematics or metaphors, but not both. This raises the question of whether America is philosophically suited for leadership in the post-industrial world—or whether this country might be in some basic way incompatible with the future.

More than any other country, the United States is a product of classical science, the science of Newton and Descartes, the science that produced the Enlightenment and the Industrial Revolution. The American political and economic system is based on the Newtonian view of the universe as a clocklike mechanism of separate parts all working together under immutable laws. John Locke's notion of the free individual existing under natural law, Adam Smith's conception of the invisible hand at work in a free marketplace—these are ideas that follow directly from the Newtonian conception of an orderly and mechanical world. But, unfortunately, the world is not that simple [any-more].

Lest the reader conclude that the dichotomy between the simple machine and the complex hologram is apropos only to the practice of management, consider Slater's (1974, pp. 29-30) critique of the practice of medicine:

It has taken more than a century for Western medicine to rediscover what witch doctors and shamans have known all along: (1) that a disease occurs in the whole organism, not, as in a machine, in one defective part; and (2) that every organism is organically related to others, and to the total environment, and hence any "cure" that does not take account of these relation-ships is likely to be ephemeral. What we stigmatize as magic is scientific inasmuch as it teaches the wholeness and intercon-nectedness of living forms. Scientific medicine, on the other hand, is irrational in that it treats the organism as if it were a machine, disconnected from its surroundings and internally dis-connectable.

Managers and consultants—all healers of human systems—will not become successful by tinkering with the parts. A vastly different approach is necessary. Organizations must be viewed as holographic images. Otherwise, managers, consultants, and re-searchers will see only a small portion of the total picture. If managers work with just the simple machine parts of the organi-zation, they will be severely limited in what they can control and manage. If consultants also examine just these parts, they, too, will be unable to help managers solve complex problems. If researchers see the organization with the same blinders, they will find it impossible to explain much of what goes on in or-ganizations. Without the holographic view, most of what goes on and of what must be managed and controlled for success would be beyond everyone's perceptual reach.

Principle 2: Complex Versus Simple Problems

Once we accept the holographic view of the world, we next must realize why a different type of problem comes into being. While the simple machine view elicits simple problems, the holographic view reveals complex problems. There is a night-and-day difference between simple and complex problems. If simple problems are approached as complex problems, the organization is wasting its limited resources—it is being inefficient. Such an approach is like assigning twelve different specialists to solve a problem that could have been assigned to just one person. On the other hand, if a complex problem is approached as if it were simple, the consequences reach far beyond matters of efficiency. The complex problem will not be solved at all. Worse yet, the organization may incorrectly believe that it has managed the problem—only to suffer dire consequences later.

If complex problems, such as determining business strategy or deciding on a new business venture, also wind up being the most important problems facing the organization, approaching such problems as if they were of the simple machine variety can prove deadly. It is only by understanding the full implications of a holographic world that we can begin to discover why the methods for solving complex problems must be drastically different from the established methods for solving simple problems.

Briefly, a simple problem is evident when one person can have all the expertise and information to solve it. In solving such a problem, it would be redundant—inefficient—to include many more experts who simply have the same talent and information. Actually, the only reason to include additional individuals is to generate commitment; this may come in handy when it is time to implement the chosen solution, but the extra persons are not needed to improve the quality of the decision. For example, a problem of choosing between two methods for costing inventory is largely an accounting problem, although even here an understanding of tax laws and corporate objectives would be useful.

Alternatively, a complex problem is evident when one person cannot have all the expertise and information to solve it. This deficiency stems from the limited capacity of individuals to possess large amounts of information and to acquire widely different areas of expertise. Simply put, each person tends to be a specialist in only one or, at most, a few areas. Some problems,

however, involve many different angles—as in a complex hologram—and require many diverse competencies. Here, several different experts must be involved in defining and solving the
problem. This diverse involvement is absolutely crucial for developing a high-quality solution. For example, the group determining the new strategic directions of the firm should include
experts from each division, department, and staff group in the
organization plus others who understand the economy, competitors, government agencies, and public opinion.

It seems that most of our contemporary organizations are
designed to accommodate simple problems. The organization
chart generally consists of the typical functional areas, such as
manufacturing, marketing, finance, human resources, and research and development (R&D). In years past, problems fit
neatly into these categories and could easily be identified as finance problems, marketing problems, personnel problems, and
so on. The same is true today for any other type of organization. For example, hospitals subdivide problems into the traditional medical specialties, and universities subdivide problems
into the long-standing scientific disciplines.

Thus, one major barrier to managing complex problems
is the perception that all problems can fit into the neat, simple
compartments that always have worked in the past. Dynamic
complexity means that the old ways of categorizing problems
may no longer be viable. It is not a question, however, of creating new simple categories. Instead, there is a need to form new
integrated categories—more product- and market-oriented than
process- or functionally oriented. Such new boxes on the organization chart would better fit with the nature of the problem—
treating a whole product or service in an integrated way.

Capra (1982, pp. 19-20) offers a provocative look into
the relationship between one's world view and how one cate-
gorizes complex problems:

We find ourselves today in a state of profound, worldwide crisis. We can read about the various aspects of this crisis
every day in the newspapers. We have an energy crisis, a health-
care crisis, high inflation, and unemployment, pollution and

other environmental disasters, the ever-increasing threat of nuclear war, a rising wave of violence and crime, and so on.

All of these threats are actually different facets of one and the same crisis—essentially a crisis of perception. We are trying to apply the concepts of an outdated world view—the mechanistic world view of Cartesian-Newtonian science—to a reality that can no longer be understood in these terms.

We live in a globally interconnected world, in which biological, psychological, social, and environmental phenomena are all interdependent. To describe this world appropriately we need an ecological perspective that the Cartesian world view cannot offer.

What we need, then, is a fundamental change in our thoughts, perceptions, and values. The beginnings of this change are already visible in all fields, and the shift from a mechanistic to a holistic conception of reality is likely to dominate the entire decade. The gravity and global extent of our crisis indicate that the current changes are likely to result in a transformation of unprecedented dimensions, a turning point for the planet as a whole.

Most social sciences are . . . fragmentary and reductionist. Present-day economics, for example, fails to recognize that the economy is merely one aspect of a whole ecological and social fabric. Economists tend to dissociate the economy from this fabric and to describe it in terms of highly unrealistic theoretical models. Most of their basic concepts—efficiency, productivity, GNP, etc.—have been narrowly defined and are used without their wider social and ecological context. In particular, the social and environmental costs generated by all economic activity are generally neglected.

Consequently, current economic concepts and models are no longer adequate to map economic phenomena in a fundamentally interdependent world, and economists have generally been unable to understand the major economic problems of our time.

For example, economists have been quite unable to understand inflation. Hazel Henderson, one of the most eloquent critics of conventional economics, defines inflation as "the sum of all variables that economists have left out of their models."

Managers and consultants are no less deserving of this critique. We must be willing to see the world in new ways—as a complex hologram. This new perception will allow us to sort dynamic complexity into more integrating categories. Otherwise, organizational decline will be the net result of all the variables left out of the proverbial quick fix.

Principle 3: Multiple Versus Single Tracks

Once we recognize the holographic view of the world with all its complexity, what implications can be derived for managing our organizational problems? Single tracks and quick fixes are to be avoided; integrated tracks and long-term solutions are to be embraced. Managers and consultants, therefore, must approach complex problems with multiple perspectives, multiple methods that affect different leverage points, and multiple action steps to act on these points.

Essentially, complex problems are made up of interconnected streams, some occurring at the water's edge and others flowing at the depths of human experience. While the systems approach has provided a better way of understanding the interdependence at the surface level—where things can be easily observed and measured—the holographic view requires diving to the depths of human psyches, elusive assumptions, and hidden cultures. Thus, integrated approaches include not only a great variety of perspectives at the surface level, such as strategy, structure, and reward systems, but also perspectives that probe the essence of human nature.

Any integrated approach to organizational success also must include a variety of leverage points in order to control—hence manage—performance and morale. A single approach that attempts to "fix" a problematic situation by influencing only one point and inadvertently or purposely ignoring all the interrelated aspects is doomed to fail. For instance, the reward system changes meant to motivate members to high levels of performance cannot counteract job descriptions that either are vague or steer behavior in the wrong direction. Similarly, if the strategic plans for the firm are not in accord with the trends in the marketplace, any reward system based on the old strategic choices will result in misplaced effort.

The five tracks to organizational success portray the principle of multiple tracks versus single tracks. The culture track, management skills track, team-building track, strategy-structure track, and reward system track cover a wide range of at-the-surface and below-the-surface barriers to success. Each track, of necessity, contains a number of leverage points so that managers and consultants can affect directly performance and morale. Chapters Four through Eight will present the multiple and integrated sequence of action steps that make up each track.

In the spirit of the holographic view, it might be useful to consider why managers and consultants are steeped in the quick fix—single tracks—rather than in multiple tracks. Essentially, we must take a serious look at our educational system to see precisely what is taught about real-world problems. Sieber and associates (1978, p. 31) have discerned what children learn in school from day one:

> There is evidence that students seldom are taught appropriate ways of dealing with uncertainty. On the contrary, they usually are taught to regard problems as having clear and determinate solutions and to look to others for the answers. [Researchers have observed] that teachers usually provide students with specific information and then expect specific "right" answers to questions about that information. Children hunt for cues to what answer the teacher expects. Furthermore, it appears that teachers do not often allow questioning interruptions from students. The results of this regimen are as one might expect: when questioned about problematic matters, students usually give simple, dogmatic answers.

As children grow to be managers, why should they suddenly adjust to dealing with complexity when all their formal training has been with simple problems? Instead, when students become managers, they look to their bosses for cues as to the right answers—the single right answers, preferably in numerical form. Professor William Hamilton, director of the Management and Technology Program at the prestigious Wharton School at the University of Pennsylvania, summed up the whole matter boldly in response to the charge that business schools "are still largely geared to turning out number-crunchers. 'One of the

Linear thinkers in an abstract world

—Proff. What do you want, is that on the test?

solutions to the Japanese threat is to export a number of our MBA programs to Japan' " (Sieber and others, 1983, p. 80).

Where and when does one learn about the third dimension, about cultures, assumptions, and individual psyches? Other than clinical psychology, psychiatry, and cultural anthropology, most scientific work on organizations remains at the surface level. One must understand the human psyche in order to appreciate why exploring below the surface is somewhat scary to most people. In fact, the idea of acknowledging unconscious forces has never been very popular.

While studying behavior in the nineteenth century, most scientists concentrated on biology, physiology, and anatomy—those aspects of the individual that could be seen or touched directly. Then Freud came along and suggested that each person had an "id, ego, and superego." These things could not be observed; rather, they were contrived—hence conceptualized—to help explain behavior that could not be explained solely by the tangible aspects of the individual. At their inception, such discussions created a furor. In time, a revolution in thought took place. Today it is generally accepted that all individuals have an unconscious being, but the resistance that people have to exploring this unconscious side of themselves has not changed since Freud's time. What cannot be seen or touched is feared by some and considered taboo by others.

Not surprisingly, this general fear of the unknown—of what lurks in the dark—continues in science and in the university today. The prevailing culture of most research programs in professional schools of business can be summed up by these unwritten rules: If it can be easily measured, it must be important; if you can easily observe it, it should be managed. Of course, the corollaries are: If you can't measure it, it's not important; if you can't observe it, don't bother. Naturally, if academics do not research and teach the hidden side of human nature and organizational life, students and managers will not learn it, unless they learn it on their own. I suspect that very few schools of business teach such courses as The Psychoanalysis of Organizations (de Board, 1978) or Teaching Companies to Cope with Evil (Mitroff and Kilmann, 1984b).

Multiple tracks to organizational success, therefore, would have to integrate all the surface aspects of organizations with the psychoanalytical, cultural, and assumptional aspects. This is the holographic approach to today's complex problems. Anything short of this, or using single, surface, quick fixes in the extreme, will miss the mark. This point is so fundamental that it cannot be overstated. I consider it naive and foolhardy for managers and consultants to try to solve today's interconnected problems (including below-the-surface aspects) with anything less than an integrated program.

Principle 4: Participative Versus Top-Down
Approaches to Managing Tracks

I have found that most people are willing to lend a helping hand if one asks nicely and sincerely. People enjoy contributing to a worthwhile cause. If there are significant problems to solve requiring an extensive cooperative effort on everyone's part, generating a team spirit will go far toward overcoming barriers and solving problems. Only in a crisis, when time is limited, is a different kind of approach called for.

It seems that viewing the world as a simple machine, however, created organizations in the mold of the Prussian army. The terminology of chain of command, lines of authority, span of control, and line versus staff has its roots in military organizations. Here, one salutes the uniform and not the man. The officers are wise and all knowing; the recruits are ignorant and just waiting to be told what to do—there to do, not to think. Stephen Vincent Benét (1927, p. 12) described the dilemma of the military model as follows:

If you take a flat map and move wooden blocks upon it strategically, the thing looks well, the blocks behave as they should. The science of war is moving live men like blocks. And getting the blocks into place at a fixed moment. But it takes time to mold your men into blocks. And flat maps turn into country where creeks and gullies hamper your wooden squares. They stick in the brush, they are tired and rest, they straggle after ripe blackberries, and you cannot lift them up in your hand and move them.

The top-down approach to management seems very akin to the military model in its style and assumptions. Executives and managers believe that one-way communication backed by the formal authority of their positions is enough to implement any decision into action. The assumption is that members lower down in the hierarchy will understand what is intended and follow through exactly as requested—like moving blocks on a flat map. If the decision is a simple instruction to be carried out, perhaps a top-down approach is fine. If the members below are eager to do whatever those above request, perhaps member compliance is automatic. If members have learned never to question their superiors, then again the members are likely to comply.

A *Business Week* article, "The Revival of Productivity" (1984, p. 100), shows that the military model is still being fought today:

> The new management and labor attitudes embodied in the Tandem [Computers, Inc., in Austin, Texas] approach are also having a big impact at Lockheed-California Co., a division of Lockheed Corp. R. P. Leifer, director of productivity, sums up what may be the most critical point in industry's drive for competitiveness: "For a long time we thought of the hourly employees as coming to work with hands and forgetting they had a brain."
> But this approach calls for companies to replace authoritarian management with a participative style, and many managers are reluctant to go that far.

WITH Little Non-Creative Thinkers

Let us return to the holographic world. Problems are complex, having many angles all subject to different interpretations. One-way communication is like the old "telephone game" in school. The teacher hands a short written message to one student, who then whispers the message into a second student's ear. The second student whispers the message he heard to a third student, and so on. When the last, say tenth, student proudly announces to the rest of the class the message he received, it is surprising to learn how much modification the initial message has undergone. In some cases, the final message is opposite to the original. In other cases, it is even on a different topic. The more complex the original message, the more distortion takes place. The more students in the communication chain, the more errors in transmission occur. Only when the original message is a simple fact can any transmission be perfect.

With complex problems, top managers do not have a monopoly on expertise and information. The nature of complexity, it will be recalled, is that one person cannot possibly have all the necessary inputs to solve the problem. Taking the top executive group as one perspective suggests that any complex problem needs the additional perspectives of the lower-level managers and employees. Since members at the lower levels are generally on the "firing line"—closest to the machinery, the consumer, and the community—they are in an excellent position to observe problems and to provide different inputs. They may even try to communicate their insights to the higher levels. If a top-down style pervades the organization, however, higher management will not listen. The lower levels become increasingly frustrated and annoyed at this posture: "Why won't they ask us about the problem? We're the ones who have to live with it. They'll probably just go ahead with their same old solution!"

Furthermore, the extent to which decisions require member commitment for successful implementation suggests that the lower-level members may not comply automatically. Especially in cases in which the problem is complex—here read "ambiguous"—members have some freedom in interpreting how any decision is put into practice. If members do not commit to the decision as intended, what finally is implemented may be a far cry from what top management had in mind. It is also possible that the decision may not be implemented at all as members interpret the top management message as "implement when and as you see fit." It never fails to amaze me how many times the lower-level members look the other way as they interpret either requests or commands from top management in this light.

Some companies are still grappling with the consequences of a top-down approach when a very different style is needed to address dynamic complexity. In a *Business Week* article titled "Texas Instruments Cleans Up Its Act" (1983, p. 57), the following observation was offered:

But even the smoothest-running planning system is worthless if the company's management second-guesses its results, and TI's top two executives have long been accused of doing just that. Company insiders maintain that Shepperd and Bucy have instituted a top-down, autocratic approach to decision-making—and the carefully nurtured TI culture is responding by telling top management only what it wants to hear.

A similar assessment of TI's leadership style was presented in a *Fortune* article a year earlier (Uttal, 1982, p. 44):

The largest fault in TI's strategic planning system probably stems from top management's reluctance to delegate authority. "The corporate fathers don't have confidence in their people," says a former . . . manager. "They're always changing strategies in the boardroom." Gradually, it seems, the formalized matrix method of planning has turned into an informal top-down approach. "By the time I left early this year," says one refugee, "lower level managers had lost a great deal of authority."

The alternative is the participative approach. Here, members throughout the organization are involved in decision making and implementation on matters that directly concern them. Their insights, expertise, and information are brought to bear on important, complex problems. The executives at the top realize that they have a limited view of the whole situation and purposely search for alternative perspectives. Member involvement in decision making also generates the commitment necessary for successful implementation.

Richard Boyle (1983, p. 21), group vice-president of the Defense and Marine Systems Group of Honeywell, Inc., suggests how an organic, nonmilitary model of organization goes hand-in-hand with a participative approach to management:

The evolution of our organization has been highly exploratory—a step-by-step process. We began by articulating a set of goals and principles for the organization we hoped to become, rather than a plan of action. Next, a plan to begin achieving those goals was developed; it has continued to develop and change as we learn more about what works and what is needed.

After several years of undergoing this process, we have a new style of participative management and employee involvement. It has dramatically changed the work environment of almost every manager and employee, and we feel it accounts in large part for the increases in the quality and profitability of our products.

When participative approaches are used sincerely, they set up extensive two-way communication. This communication pattern prevents messages from being distorted. For complex problems, it is absolutely essential for all available information to be processed and understood. Accurate information from different experts is the key resource for solving complex problems.

In a holographic world that elicits complex problems continuously, not only are totally integrated approaches for management required but these approaches—multiple tracks—must be conducted in a participative manner. The latter is the only style for collecting and acting on information that is likely to generate quality decisions and commitment to these decisions. To look at a complex problem from one perspective with limited information is to guarantee surprises rather than solutions. If single-track efforts are coupled with top-down approaches to implementation, it is just a matter of time before the solution backfires. Something gets overlooked as the top-down executives impose their limited view on a complex situation. Such approaches to complex problems always seem to come back to haunt the organization and its top-down decision makers. A vicious cycle is evidenced when such failures result in an increased effort at top-down control so that "this time we'll get it right!" However, rather than more of the same, top management should try a different approach altogether—the participative one.

In sum, the principle of participative versus top-down approaches to managing tracks recognizes that "flat maps" no longer exist for travel in a world of dynamic complexity. Rather, this new terrain is more like turbulent oceans: The land has been washed away. As a result, the old ways of collecting information and making decisions will no longer work in this geography.

I ASKED what Time it was
: they changed me I am
to teach me how to
WIND my watch

*Principle 5: What Managers Can Do with Consultants
Versus Without Consultants*

As suggested several times now, tackling complex problems requires a broad range of expertise and information. With a participative approach, the organization has full access to all its members. Is that enough? What if the members affected by the problem do not have all the necessary inputs and skills to proceed? Should management search outside its boundaries? Certainly, for its most important problems, the organization should not restrict itself to the talents and insights of only the membership.

Let us define two types of consultants: internal and external. Internal consultants are employed full time by the organization and reside in various staff groups or in a department of human resources, personnel, organizational development, quality improvement, corporate development, or organizational planning. Any of these departments may include individuals who are trained in diagnosing and solving organizational problems—working on either business-related problems with technical expertise or systems-related problems with behavioral science and management expertise.

An external consultant, as the distinction suggests, is not an employee of the company. Such consultants are drawn from consulting firms, independent practice, or university settings. These individuals do not have an intimate knowledge of the business side of the organization. However, they are probably more objective in their approach because of their separate employment relationship.

External consultants are needed most when top management wants to collect information about problems the membership experiences, particularly if these problems involve the way the organization is managed. It is very unlikely that members will tell their superiors about severe management style problems before the five tracks have been implemented. Even internal consultants from the personnel or human resource department might have difficulty in getting members to open up about such delicate matters for fear that this information could travel back to their bosses. If anonymous questionnaires are distributed as a way of collecting member perceptions, some people still will be reluctant to present their true feelings. Here, members may fear that their questionnaires are coded to identify respondents. Therefore, both managers and internal consultants may be unable to gather diagnostic information when the topic—management and organizational problems—is too close to home.

An external consultant, however, is more likely to develop the rapport with the membership necessary to gather such information. Naturally, confidentiality must be stressed and precautions must be taken, and there always will be a few persons who will not open up under any circumstances. But external consultants are in the best position to argue for trust, confidence, and professionalism because of their independent, more objective posture.

Besides collecting delicate information regarding the diagnosis of the organization's problems, consultants are better than managers at dealing with interpersonal problems, group feed back sessions, and troublemakers. These topics always bring ego defenses and conflicted psyches to the forefront. It takes a specially trained consultant to work with these delicate aspects of human nature. Likewise, external consultants are better than managers at bringing the hidden cultures to the surface, since these cultures may not portray what top management was hoping to learn. Similarly, consultants may be best at guiding the process that uncovers hidden assumptions. Often a fair amount of stress is involved when managers first see their outmoded assumptions face-to-face; a skilled consultant is needed to help managers work through such confronting moments. As each of the five tracks is covered in detail (Chapters Four through Eight), I will indicate the points at which using consultants to conduct various tracks or portions thereof is better than leaving managers to act on their own.

Weinshall (1982, pp. 53–54), in an article titled "Help for Chief Executives: The Outside Consultant," eloquently summarizes why managers cannot conduct all five tracks by themselves:

The question is whether managements need, and can be helped by, outside consultants. . . . The answer to this question is definitely in the affirmative. Managements in all organizations suffer from a condition referred to as the "no-full-disclosure disease." This disease manifests itself through people within the managerial hierarchy who do not reveal to their colleagues all their concerns about the organization. They worry that the things threatening them may come to the notice of those who affect their position in the organization. They worry that their immediate superior may hear things which will be detrimental to their own advancement or beneficial to the promotion of others. They worry about their peers, with whom they compete for the favor of a common superior. They worry about their subordinates, younger and more recently trained and educated, whose acquired knowledge of the organization may soon rival their own and thus destroy their own area of superiority. . . .

The no-full-disclosure disease is a universal one and no organization is free from it. Most managers who first hear of its universality are surprised, thinking that it only affects their organization and themselves—a phenomenon known as the "fallacy of uniqueness." This disease is the cause of grave pathologies among managements, referred to as "undisclosed feelings" and the "hierarchical communication gap." Curing these ailments, and the no-full-disclosure disease which causes them, can be done only by outside consultants, who can help managers to open up, [and] bridge the communication gap.

In a holographic world, it is necessary to look deeper into the issue of what managers can do, with or without consultants. Essentially, it is an issue of managers seeking help, how they feel about doing so, and how this affects their own image as self-sufficient individuals. In some circles, seeking help is a sign of weakness. I remember one top executive who remarked how proud he was that his organization had weathered the storm without anyone else's help! I have consulted with some companies that initially were ashamed to admit that they needed help from consultants: It was taken as a sign of failure. As a result of such attitudes, consultants often arrive on the scene too late or when the crisis is already at hand. It is very difficult to implement a participative approach to solving complex problems when the ship is sinking.

For some managers, going to various staff groups for help

or to external consultants is like admitting to being alcoholic. As a result, managers often attempt to solve problems on their own. Actually, if a senior executive has difficulty in asking for help from either internal or external consultants, he will also be reluctant to use a participative approach with the membership. The reason is the same in both cases: It is tough to admit to oneself that one does not know or control all that goes on. In viewing the world as a simple machine, perhaps it is possible to know and control the whole system. In a holographic world, however, it is quite impossible to have tight control over dynamic complexity and human nature.

If all managers and executives realized that the nature of the world has changed and that they no longer can expect to be on top of every situation, perhaps this might take some of the pressure off. It might encourage them to collaborate, to seek more help from the membership, from internal and external consultants, from the community—in short, from anyone anywhere. This is the name of the game in the holographic world. The age-old barriers of pride, macho images, and self sufficiency must be overcome. Instead, in order for success to be achieved, these barriers must be transformed into channels of self-acceptance, reciprocity, and interdependence.

The most enlightened managers today are those who take pride in reaching out for help from whomever they can get it. These managers know their limitations and accept them as part of their human makeup. They are the first to recognize what they can do effectively by themselves and when they need to enlist the aid of others. It is not a matter of massaging egos—it is a matter of doing what is necessary to solve complex problems. The enlightened manager looks for diversity of inputs as a natural and recurring part of his job.

Principle 6: Books to Study Versus Books to Skim

This last principle has to do with the way this and other books are read. The philosophy of cookbook formulas for managers encourages the essential principles to be boiled down into very simple statements: The art of management is reduced to slogans, rules, reminders, and "one-minute" activities. These guidelines may work in the world of the simple machine, but they will not work in a holographic world. On the contrary, using such simple guidelines for complex problems will surely boomerang.

This book is one that must be studied, not skimmed—there is no way around it. I am not suggesting that the material is so difficult that it will take weeks and months to digest, but I do feel that it takes a thorough reading to learn what is being said; by skimming, one will miss the major points. I also ask the reader not to study the chapters out of order, as there is a certain building process that takes place. This is especially the case with the five tracks. As mentioned earlier, the five tracks are integrated in a particular sequence and should not be implemented out of order. The same goes for learning the conceptual linkages in the first place.

I have taught many executive programs during my dozen years at the University of Pittsburgh (Pitt). These programs have been conducted at Pitt, at other leading universities, and in-house at major corporations. I have relied on the material I am presenting in this book to transmit an understanding of the five tracks and of how managers can implement them for organizational success. Let me briefly summarize what I have learned from these executive programs to illustrate how readers can learn what is in these pages.

All the material in this book is readily understandable in a lecture/discussion format. Managers are not left confused and guessing. However, because the reader does not have the benefit of dialogue, a special effort to learn the principles and the tracks must be made. I have found that when a group of executives first reads the material presented in this book and then discusses it among themselves, the group members benefit greatly from the exchange of ideas. They supply their own examples of the quick fixes that are used again and again in their companies even though the fixes fail to solve the problem. Sometimes they have had experiences with applying more than one track and have learned the value of multiple tracks. The ideal response I have heard from executives is: "While I did have to read carefully to see how the five tracks all blend together, I now see my organization and my job as a manager in a new light. I have learned a new way of thinking about and coping with complexity."

One question that is asked frequently is: Why should managers learn about aspects of the organization that they do not control? This question often focuses on strategy and structure. My response is in three parts. First, it helps if one knows the impact of those things he does not control; in this way, he at least will not blame himself for something that is not his doing. Second, a person may feel that he has little authority for conducting one or more tracks, but he still may be able to influence how the tracks proceed; even strategy and structure can be affected by comments made to superiors or by the way arguments are offered during discussions on the firm's mission. Naturally, after the five tracks are implemented, all members will have more influence over each aspect of the organization. Third, as one climbs the management hierarchy, he will gain more power from his position to affect such things as strategy and structure. Some of this material, therefore, is as much for a person's future position as it is for his present job. In any event, knowing what affects performance, how to help in directing one's influence toward tracks that currently seem out of reach, and preparing oneself for the future should be reasons enough to learn this material.

I have little patience for up-and-coming managers who, after hearing these discussions on the new dynamic complexity of the world, still want simple formulas: They cannot think or act without the quick fix. I can only assume that as children they must have received a strong dose of the regimented education cited earlier in this chapter, which must have been reinforced in their home life as well. Their blind compulsion to be certain, secure, and accurate at all times prevents them from listening to (or reading) material that speaks to uncertainty, insecurity, and imprecision.

All institutions need some stability and tradition. But who will make sure that complexity and change are being managed? To learn this new way of managing requires a dramatic break from the past. It also requires a thorough study of this material and not just a quick reading. A quick reading is no different from a quick fix. It just will not work anymore.

Conclusion

The first item in each of the six principles represents what is needed for managing dynamic complexity. One must recognize a holographic, three-dimensional view of the world. Such a world view reveals complex problems that can be solved only by multiple tracks. Since a great diversity of expertise and information is needed to implement multiple tracks effectively, a participative approach is the only way to bring forth the necessary inputs *and* commitment for success. Further, this critical need for diverse information very well may transcend the conventional boundaries of the problem. Both internal and external consultants often are needed to do what the managers cannot or should not do on their own—collect sensitive information about management and organizational problems, confront the organization's troublemakers, and seek honest feedback about their team's functioning. Lastly, in a holographic world, new perspectives and insights cannot be learned overnight. They must be studied and discussed before the five tracks can be brought to any organization.

The outdated alternative—the simple machine world—is to continue searching for the quick fix. A top-down style of making decisions and implementing solutions works well in such a world. With a simple machine view, there is little need for additional expertise either inside or outside the organization. Besides, with strong, single-minded leaders, it would be a sign of weakness to admit to not knowing all aspects of the problem. Finally, quick fixes can be learned quickly. That is the beauty of simplicity.

These principles and their sharp distinctions will reappear throughout the remaining chapters of this book. When we travel through the material for each of the five tracks, the reader will be reminded of the holographic view, complex problems, integrated tracks, participative approaches, and consultants. These are inescapable if we are serious about creating and maintaining organizational success. When the next era begins and the world is no longer complex, when problems are once again simple, and when single tracks are sufficient for success, the tide may turn. Or, a new dimension will be born, followed by a new image of the world.

CHAPTER TWO

Theory Behind the Five Tracks

Theories are nets cast to catch what we call "the world": to rationalize, to explain, and to master it. We endeavor to make the mesh ever finer.

—Popper, 1959, p. 59

A model is a simplified picture of a part of the real world. It has some of the characteristics of the real world, but not all of them. It is a set of interrelated guesses about the world. Like all pictures, a model is simpler than the phenomena it is supposed to represent or explain. . . .

. . . models are central to science, history, and literature. They are also a part of normal existence. We are constantly forming partial interpretations of the world in order to live in it. Because we do not always label our daily guesses about the world as "models," we sometimes overlook the extent to which we are all theorists of human behavior. The activity is not mysterious.

—Lave and March, 1975, pp. 3, 4

Behind every approach to organizational success is a theory. This theory proposes how a change in one set of variables will bring about change in a second set. The first set of variables usually includes leverage points that are directly controllable by managers and consultants; the second set is the intended result—organizational success.

The theory that supports a quick fix states that a change in *one* independent variable, such as strategy, is enough to change a desired outcome, such as performance. This type of theory is as simple and machine-like as the quick fix itself. The theory that supports an integrated approach states that changes in *several* interrelated variables, such as strategy, structure, and culture, are necessary to achieve the intended results. The theory behind the five tracks, therefore, must show the complex relationships among many different kinds of variables.

A theory can be left implicit by never being written down or discussed; this serves to protect the theory from closer scrutiny. Alternatively, a theory can be made explicit by being developed into a formal model. Having such a model enables the theory to be examined, debated, and, if necessary, revised or replaced. This scientific process helps keep our theories and the practice of management up to date.

If the theory behind every quick fix were made explicit, the folly of the single approach for solving today's problems would become evident. However, it is not enough just to show that the quick fix is an impossible solution to complex problems: In order for managers and consultants to move beyond the simple machine approach, an alternative theory must be provided. This alternative theory must include a wide range of variables—those in the open system as well as those suggested by a holographic view of the world. Furthermore, as noted above, this theory must be made explicit so that it will be subject to criticism and change. Not until the implicit theory behind the quick fix is replaced by an explicit holographic model will managers and consultants adopt an integrated approach.

The Barriers to Success Model

Figure 1 shows the theory behind the five tracks in the form of a model. The model consists of five broad categories representing the open systems aspects of an organization plus,

Figure 1. Barriers to Success.

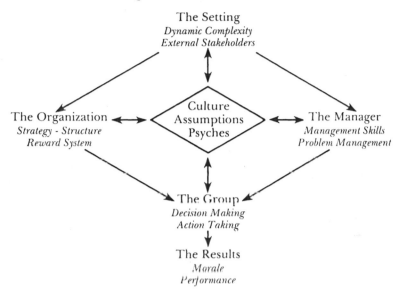

at center stage, three holographic aspects that add the dimension of depth. The five broad categories are the setting, the organization, the manager, the group, and the results. The three holographic aspects are culture, assumptions, and psyches. The double arrows surrounding the "holographic diamond" signify the strong reciprocal influence between the three below-the-surface aspects and all the other categories. Similarly, the single arrows show the primary (but not exclusive) impact one category has on another, particularly how several categories combine to determine decision making and action taking, as well as morale and performance. The purpose of the holographic model is to understand and master all these "interrelated guesses."

The model is referred to as "Barriers to Success." This title emphasizes how the organization will be plagued with barriers that stymie both performance and morale if it does not adapt to its surroundings. If managers and members feel thwarted in their efforts to create and innovate, one or more barriers are holding them back. If managers cannot get the information they need to make important decisions, another barrier is restricting their efforts. If the organization must respond to market changes

or customer requests quickly yet the members first have to follow many time-honored procedures, again some barrier is
blocking adaptiveness. If work groups put pressure on their
members to do the minimum to get by, another barrier is hurting the organization. Lastly, if members generally feel out of
control, helpless, and inept, more barriers are wasting away the
firm's human resources.

The Barriers to Success model systematizes the variety of
barriers that must be managed in today's organizations. Several
of the barriers shown in the model are directly controllable by
the managers and members through specific leverage points and
the five tracks. However, other barriers are not subject to direct
control by anyone. At best, these uncontrollable barriers must
be monitored so that they can be responded to with the most
up-to-date knowledge available. If all barriers can be controlled
and monitored effectively, what was once a barrier becomes a
channel for success.

Regarding the *un*controllable barriers, each organization
has three "facts of life." The first is the setting in which the organization exists. While dynamic complexity can be monitored,
it must be taken as a given. The second uncontrollable barrier
is the human psyche—deep-seated, relatively fixed styles to
cope with life's problems. The third such barrier is assumptions
—the unstated beliefs behind decisions and actions. While assumptions are hidden from view, they can be updated to reflect reality with proper management skills and a supportive
culture.

Regarding the controllable barriers, each organization has
five leverage points that can affect morale and performance: (1)
the firm's culture, (2) the managers' skills for solving complex
problems, (3) group approaches to decision making and action
taking, (4) strategic choices and structural arrangements, and
(5) the purpose and design of the reward system. There also
may be a number of other leverage points whereby the organization can be "touched" directly, but these other points tend to
provide quick fixes (such as replacing personnel or reclassifying
jobs) rather than long-term solutions to complex problems.

The five tracks to organizational success were designed to

act on these five leverage points—to transform all controllable barriers into channels for success. The culture track is a series of planned action steps to identify an outdated culture, develop the new culture that will move the organization forward, and then implement the new culture into each work unit. The management skills track, as a series of action steps, provides managers with the new skills necessary to address dynamic complexity— skills for surfacing, examining, and then updating assumptions. The team-building track does three things to improve the quality of group decision making in a series of action steps: (1) keeps the troublemakers in check so that they will not disrupt cooperative team efforts, (2) brings the new culture and updated assumptions into the day-to-day decision making of each work group, and (3) enables cooperative decisions to take place across work group boundaries, as in multiple-team efforts. The strategy-structure track goes through a step-by-step process to determine (or confirm) the new strategic directions of the firm, including the organizational structures that would most support the accomplishment of the firm's mission. The reward system track goes through its action steps to design the compensation and performance appraisal system necessary to sustain the benefits from all the other tracks.

The following discussion will define each category in the model in more detail. After that, I will describe the important linkages among them. This will show the key implications and benefits of working with a holographic model rather than concentrating on only one or two parts, as is done with the quick fix. Actually, the beauty of such a model is the way it enables the viewer to systematically see, understand, and control more with it than without it. In addition, the model will show why a completely integrated program, such as the five tracks, is the only way to organizational success.

In order to illustrate both the separateness and interconnectedness of the categories shown in Figure 1, examples about the recent transformation of the American Telephone and Telegraph Company (AT&T) will be given throughout the chapter. This case is powerful because it requires an unprecedented break from the past by the world's largest company. Simply put, the future success of AT&T requires a radical change in every category in the model. Furthermore, if all the categories in the model are not realigned in an *integrated* fashion, the new AT&T companies will be fraught with recurring barriers to success. As discussed in Chapter One, it seems that an organization's size, age, and prior success do provide the mightiest challenges to future success when dynamic complexity plays its hand. The barriers to success become as large and formidable as the organization itself.

The Setting

At the top of the figure is the broadest category of all. It includes every possible event and force that can affect the survival of the organization. Even if many of these possible events are generally irrelevant, they can become a significant factor for the organization to consider at any time. For example, the world can be caught in an economic recession that ultimately affects organizations in every industrial nation. Similarly, an energy crisis, such as the one in the 1970s, can affect many countries, including their economies and political strategies. The term *dynamic complexity,* which was first introduced in Chapter One, summarizes the two qualities that are having increasing impact on all organizations: rapid change and interdependence.

A useful way of looking at the setting of the organization is through the concept of *stakeholder*: any individual, group, organization, or community that has some stake in what the focal organization does (Mitroff, 1983). While stakeholders can include persons and groups inside the organization, for present purposes we will consider only those outside the organization. The advantage of the stakeholder concept is that the relevant parties listed can vary tremendously, depending on the organization being studied. While most organizations would consider similar stakeholders—such as the government, stockholders, competitors, and financial institutions—as relevant to their setting, different strategies and different products and services (markets) result in very different stakeholders. Further, new stakeholders—such as new competitors with improved products, new government agencies with new regulations, new research groups developing new production methods and technologies, and new consumers with different tastes—can enter the organization's setting at any time.

Consider the case of AT&T. Once the largest company in the world, AT&T existed within a very stable, regulated, monopolistic setting. In the early 1980s, AT&T suddenly found itself in the throes of dynamic complexity. This dramatic shift took place as a result of just two decisions by two external stakeholders: (1) The Federal Communications Commission (FCC) required AT&T to form a separate, unregulated subsidiary to provide new telephone equipment at customer locations, effective January 1, 1983. (2) After an eight-year study, the Department of Justice decided to break up AT&T's monopoly as a telephone company, effective January 1, 1984.

W. Brooke Tunstall (1983, p. 17), assistant vice-president and director of corporate planning of AT&T, aptly describes how the decisions of two stakeholders can so powerfully affect the very soul of the organization and its members:

> Essentially, AT&T is moving from its former geographical profit centers (Bell Operating Companies) to nationwide lines of business serving discrete markets. As with the regional companies, this involves a radical change in many aspects of the way the company operates, including its culture. Its "interconnectedness" with its former operating subsidiaries will be through tie lines and contracts, as opposed to structure and culture.
>
> While the critical research, manufacturing, and long distance operating capabilities of AT&T remain intact, it must be recognized that the two government mandates will mean the *disintegration* of the Bell System as the nation has known it. This, of course, strikes at the heart of Bell's historical legacy—*its sense of unification* over the course of a century.

The "culture shock" created by these changes is difficult to exaggerate. In fact, when Bell System people began to verbalize their feelings on January 8, 1982 (the day divestiture was announced), they spoke in metaphors of personal grief, almost as if they had been deserted or there had been a death in the family. Gradually, the initial shock began to abate, helped along by occasional flashes of grim humor. "My initial reaction," one company president said, "was that my best horse had just been shot out from under me."

It should be strikingly apparent that most problems that beset organizations stem from the actions of various stakeholders in its setting. Stakeholders change their plans, alter their decisions, modify their demands, and adapt to changes in their own environment of stakeholders. These dynamics foster stresses, strains, conflicts, and, hence, problems. Consequently, any organization existing in a complex and changing environment will face a continual stream of dilemmas no matter how perfectly the organization is designed and managed internally.

As will be emphasized throughout the rest of the book, keeping a close watch on the movements of stakeholders, including the entry of new stakeholders and the exit of old ones, is the surest way to keep tabs on dynamic complexity. Because it involves future events and unknown facts, this monitoring process is rooted in the assumptions the organization makes about its stakeholders: Managing dynamic complexity in the organization's setting amounts to updating assumptions regarding all relevant stakeholders. In this way, the uncontrollable barrier represented by the organization's setting can be understood—perhaps even anticipated—so that it can be acted upon.

The Organization

The formally documented systems of any organization include strategy, structure, and reward systems. Strategy is the way the organization positions itself in its setting in relation to its stakeholders given the organization's resources, capabilities, and mission. This strategy can be broken down further into specific objectives, policies, and plans as guides to all decisions and actions. Structure is the design of divisions, departments, and work groups, as shown by an organization chart. In addition, structure includes the more detailed job descriptions, rules, and work procedures that guide task activities within each unit in the organization. The reward system includes all methods to attract and retain employees, but particularly to motivate employees to high levels of performance. All approaches to performance appraisal would fit into this category as well.

In general, the organization in the model represents all the formal mechanisms that are under the immediate control of the managers. Naturally, as the setting of the organization changes, new stresses, pressures, conflicts, and problems are created. Alterations in strategy, structure, and reward systems may be necessary for organizational success. A critical problem, therefore, is to adjust the organization—with all its formally documented systems—to keep it on track with its setting—the changing demands and requirements of external stakeholders.

The critical decisions by the government that affect AT&T require sweeping changes in strategy and structure. If these documented systems are not realigned with AT&T's new mission (to be competitive in the telecommunications industry, for example), these formal systems can become massive barriers to success.

Since it agreed to divestiture on January 8, 1982, AT&T has moved at breakneck speed to complete the reorganization the largest corporate breakup in U.S. history. "We've just about pulled off the most complex restructuring job by any business anywhere," boasts AT&T Chairman Charles L. Brown. In just 20 months, the phone company has essentially completed the Herculean task of dividing nearly 1 million employees and $148 billion in assets among itself and the new holding companies. Beginning on October 1 [1983], the eight companies will start a dry run of their independent structures. Now, says Brown, "We must set a course that redirects a great business onto an equally great new path . . ." ["Changing Phone Habits," 1983, p. 68].

Critical to the new shape of AT&T is its division along business lines. Before divestiture, the phone company was organized according to function—Bell Labs did the research and design, Western Electric did the manufacturing, and the local operating companies installed and operated the equipment. The new lines of business, on the other hand, will generally be self-contained, each with as much research, manufacturing, and marketing strength as it requires. AT&T Communications, for example, has its own network designers, operators, and marketing force. And each line of business will be responsible for its own profits and losses ["Changing Phone Habits," 1983, pp. 68, 69].

But these radical changes in structure ultimately will have to be supported by a new reward system that encourages a market orientation. If risk taking is desirable, managers will have to be rewarded for taking chances, recognizing that mistakes will be made. The reward system can be designed so that employees will be encouraged to make the mental and behavioral switch to the new organization. At the same time, the reward system can discourage employees from living in the past.

Western Electric's Government Sales unit is experimenting with incentive pay for second- and third-level sales managers. Managers of other groups—including Network Systems and Consumer Products—are considering profit-sharing plans. . . .
Even those executives who welcome the chance to take risks are impatient with what they see as top management's slowness to institute change. Says Steven M. Bauman, a product planning manager at AT&T Information Systems: "We need to dramatically reward people who are making things happen and dramatically punish people standing in the way" ["Culture Shock . . . ," 1983, pp. 114, 116].

Realigning the structures and reward systems with AT&T's new strategic directions is absolutely critical for the future success of the newly formed companies. However, even if all the formally documented systems have been updated and implemented, will the managers fit into their new organizations? Or do they need to go through a radical reorientation as well?

The Manager

While employees are certainly an important part of the membership, the Barriers to Success model emphasizes the special role played by the managers, those who have the responsibility for what takes place. As one management principle states: You can delegate authority but not responsibility. Also, as many have stated, managers are paid to take the blame and to get the glory for what transpires. It is the managers who are entrusted with making decisions and taking actions, whether they decide to do this in a participative way with their employees or in a top-down manner.

The aspects of managers that are emphasized in Figure 1 concern management skills and methods for problem management. Skills include the whole host of technical, conceptual, analytical, administrative, social, interpersonal, and motor skills that have been studied. Depending on the nature of the organization's setting and the responsibilities assigned, the required skills for each management position can be outlined. Whether these skills are present due to selection or training is another matter, but it is essential to understand the skill requirements of any job and especially how these skills may need to be changed in response to a new setting. The greater the changes in the setting, the more the appropriateness of current or prior skills may have to be questioned and reexamined. Stated differently, a major problem for organizations facing shifting stakeholders is to update the various skills of their managers. Furthermore, technical skills tend to be updated more regularly and proactively than are conceptual and analytical skills, since the latter are seemingly harder to pinpoint and specify. However, given the dramatic changes that have occurred in the setting of most organizations, some of these "fuzzier" skills have become more and more relevant to managing complex problems—those that involve much more than technical knowledge.

The term *problem management* refers to a very special class of skills needed by managers for today's complex problems. Until recently, managers have been thought of primarily as decision makers—persons who must choose among a set of given alternatives to arrive at an optimal or satisfactory solution. This is all well and good if the alternatives are already determined and the rules for choosing among the alternatives are clearcut. With dynamic complexity, however, it is not even clear what the essential problem is, let alone what the alternative choices are. Today's managers have to be problem managers even more than decision makers. This entails learning methods to monitor and revise assumptions regularly.

As AT&T switches from a highly regulated to an intensely

competitive setting, its managers face very different kinds of problems. Can AT&T's managers make the transition?

The split-up of the Bell system not only represents the biggest breakup in corporate history but also the most enormous task of reorienting managers that any company has ever had to face. The surviving American Telephone and Telegraph Co. and the seven regional operating companies that will go their separate ways . . . must redefine managers' jobs, teach them new skills, and—most important—change their mindsets. . . .

In fact, some critics charge that senior management is the biggest obstacle to change. "The dilemma the company faces is having to move fast and having a group of executives who have not grown up with the skills they need," says a consultant who has worked with AT&T since the 1970s ["Culture Shock . . . ," 1983, pp. 112-113].

What new style of management is necessary for an organization that was literally thrown into dynamic complexity overnight? What new skills must these managers acquire? Will managers realize that they need a whole new outlook and approach to their jobs? According to Tunstall (1983, p. 21):

As AT&T moves toward a more competitive environment, its management style must adapt accordingly. In the process its managers must recognize that marketplace uncertainty will replace regulatory uncertainty, and that cultural mores will change to value more entrepreneurial types of managers than in the past. Attitudes toward risk-taking vary considerably among corporations and are an essential ingredient to the total makeup of the corporate culture. Regulated firms like AT&T, with their more predictable forecasts of sales volumes, are not prone to promote risk-taking as a valued managerial attitude. This is not a pejorative statement; indeed, it would be foolish to take risk where the rewards are not compensatory. However, in competitive industries which experience sharp shifts in market share and in which greater sensitivity to economic conditions prevails, conservatism is tantamount to default in the marketplace. Unquestionably, AT&T's managers of the future will be more inclined to risk taking than care taking.

Care taking, as a management style, seems to fit well with the simple machine view of the world—proper maintenance of all working parts. Risk taking, in contrast, is mandatory in a world characterized by dynamic complexity.

The Group

The lower part of the model portrays the decisions and actions that follow from group efforts. While individuals do make decisions and take actions on their own, today's holographic organization requires multiple inputs from members of one or more groups on all complex problems. Groups can be nominal—existing in name only—as information is not even discussed among the members. Worse yet, in some groups information is kept secret, as with powerful cliques. Alternatively, groups can be teams—highly interactive, cohesive sets of individuals all working toward the same objectives. Generally, it is the team approach that will provide the most comprehensive source of expertise and information to solve complex problems, where synergy enables the team to contribute more than the sum of its members.

Certain individuals, referred to as troublemakers, make it difficult for information to be shared openly. These individuals, because of internal conflicts that have not been resolved suitably, are overly aggressive, self-serving, vindictive, and harmful to others. As a result, these troublemakers can be a major barrier to success. When an organization is undergoing significant change, it seems that troublemakers come from out of nowhere to cause everyone difficulty in moving ahead. Not until the disruptive behavior of these individuals is under control will others in the organization be willing to risk the open sharing of information.

Next, of utmost concern is the *quality* of the decision the group renders and its *commitment* to implementing the decision as intended. In most cases, particularly for complex problems, the greater the diversity of knowledge and information discussed, the higher the quality of the decision. Further, if members have been actively involved in providing information and making the decision, they generally will be more committed to carrying it out. Only for simple problems can the decision making be delegated to one or only a few persons. Only in the simple machine view of the world can one ignore the importance of member commitment to follow through on the decision.

Moreover, since groups in the organization are not entirely independent of one another, several groups may have to join together to solve some particular problem. If information and expertise do not flow between these groups, again the quality of any decision will be negatively affected. Similarly, if the groups maintain their vested interests regardless of how the final decision turns out, it is unlikely that the decision will be implemented as intended. Instead, each group will interpret the plan of action to its own advantage. Here, the organization does not benefit from its joint group efforts. Only if the groups have learned to break down their artificial boundaries and look at the larger picture will the organization benefit from such interteam activities.

The tremendous changes taking place at AT&T demonstrate how the group becomes a catch-all barrier to success—a combination of all the other unresolved barriers still needing to be transformed into channels. Further, because of the dynamic complexity now facing AT&T, it is imperative that all groups work together to solve complex problems that otherwise will fall between the cracks. Nowhere is this more evident than in the problems created by switching from a manufacturing to a marketing orientation. During such a major transformation, it will be recalled, various troublemakers come to the forefront.

Manufacturers, not marketers, have moved into the corporation's pivotal jobs under a top-level reorganization in December [1983], consolidating their hold on strategy, new-product introductions and day-to-day operations. . . .

The most recent battle between the manufacturers and marketers has centered on AT&T's coming entry into computers. "We're talking World War III," quips one manager who was involved in the battle. When the battle ended a month ago, the manufacturing side had won control of computer pricing policy, computer distribution channels and even the marketing arm's product task forces.

"There is some concern over which fish is swallowing

which fish," admits Charles Marshall, the president of AT&T Information Systems, the marketing arm of the company. Jack M. Scanlon, the head of AT&T's computer systems unit, adds, "There'll always be internal tugs of war." But a supervisor who has been with AT&T for 12 years says, "Political infighting has become so intense it's like cannibalizing your own children."

Such internal strife, with manufacturers continuing to gain ground at the marketers' expense, may hurt AT&T in moving into the deregulated future. As time goes by, AT&T will increasingly compete against the likes of International Business Machines Corp. and other high-tech companies that react quickly to consumer demand. . . .

. . . Adds William McKeever, an analyst at Dean Witter Reynolds Inc., "IBM will flatten AT&T in the automated office and computer business unless the marketing types gain more control. . . ."

"Ultimately, whether it's silicon chips, computers or plain respect, the marketers feel they're not getting enough from the manufacturers," a former marketing manager says. Mr. O'Donnell [formerly division manager of corporate development at Information Systems] adds, "There's so much mistrust and anxiety among the executives that the ranks feel it now." Mr. Bosomworth [president of International Resource Development Inc.] calls the present situation of manufacturers dominating marketers a "ticking time bomb" [Langley, 1984, p. 1].

These accounts might lead one to conclude that the problem is simply a matter of some manufacturing executives achieving a workable resolution with the marketers. On the contrary, a holographic view shows that the "ticking time bomb" reflects a very uneasy and unstable transition of AT&T's culture, management skills, strategy, structure, and reward system. All these aspects jointly affect the relationships among people within and between the work units. As Figure 1 shows, the group is directly affected by all the previous categories in the model (indicated by the arrows). If these tangible and intangible properties of the organization result in a multiplicity of barriers to success, it will be most difficult for any group to render high-quality decisions and actions. The group will be caught in a bureaucratic grip even before it begins discussion on any complex problem. The same will be true for any multiple-group effort.

The Results

The two primary outcomes that interest organizations have been referred to most frequently as morale and performance. *Morale* is the human resource side of the equation, the extent to which members have a positive feeling about and commitment to their work and their organization. Morale includes job satisfaction and satisfaction with one's work group, superior, physical surroundings, salary, and fringe benefits. *Performance* is viewed in many different ways, depending on which stakeholder is being considered. For example, stockholders emphasize return on investment, consumers emphasize quality and reliability of products, and the community emphasizes more jobs and clean air. *Organizational success* is creating and maintaining high performance and morale for all or most stakeholders over an extended period of time.

There are two major reasons for distinguishing decisions and actions from morale and performance. First, each decision and action does not translate directly into specific increments in morale and performance. Measurable changes in the latter occur from numerous decisions and actions combined in a very complicated way. Sometimes it takes a long series of decisions and actions to make a noticeable difference in these results; at other times, one critical decision or action can make or break performance and morale. Second, there is generally a time lag between decisions and actions on the one hand and performance and morale on the other. It simply takes time to build morale, while it may take little to destroy it. Regarding performance, it takes time to develop new products and bring them to the marketplace; however, one bad decision can affect many stakeholders in a short time.

One might expect that the abrupt changes at AT&T have had a devastating effect on morale, especially on those persons who were most comfortable with the proven ways that worked in the old regulated setting.

After 38 years of helping to build the best telephone system in the world, Richard L. Conway, 61, views the split-up of the Bell System with considerable anguish. Like scores of veteran managers who cannot or will not adjust to the new environment, Conway decided "it wasn't worthwhile hanging in." So Conway, district manager in American Telephone & Telegraph Co.'s General Depts., retired on Sept. 9 [1983] even though the company still needs his expertise. "All of us took a certain pride in where we had come from. It doesn't give you satisfaction tearing it apart," he explains ["Culture Shock . . . ," 1983, p. 114].

Regarding performance, it is still too early to tell what impact the AT&T divestiture will have on long-term results. In the short term, however, the transformation is very costly.

The American Telephone and Telegraph Company yesterday reported a loss of $4.9 billion for the fourth quarter of 1983, by far the biggest ever by any company, because of extraordinary charges related largely to the breakup of the Bell System. . . .
"These results will be surprising as well as confusing to many investors," AT&T's chairman, Charles L. Brown, said in a statement. "I therefore want to stress that, in the main, they reflect one-time, one-of-a-kind events which are a consequence of the breakup of the Bell System."
He added, "These results by no means are an accurate measure of current operations and they are certainly not predictive of the future earnings performance of AT&T and the Bell Companies" [Pollack, 1984, p. 25].

The Holographic Diamond

Finally we get to the uniquely holographic aspects that blend everything together, supplying the third dimension to our analysis. Three below-the-surface aspects are distinguished: culture, assumptions, and psyches. This ordering reflects the relative depth of these concepts. Thus, culture represents the collective unconscious of the organization, although it can be brought to the surface rather easily: Culture has leverage points. Assumptions, however, occupy a somewhat deeper level in the organization. Actually, a supportive culture is a prerequisite to individuals' willingness to expose their assumptions. However, once willing, individuals must acquire methods and skills for working with those assumptions. Finally, individual psyches represent the deepest layers of the mind. Since psyches are quite unconscious and fixed, there is no need to monitor them per se. However, an understanding of how individual egos affect supposedly rational organizations is essential for a realistic understanding of why the five tracks are needed and how they work.

Culture

Culture is the invisible force behind the tangibles and observables in any organization, a social energy that moves the membership into action. Culture is to the organization what personality is to the individual—a hidden yet unifying theme that provides meaning, direction, and mobilization. Strategy, structure, and reward systems are just not enough to get members working together in the right direction. Besides, formally documented systems cannot specify everything in advance, especially in a rapidly changing world.

Operationally, culture is defined as *shared* values, beliefs, expectations, attitudes, assumptions, and norms. These are seldom written down or discussed; rather, they are learned by living in the organization and becoming a part of it. As will be discussed later in this book, culture fills in the gaps between what is formally decreed and what actually takes place. Culture thus determines how formal statements are interpreted and provides what written documents leave out. This affects all decision making and action taking, which in turn affects morale and performance. Of special concern is how culture can steer behavior in the exact opposite direction from what is "requested" by the formally documented systems or by top management. This is when culture becomes a barrier to productive efforts instead of a channel for organizational success.

The role of culture in managing change and transition has become a major problem for AT&T. Just acknowledging the cultural aspects of the reorganization is certainly a step in the right direction. The next step is to manage culture explicitly rather than to assume that it will take care of itself when the other leverage points are being addressed.

It has been said that the Bell System contained all the necessary attributes of a nation: territory, idiomatic language, history, culture, and government. The assertion may have been slightly exaggerated, but its cultural component was unarguably accurate. That culture, in fact, generated the energy to drive the enterprise to become the world's largest—in terms of both assets and employees. . . .

Clearly, the culture must be reshaped, adapted, and re-oriented to bring the value systems and expectations of AT&T people into congruence with the corporation's new mission and to prepare them for the competitive telecommunications battles looming ahead. Yet no AT&T manager is charged specifically with the management of the corporate culture. No task force is studying its dimensions. No committee is planning approaches to altering its underlying aspects.

The reason is that the culture is as broad as the enterprise itself, as pervasive as a value system that evolved over a century of service, and as amorphous as the attitudes and expectations of one million employees. Managing the required changes in culture is not an event underlying divestiture; rather, divestiture is one of the causal factors underlying change in the culture. No one manager is assigned responsibility for managing the change because all managers must be responsible for it. . . .

With divestiture, AT&T will experience a metamorphosis that would challenge the most boastful caterpillar. The organizational, technological, and operational complexities to be faced are literally without parallel. Yet, more than one informed observer maintains that changing the corporate culture is still the most difficult task facing management [Tunstall, 1983, pp. 15, 18, 25].

A similar view was expressed in "Changing Phone Habits" (1983, p. 71), emphasizing the critical role played by the invisible force behind the organization:

Whether AT&T can succeed in its new competitive environment remains an open question. Some observers are convinced that the phone company will find it impossible to change its monopolistic ways. "The toughest thing to change is corporate culture, and AT&T's corporate culture was not designed for competition," maintains a former AT&T executive.

As the subsequent material on the five tracks will demonstrate, culture change is the first track and probably the easiest one to manage. But culture change will not be sustained if it is not accompanied by the systematic implementation of all the other tracks. Making all managers responsible for managing the culture change is no different from ignoring it; such diffused responsibility will ensure that culture is managed by none.

Assumptions

The holographic view places assumptions at the second level of depth, after culture. Simply put, assumptions are all the beliefs that have been taken for granted to be true but that may turn out to be false under closer analysis. Underlying any decision or action is a large set of generally unstated and untested assumptions. If some of these assumptions turn out to be false, then the decisions and actions taken are likely to be wrong as well. Assumptions drive the validity of whatever conclusions are reached. We should not let our important decisions be driven by things that have not been discussed or considered. Assumptions need to be surfaced, monitored, and updated regularly.

For example, managers may be assuming that the following unstated beliefs are unquestionably true: No new competitors will enter the industry; the economy will steadily improve; suppliers for raw materials will not significantly raise their prices; the government will continue to restrict foreign imports for the industry; another firm will not develop a new product that renders the firm's current offering obsolete; the consumer will buy whatever the firm produces; the availability of capital will remain the same; corporate headquarters will continue to support the growth of the company; the culture that worked in the past will work equally well in the future; employees will continue to accept the same compensation package and benefits plan; yesterday's structures are best for solving today's problems. In short, all previous decisions and actions may have been based more on what worked in the past.

If the organization's setting is entirely stable and the past always flows smoothly into the future, then prior assumptions, if true, will be correct assumptions for the future. However, if the setting has been undergoing marked changes, then the assumptions that guided the past may be wholly inaccurate for the future. Worse yet, if assumptions are not examined and discussed, managers and organizations may wrongly assume that their tried-and-true ways are still appropriate—a case of erroneous extrapolation. This sort of thinking is dangerous for the modern organization. In essence, the Barriers to Success model directs special attention to the hidden barrier created by unexamined assumptions. When these assumptions are exposed, tested, and then revised, the new assumptions become the channels to guide all important decisions and actions.

Tunstall (1983, p. 23) has suggested the rippling effect a change in one government regulation has had on the entire belief system of AT&T:

The new AT&T organization will, of course, reflect the separation of the detariffed portion of the business from the remaining portions (as required by Computer Inquiry II). It will also influence virtually every *assumption, expectation, and belief system* of AT&T's employees concerning the company and their positions within it. [Emphasis added.]

The need to expose and update all assumptions is essential for high-quality decisions. Even *one* outdated assumption can result in a poor or unrealistic decision. If a decision is vital to the success of the firm, failing to revise all relevant assumptions can be perilous.

In 1980 and 1981, AT&T installed a new management team at PacTel [Pacific Telephone] with the mission of straightening out the company's battered finances and polishing its lackluster image. John Hulse, the first executive in a Bell operating company to bear the title of chief financial officer, moved to PacTel from Northwestern Bell Telephone Co., where he had served as chief executive of its South Dakota and Minnesota units. He came at the request of new PacTel Chairman Donald E. Guinn, a strong believer in strategic planning who headed network services at AT&T for two years before moving to PacTel in late 1980.

Guinn and Hulse arrived to find a company whose strategic plan was based on unrealistic financial assumptions. The three-to-five-year plans, which called for increasing capital expenditures 55%, to as much as $4 billion per year, by 1984, "clearly were based on unreasonable regulatory expectations," says Hulse. "This was a company that hadn't had a major rate increase" since 1974 "but whose plan assumed it would be able to obtain $1 billion to $1.5 billion from the commission" ["How One Bell Baby Struggled to Its Feet," 1983, p. 118].

One can bet that most complex problems involve more than financial assumptions: There are legal, economic, political, technical, human, and organizational assumptions to be considered as well. In fact, for every stakeholder there is a different set of assumptions. During the management skills track, managers acquire the necessary conceptual and analytical skills to analyze and update their assumptions.

Psyches

The third of the holographic aspects of organizations is also the deepest: the innermost qualities of the human mind and spirit. While psyches are not considered a leverage point for affecting morale and performance, an accurate understanding of human nature is essential in order to design strategy, structure, reward systems, cultures, and the implementation of all business decisions. In essence, the assumptions members make concerning human nature—what people want, fear, resist, support, and defend—underlie the eventual success or failure of all these systems and decisions. Probing the depths of the human psyche will allow us to make more realistic assumptions about how people think and act in today's organizations.

Specifically, more accurate assumptions about human behavior would reflect the following qualities: (1) Human beings are not entirely rational—they make decisions based on limited information and can analyze only a few variables at one time. (2) Human beings have limited memory and tend to distort the recall of events according to their psychological needs. (3) Human beings are often insecure—their negative feelings of self-worth and confidence result in numerous defensive reactions and dysfunctional coping styles. (4) Human beings may have strong desires for power and control—to minimize their fears of dependency stemming from discomforting childhood experiences. (5) Human beings do not like massive change, since their security and position in life will be altered. (6) Human beings do not universally have the ability to learn—sometimes all they can do is fight to survive. (7) Human beings have a strong need to be accepted by a group, stemming from their early family experiences—they are, therefore, susceptible to doing what the group decides in exchange for group membership.

Once we have a more up-to-date understanding of human nature, we will be more successful in designing organizations and making all kinds of business decisions. Only when we make naive assumptions about psyches—that human beings are all rational, all knowing, honest, good, and pure—are we surprised and shocked regularly as the membership, or any stakeholder, acts differently from what we expected.

Key Implications of the Model

Most of the problems organizations now face can be linked directly to dynamic complexity and the shifting nature of external stakeholders. The Barriers to Success model shows the major categories (variables) that need to be monitored or controlled for organizational success. The beauty of the model comes from the interrelatedness of all its categories. Understanding the highly interrelated nature of today's organization is a prerequisite to mastering it. As such, the holographic model allows us to derive some rather startling implications about what it takes to manage organizations.

The Barriers to Success model is not a simple machine. If it were, it would not have morale as an outcome variable—only performance. Culture would not even be considered—it is too intangible and fuzzy. Furthermore, the setting would consist of well-ordered input/output transactions between the organization and its environment without considering, and therefore not listing, managers and their skills in making such transactions. In the extreme case, the simple machine represents the organization as a single decision maker—all knowing, always rational, and highly predictable, as in modern economic theory. Actions are expected to follow decisions automatically and without hesitation. Assumptions and psyches do not count.

The model is more than an open system. If it were just an open system, it would not consider culture—nor would it include assumptions on the part of the managers. Further, the membership would not include troublemakers who could, because of their intrapsychic conflicts, do harm to other individuals. Morale would be included as an outcome measure as long as it could be measured easily. Also, actions would not have to be distinguished from decisions, since it would be irrational to resist, distort, or deny a decision after it has been conceived and agreed upon in a rational manner. Lastly, decisions and actions would lead logically and exactly to changes in morale and performance.

The model is a complex hologram. It contains culture and psyches—the collective and individual unconscious—as well as the more traditional and rational elements. It recognizes that actions do not necessarily follow decisions. Morale is a complex, elusive outcome in its own right, but it is real enough even if it cannot be measured as precisely as sales or profit. Assumptions about a complex set of stakeholders are acknowledged explicitly, even though managing assumptions is anything but a well-structured and predictable activity.

Although the model shown in Figure 1 is rather general and vague as it stands, it does capture the multiplicity of angles demanded by a holographic view of the world. The views of the world as an open system and as a simple machine are simply too restrictive to sort the complex problems of today and tomorrow. As will be shown later in the book, we cannot take any chance that one or more views of an organization's problems are overlooked or ignored. This happens when the implicit theory or model directing our attention serves to exclude certain categories of problems from our consideration. With dynamic complexity, every possible view must be included and examined.

Now we will consider the key implications that derive from a holographic model. To begin with, might it be that organizations are continually applying the same simple theories and models to manage problems when in fact these no longer capture the way the world has become? The solution is not, therefore, a matter of using the old models better but of adopting an altogether new kind of filter. This is the whole point of the Barriers to Success model. When the time comes that the holographic view of the world no longer portrays the sorts of phenomena the world now creates, it will be necessary to create new models to guide our efforts. Only by making our theories explicit in the form of models, including the assumptions that drive these models, will we be able to disband old models and move onward.

Moreover, have our systems of organization, management skills, assumptions, and cultures kept up with the world as a complex hologram? It does not seem so. The major problem facing organizations is change in response to new problems imposed by new stakeholders. In the past ten years, there has been a great need for organizations to examine and alter their strategic directions. At the same time, there has been a great need to consider how strategic changes will be implemented as changes in the formally documented systems. Similarly, it is necessary to consider whether management skills have kept up with the increased complexity in the world. Now, however, it may be absolutely crucial to examine whether organization cultures and assumptions coalesce into action for the past or for the future.

Specifically, how will the structure of divisions, departments, groups, and jobs be altered to implement changes in strategy? How will reward systems be altered so that the desired shift in strategic focus will be supported by the formal assessments and rewards members receive? Do managers need to be trained in problem management and assumptional analysis methods so that they are equipped to see the world and their problems in a new light? Can managers be trained to define and solve problems differently? How can managers develop the skills to work with employees in a way that supports the generation of information that is needed to tackle these new problems?

Continuing, can the culture of the organization be managed and controlled? How can the membership create the culture that is suited to the future rather than impose the will of the past? How can group efforts be made more effective so that a wide variety of expertise and information is brought to bear on complex problems? Can members from different work groups realize the importance of sharing their knowledge and talents across group boundaries so that complex problems do not fall between the cracks? Is a systematic and comprehensive change along all these lines possible so that high-quality decisions will lead to effective action, which subsequently will result in high performance and morale? What combination of all these changes will ensure high performance and morale as continual change occurs in the organization's setting?

These questions describe the variety of problems that come up again and again while managing organizations. Naturally, there are differences from one organization to another; there always are some unique circumstances or histories that moderate the extent and variety of these basic questions. However, I wish to emphasize the almost uncanny pattern that has emerged in all the research and consulting I have done in organizations. Very rarely do I find that the formally documented systems *alone* need readjustment for organizational success. Rarely do I find that managers' learning of new skills about complex problems will *by itself* solve the organization's performance and morale problems. I have never encountered a case in which only the culture had lagged behind and an effective "organization" was already in place, with managers applying up-to-date skills. The culture problem *always* has been associated with problems in the organization, the group, and the manager as well.

These general findings really are not that surprising. Even viewing the world as an open system requires that we recognize how every aspect of an organization is interdependent with every other aspect, including its setting. Therefore, a problem in one area automatically creates problems in other areas, just as a change in one category in the model causes secondary and tertiary effects in other categories. Only in the image of the world as a simple machine could one expect to alter one component part without disturbing the functioning of another.

The world as a complex hologram not only includes this interrelated view of the open system but adds an assortment of

unconscious (individual and collective) and nonrational aspects
of human life. Given all this, what is the likelihood that today's
organizations can cope with a new world by adjusting only one
category in the Barriers to Success model? It is very unlikely
indeed. What about the possibility of adjusting most but not all
of the categories shown in Figure 1? That is just as unlikely,
sorry to say. Rather, it seems that all categories have to be considered and acted upon in all cases. This is the new rule of organizational change, not the exception. Management development, organizational design, and culture change, all with an
enlightened view of the world and all its stakeholders, are necessary to revitalize our organizations. Otherwise, the extent and
variety of complex problems will continue to impose troublesome barriers to organizational success.

Consider the unparalleled challenge facing AT&T as its
strategic shift must be supported by fundamental changes in all
the other categories in the Barriers to Success model.

The AT&T example clearly demonstrates the need for a
company to examine its existing culture in depth and to acknowledge the reasons for revolutionary change, if changes must be
made. As AT&T learned from its earlier attempt to sell specialized services, change cannot be implemented merely by sending
people to school. Nor can it be made by hiring new staff, by acquiring new businesses, by changing the name of the company,
or by redefining its business. Even exhortations by the chief
executive to operate differently will not succeed unless they are
backed up by a changed structure, new role models, new incentive systems, and new rewards and punishments built into operations ["Corporate Culture," 1980, p. 151].

This need for a multiple—if not a fully integrated—approach to
AT&T's organizational success was reported several years *before*
AT&T was deregulated and split apart. The handwriting was already on the wall. In just a few years, we will know if AT&T
was able to overcome its barriers to success.

Conclusion

The Barriers to Success model focuses attention on some
very different types of variables that determine organizational

success. These types include external contextual factors (the setting and its stakeholders) and internal individual aspects (assumptions and psyches) that cannot be controlled but can be monitored and understood.

Other types of variables include leverage points that are of the organization (strategy-structure and reward system), the manager (management skills and problem management), and the group (decision making and action taking). While culture is an intangible, below-the-surface aspect of organizational life, it, too, has a leverage point and can be managed directly.

The complex interrelationships among all these categories and variables constitute the theory behind the five tracks. As long as the Barriers to Success model continues to capture the nature of problems that confront today's organizations, it is essential to use this model to guide efforts at organizational success. With further experience and research, this model may become more detailed and elaborate; but when it no longer describes new problems and methods of change, it will be time for an altogether new model. In the meantime, however, we will use what we have and keep the conversation going.

CHAPTER THREE

Practice
Behind the
Five Tracks

Planned change is a method which employs social technology to solve the problems of society. The method encompasses the application of systematic and appropriate knowledge to human affairs for the purpose of creating intelligent action and choices. Planned change aims to relate to the basic disciplines of the behavioral sciences as engineering does to the physical sciences or as medicine does to the biological disciplines. Thus, planned change can be viewed as a crucial link between theory and practice, between knowledge and action. It plays this role by converting variables from the basic disciplines into strategic instrumentation and programs.

—Bennis, 1966, p. 81

Practice is a deliberate attempt to influence a person or situation, to intervene in the course of natural events. The goal of practice is to alter outcomes, to accomplish something—such as organizational success—that will not occur on its own. Practice is the alternative to evolution and chance. Indeed, practice is more similar to revolution when all the tangible and intangible aspects of the organization are purposefully altered in order to break from the past.

Just as theory is useless without practice, practice is aimless without theory. The theory behind the five tracks pinpoints which barriers block performance and morale and thus serves to focus attention on what needs to be altered. Focus by itself, however, is not enough; the practice behind the five tracks must also specify *how* all identified barriers can be transformed into channels for success.

Furthermore, any practice that attempts to influence people and situations will not be automatically effective. Rather, practice must be guided by a well-conceived plan of action—a program of planned change—that is implemented skillfully and carefully. In order to revitalize an organization, such a program must take into account everything known about introducing and managing change in organizations (the *how*) as well as the particular leverage points that should be altered (the *focus*). Ideally, a change program also specifies the sequence of stages by which managers and consultants can engage in the practice of organizational success.

The Five Stages of Planned Change

Figure 2 shows the five stages of planned change that constitute the practice behind the five tracks: (1) initiating the program, (2) diagnosing the problems, (3) scheduling the tracks, (4) implementing the tracks, and (5) evaluating the results. To be successful, all integrated programs for improving organizations must devote sufficient time and effort to complete each stage. Movement from one stage to the next, shown by the single arrows, should not take place until all the criteria for the earlier stages are satisfied. Otherwise, any glossed-over stages will come back to haunt the organization. Also, continual recycling through all five stages, without success, will eventually wear the organization down. It is desirable, therefore, to halt the entire change program until a particular stage can be conducted properly; or, if it seems that the nec-

Figure 2. The Five Stages of Planned Change.

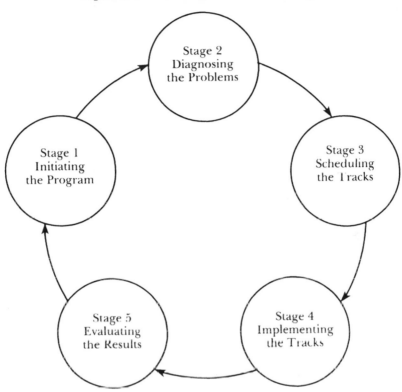

essary commitment and learning are unlikely to develop, the entire program should be terminated. There is simply no reason for managers and consultants to go through a long and difficult process if success is not possible.

The first stage, initiating the program, begins when the organization realizes that its old ways of addressing problems are no longer effective. At this point, the managers contact external consultants who can provide a fresh approach. If both the managers and consultants believe that there is sufficient basis for proceeding—including sincerity, commitment, resources, and talent—the sequence of action continues. The second stage, diagnosing the organization's problems, is ideally performed by the consultants, independent of the managers' previous assessments. It is best for the consultants to interview a representative sample of members throughout the organization to discover the full extent and variety of problems. The third stage, scheduling the tracks, first selects the particular techniques that will make up each of the five tracks. These techniques are chosen (or developed) to address the specific problems that were identified during the earlier diagnosis. The third stage concludes as the five tracks are scheduled for implementation—in a planned sequence of activity. This sequence is what makes the five tracks a completely integrated program. The fourth stage implements the tracks as planned, although numerous adjustments take place as more is learned about the organization and its capacity to change. The fifth stage evaluates what results have occurred due to the program. Based on various evaluations, additional activities may be scheduled and implemented for one or more tracks, and the cycle of planned change continues.

This chapter describes planned change as a collaborative effort among managers, members, and external consultants; this is the best way I know to guarantee the success of the whole program. In many cases, however, top managers may prefer to practice the five tracks on their own, just as they ordinarily make decisions and take .action. Every top manager will have to make up his own mind on this issue. But I do caution managers not to conduct single-handedly those aspects of the program that are clearly beyond their skills and experiences. It is to be hoped that managers can recognize their limitations.

For example, it helps to have external consultants for collecting sensitive information about management and organizational problems, surfacing cultural norms, exposing outdated assumptions, confronting the organization's troublemakers, and helping the managers hear honest feedback about their team's functioning. Therefore, the diagnostic stage—and major portions of the culture, management skills, and team-building tracks—should be guided by consultants. The strategy-structure and the reward system tracks can be conducted primarily by the managers, although even here consultants can help foster a more participative approach than managers by themselves tend to utilize.

As a result of this chapter, the reader should appreciate the essential difference between theory and practice. Theory can be studied and learned in a classroom and by reading the major textbooks in the field. Practice can be learned only by doing, by being actively involved in the process of change itself, and by taking responsibility for what happens. The latter approach to learning and change is exemplified by the Synthetic Fuels Division (SFD) of Westinghouse Electric Corporation—a division that took part in an integrated program of change via the five tracks. Not surprisingly, given the holographic nature of the world, SFD engaged in planned change under conditions of dynamic complexity and shifting stakeholders. As each of the five stages of planned change is presented below, a relevant segment of the SFD story will be told. Similarly, at the end of each subsequent chapter on the five tracks, we will again return to a portion of the SFD story. This will illustrate how the theory behind the five tracks is put into practice.

Initiating the Program

The program of five tracks can be initiated only after one or more members of the organization realize that something is very wrong and that they do not know what else to do. They may have tried a number of approaches or solutions in the past, but the problem that confronts them just has not gone away. In many cases, top managers may have discussed the problem with their advisers, but they all have run out of quick-fix alternatives. It is at this point that one or more managers suggest that outside help is needed to look at the situation in a new light.

It is important to appreciate the deeper reasons why an organization might seek outside help. The best possible case is when the organization is sincerely committed to change, is clear about the need for an integrated program, and then contacts consultants who share this view. The worst possible case is an organization that feels the need to go outside for help but really does not trust outsiders, is not convinced that a problem really exists, or feels pressured by certain inside groups to do something about the problem—if only as appeasement. In some of these worst possible cases, the consultant is contacted for political reasons: to help the top managers prove that their approach has been right all along. In other cases, between the best and the worst, the managers have decided what the problem is and have contacted consultants to solve it for them, using the consultants' proven methods in this area. In this in-between case, at least the managers are sincere, even if they are unfamiliar with the change process and the need for an independent diagnosis.

Generally, one or two key managers take the initiative to search for outside help. These key managers should be aware that a team of consultants not only has a broader range of talent than any one consultant but also provides the manpower necessary to work with a large organization. Further, these key managers also play a pivotal role during the remaining stages of planned change: They are the chief advocates of the program and those who feel a special responsibility for its success. Implementation, for example, is helped immensely if these key managers also happen to be the senior executives of the firm. Having the power of the hierarchy behind the change program—from beginning to end—helps ensure a successful outcome.

The consultants who are contacted should be most interested to learn if the organization is ready for change. While managers can voice their commitment, the real test is subsequent action. At best, the consultants attempt to infer from several indicators the existence of true commitment. For example, do the managers openly acknowledge their role in the creation of the problem? Do they consider alternative perspectives and approaches? Do they seem receptive to a full diagnosis by the consultants? Do they realize the extensive and involving nature of the program? Or do they hope to find another quick fix? If the consultants do not believe that sufficient commitment exists for an integrated program of change or that it is likely to be generated, I recommend sharing this with the top management group as the primary reason for terminating the project. Nobody needs a failure experience.

If there appears to be sufficient basis for continuing, the consultants meet with more managers (including the top management group) to share objectives and expectations more widely. Much like the formation of an interpersonal relationship, the consultants and the organization see if there appears to be a fit. If this rapport does not develop, it may be due to an interpersonal quirk or to a true difference in style. Regardless, I have not heard or read of a successful case of change in which the client and consultant did not "hit it off." A difficult process of change must be rooted in a firm foundation of trust, liking, and mutual respect.

The SFD story illustrates how a change program is initiated, often amidst dynamic complexity and great uncertainty. Rarely do consultants and managers come into partnership under very stable and secure conditions. It seems that the organization has to be *hurting* before the call for a new approach will be sounded and accepted.

In 1980, Westinghouse Electric Corporation formed the Synthetic Fuels Division (SFD). A coal gasification technology, which began in 1972 within an R&D group, had made sufficient technical progress to justify efforts toward commercialization and, hence, divisional status. By 1982, however, it was evident to SFD's top management that the transition from technology developer to commercial division was lagging. It seemed that the strategic shift was being held back by a culture that preferred the more comfortable life of a funded R&D group to the unfamiliar, riskier life of a profit center.

SFD's transition was accented by three impending uncertainties: (1) Would SFD's funding from the federal government continue? It seemed that the energy crisis that had stimulated the government to invest in alternative energy sources was no longer a crisis. Oil prices had fallen, thereby decreasing the comparative advantage of synthetic fuels. The apparent oil glut also seemed to demotivate the earlier rush to develop alternative fuel sources. (2) Would the demonstration project for SFD's technology, on which its entire commercial effort was based, be successful? There were still a number of design problems that had to be solved before such a scaled-up version of SFD's pilot plant could be demonstrated. (3) Would corporate Westinghouse commit the required funds for the demonstration project? The core of SFD's technology is based on process or chemical engineering capability, not electrical, mechanical, or nuclear. The latter is mainstream Westinghouse; the former is not.

In spite of, yet because of, these difficult times, the top managers knew that they had a serious internal problem. If they could not pull the division's efforts and talents together, it was unlikely that SFD could tackle the obstacles and challenges that lay before it. The top managers decided that they needed some outside expertise to solve their culture problem. They did not know what else to do.

In September 1982, Tom Kelley, manager of personnel relations, invited me to present my methods for culture change to the top management staff of SFD, including the general manager, Bill Peace. At our meeting, the staff first reviewed SFD's ten-year history and concluded by highlighting the need for a culture change. While I appreciated this view of the situation, I emphasized that I would have to conduct my own diagnosis.

I then outlined my approach to consultation: to make sure the division solves the "right" problem rather than the "wrong" problem. If, after a systematic diagnosis, an outdated culture proved to be the only problem, then a culture change project could be initiated. Alternatively, as is most often the case, the diagnostic results might indicate additional problems besides culture that needed attention. This is why the program of five tracks is the rule rather than the exception for organizational success.

Top management agreed that the interviews were to be scheduled and conducted during November. I and one or more of my associates would conduct the interviews. After the results from these interviews became available, the top managers and the team of consultants would jointly decide whether the program should continue and, if so, what the next steps would be.

While the top management group felt that the problem was already defined as a culture problem prior to this initial meeting, they now seemed to appreciate the reasons for an independent assessment. I also sensed minimal defensiveness on the part of the managers. They were very frank about their troubles and wanted to get to the heart of the problem. The meeting ended on a very positive note.

Diagnosing the Problems

This phase is very much guided by the consultants, who have to be sure that the diagnosis is based on their assessments independent of the initial reasons that brought them into the organization. The consultants, with the aid of the managers, develop a plan to identify the organization's problems. In most cases, this is accomplished by having the consultants interview members throughout the organization. The objective is to sample each level in the hierarchy—and each division and department—so that a representative view of the organization is obtainable. I always insist on interviewing all persons in the top management group simply because their views, and especially their commitment to change, are so critical to the program. If there are as many as 5,000 members in a division or organization, interviewing approximately 100 members should provide enough information to help define the organization's problems. For smaller organizations or divisions, forty to sixty interviews should be sufficient.

Each one-on-one interview with a member begins with the consultant briefly reviewing the background and expectations of the meeting. He outlines the specific questions he will be asking and indicates what will be done with the information he collects. The consultant takes the time to explain what a change program is like and responds to any questions the interviewee may have. The consultant emphasizes that he cannot do his job if he does not find out what is really going on in the organization.

The consultant then should express his awareness of the doubts the interviewee must be having about their meeting. For example, the consultant may suggest that it is quite natural for the interviewee to wonder if the consultant is working only for top management, to question whether the consultant can really learn about the unique problems of this organization, to worry about how the information will be reported to top management, to feel that nothing of real significance will come from the program—as has been the case, perhaps, with other change efforts. Often, by explicitly voicing what the interviewee must be feeling, the consultant gives the interviewee the confidence to reveal the organization's problems. The interviewee begins to feel, "If this guy senses what I'm concerned about, he must have done this many times before and must know what he is doing. I'll give it a try."

Once all the interviews have been conducted, the consultants organize the variety of problems they have discovered by sorting these onto the Barriers to Success model (discussed in Chapter Two). This helps systematize their findings according to the full range of individual and organizational barriers. Using the model helps ensure that no category is overlooked or ignored. Thus, a holographic view is taken.

The consultants then prepare a report, which is presented first to the top managers. Although these top managers may have accepted the fact that their problems required outside help, they may not have sensed the extent and seriousness of these problems. Often surprise and shock follow the presentation of the report, and much more discussion is needed before the top managers can move forward. There may even be strong defensive reactions, which serve to deny or minimize what the consultants have reported. Some of this defensiveness is quite natural, since the managers are feeling somewhat guilty for being a part of the identified problems. If their egos are bruised, it will take some time for them to move past the defensive stage and on to the acceptance phase. This can take a few days or even a few months. The consultants can help by articulating these normal human reactions and by indicating how managers in other organizations have struggled with these same feelings. Sometimes these open discussions about hurt egos take the incredible burden off the top managers, who have come to see themselves as all knowing, all powerful, and, therefore, all responsible for anything and everything that happens to their organization. As their human nature is affirmed, it becomes easier to get on with addressing the organization's problems.

When the top managers accept the general diagnosis provided by the consultants, it then becomes desirable to share these findings with the entire membership. Naturally, it takes conviction for the top managers to be willing to share the diagnosis with others. But this willingness is critical for demonstrating commitment to the membership. The act of top managers acknowledging problems to themselves and to others, while painful, is an important event in the life of an organization.

The membership can be made aware of the consultants' diagnostic report either by memo, with the full report attached, or in employee meetings, in which everyone can hear and discuss the results together. At times, it may not be feasible to reach everyone in person, particularly in a very large organization. However, active participation, including the opportunity to question and learn from the consultants directly, is generally the most effective approach. A written report, no matter how well conceived and written, is simply not as rich and engaging as a face-to-face conversation. While I recognize the real-world constraints of time and budget, I have to emphasize the importance of participation—the more the better. I have yet to encounter a situation in which too much participation was encouraged during a change effort.

As planned, SFD's problems were diagnosed in November 1982. Because of dynamic complexity and the strategic shift from a technology developer to a commercial division, culture was not the only barrier holding the organization back. As is typical, a great variety of problems—barriers to success—were identified.

A representative sample of employees across all departments and levels in the division was interviewed by myself and my associate, Mary Jane Saxton. During these interviews, we explored (1) employee perceptions of SFD's problems, and (2) whether there was sufficient commitment in the division to undergo a change program.

By early December 1982, forty-one interviews had been conducted, representing the 217 employees in the division. As agreed, the consultants presented the results to the top manage-ment group. We first listed the "driving forces" that would en-courage and support change. Quite consistently, the interviews revealed that employees want to work, to contribute, and to enjoy what they do. There was an overwhelming dedication and commitment to the technology. We heard over and over again: "It is the best technology in the world!"

The interviews also revealed, however, significant "re-straining forces" that were holding the division back. Em-ployees felt blocked, frustrated, and hopeless. Again and again it was said: "The system is in the way. Management is not com-mitted." Numerous barriers to success were expressed repeat-edly. Nevertheless, every scheduled interview took place on time. Many employees even arrived early. While they were very upset by "what had been going on for years," they still cared enough to let the consultants learn about their problems.

Through vivid descriptions and stories, we learned how SFD had allowed itself to fall into a rut. During an extended period of transition, it seemed that management had stopped challenging, communicating with, and caring for the employees. This became manifested in an apathetic performance appraisal system. Unofficially, groups assumed some of the leadership role that had been abdicated and built strong protective bar-riers around themselves. Cliques, not work-oriented teams, now called the shots: when to work, how hard to work, when to duplicate work, when to share information with other groups, whether to communicate with management, whether to trust management, and what stories to tell any newcomers in order to teach them the ropes. This evolution was not purposeful, nor was it supported by every manager and employee. Nonetheless, such bad habits had formed and gradually had become the norm.

The culture problem was thus more complex than the top managers had thought: More than culture had to be changed in order to solve the division's problems. In fact, SFD's problems were easily sorted onto the Barriers to Success model. There was a significant problem in every category. Consequently, the consultants recommended that the complete program of five tracks be implemented—to transform SFD's many barriers into channels for success. In addition, the consultants asked for the freedom to conduct whatever related activities were needed to move the program along.

Although top management was a bit surprised by the ex-tent and variety of the division's problems and the way in which these problems had formed, they seemed to accept this diagno-sis. Of greatest concern to the general manager and his staff were the repeated statements in the interviews that top management did not recognize these problems. In fact, quite a few interviewees expected that top management would screen the results and that only the positives would be reported back to the whole division. After a somber discussion, the top managers agreed that if they did not address these problems now it would be impossible to gain the support of the employees in the future. They decided to proceed with the recommended program of five tracks.

To test top management's apparent commitment to the program, I drafted my ideal conception of the memorandum that should be sent from the general manager to the whole division; this memorandum should acknowledge the severity of the problems that had been uncovered, the specific nature of the problems, and management's commitment to seeing the entire program to its completion. If the top managers could not admit to these problems in this way, it was unlikely that the program would have their full support and commitment.

These managers not only passed the test but went beyond it. This gave me a strong indication that this change program would be successful. Bill Peace strengthened the idealized memorandum I had prepared. First, the memo was revised to state that every employee of the division would be given the opportunity to hear the full diagnostic report during the next two weeks, directly from the consultants. Second, adding on a separate paragraph, Peace stated that this change program would take priority over all other improvement programs now under way. The new memo was signed by the general manager and a copy was sent to all SFD employees.

When all the departments and work groups in SFD met separately to learn the diagnostic results, they were surprised to hear the "truth" straight out, with no attempt to hide the problems and emotions that had been expressed during the interviews. This gave them the distinct feeling that something different was going to happen with this change program in comparison with the many quick fixes they had experienced in the past.

The consultants felt that the required level of commitment to embark on the full program was present for both top management and the members. But it was also clear that the road to success would not be easy.

Scheduling the Tracks

This stage involves (1) selecting the techniques (methods for bringing about change) that will make up each of the five tracks to address the specific problems identified during the diagnostic stage, and (2) scheduling the five tracks into a timed sequence of activity in order to promote effective learning and change. Once a plan for action is formalized in this stage, managers, members, and consultants will work together to implement it in the following stage.

What makes each application of the five tracks different is the particular techniques used in each track. Just as the diagnosis varies, so does the choice of technique to address each identified problem. While Chapters Four through Eight discuss the techniques used most frequently in each track to manage today's dynamic complexity, there are still a great number of other techniques to tackle each unique problem. For example, in some cases the management skills track will include material on leadership styles, conflict-handling modes, and ways to minimize defensive communication. In other cases in which the managers have already acquired these skills, management training moves directly to teaching assumptional analysis and methods for managing complex problems. Clearly, the consultants and the managers should be aware of the diversity of techniques that exist (or can be constructed) so that they can choose the ones that best fit the problems in their organization. (See Huse, 1980, and Beer, 1980, for the variety of techniques that have been developed and used for planned change.)

The one thing that most distinguishes the five tracks from the quick fix is the integrated nature of the program. The five tracks and their host of techniques are not scheduled in a random order, nor is a shotgun approach used (in which all tracks are implemented haphazardly or indiscriminately). The guiding principles in organizing and sequencing the five tracks include the capacity of members and their organization to change, what change is easiest and best to accomplish early, and what change should be left to occur later.

The culture track is the ideal place to start the program, for several reasons. It is enlightening to openly discuss what previously was seldom written down or mentioned in any conversation. Members enjoy—even laugh at—the revelations that occur as dysfunctional cultural norms are brought to everyone's attention. It is also much easier to blame norms than to blame oneself or other people. As long as members take responsibility for change, it does not really matter if blaming norms takes some of the pressure off their egos. Of prime significance, however, is that without an initial culture change, it is unlikely that the other four tracks can be successful. In many cases, cultural norms pressure members to (1) keep information to themselves, (2) distrust managers at the next highest level, (3) disbelieve that anything will really change, and (4) discourage any new behaviors without question. It would be most difficult to teach managers and members new skills if these attitudes and beliefs guided everyone's motivation to learn.

After the culture track has begun and made some progress, the management skills track can start. In most cases, the managers have contributed substantially to the organization's problems, even if unintentionally. The managers usually have not kept up with the changed setting and its new types of problems. They often have not developed the skills necessary to manage in an altogether different kind of world. If the managers can acquire some of these new skills and bring them back into the work place, everyone will sense additional feelings of success with the program.

As the culture track and the management skills track are providing some early successes, the next effort lies in transferring these learnings to the decision making and action taking of intact work groups. The team-building track brings managers and their subordinates together so that they can approach their problems more effectively—with a more functional culture and with some new skills for managing complex problems. As the culture opens up everyone's minds as well as their hearts, work groups can examine, maybe for the first time, the particular barriers that have held them back in the past. Through various feedback sessions, the work groups become more effective teams.

Eventually it becomes time for the membership to take on one of the most difficult problems facing any organization in a dynamic and complex setting: aligning its formally documented systems. One might think that the mission of the firm should have been the first topic addressed. Why should the organization proceed with culture changes, changes in management skills, and improvements in team efforts before the new directions are articulated and formalized? Isn't it logical to first know the directions before the rest of the system is put in place? Yes, that is logical. But there are other things operating in a complex organization besides logic. If we understand cultures, assumptions, and psyches—the holographic view of the world—we recognize that it makes little sense to plan the future directions of the firm if members do not trust one another and will not share important information with one another, expose their tried-and-true assumptions, or commit to the new directions anyway because the culture will not allow it. Not until there is widespread trust will the membership be able to have a meaningful discussion about things as important and close to home as strategy, structure, and reward systems.

Rather than wait for each track to achieve its objective, some tracks can be conducted while other tracks are still in progress. For example, as long as some progress has been made in developing a supportive and open culture, managers can begin the management skills track. Besides, as new skills are learned, the culture track will be facilitated by the use of effective leadership styles. Similarly, the team-building track can start when the culture and management skills tracks have made sufficient progress, even if there is still more room for improvement. However, it will be difficult to start the strategy-structure track if the organization has not moved through most of the preceding tracks; the old culture, skills, and cliques will serve to reinforce the security offered by the old structure. Likewise, the reward system track should not begin unless the new directions of the firm and the corresponding structures are in place.

One difficult question is always asked: "How long will the whole program take?" And it is asked repeatedly, not just once. My response is: "I can't say exactly; I can only suggest some rough guidelines from my prior experience." These guidelines consider the size and age of the organization, the complexity of the problems that were uncovered, the severity of the problems, the time available for conducting the five tracks, and the desire on the part of both managers and all members to learn and change. Since the organization cannot shut down its operations just to engage in a change program, the five tracks have to be conducted as other work gets done—even during crises and peak seasons.

In general, one can expect most change programs to take anywhere from six months to five years. Less than six months might work for a small division, in which the formally documented systems need only a fine tuning. However, a program taking more than five years might be necessary for a very large, old organization involving major breaks from the past in every way. If the program were to take more than ten years, I would assume that there was insufficient or intermittent commitment over this period, which prevented the momentum for change to prevail.

At SFD, the consultants selected a variety of techniques to make up each of the five tracks. Once the composition of the five tracks was determined, the consultants had to schedule them, in sequence, prior to implementation. Figure 3 shows

Figure 3. Scheduling the Five Tracks.

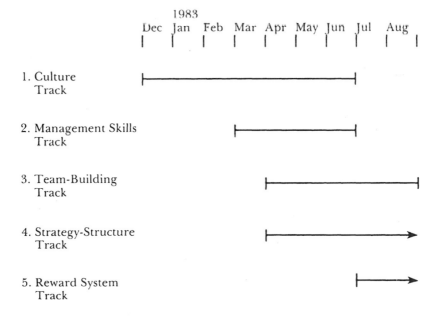

the actual nine-month schedule presented to SFD's top management group.

Based on their diagnosis, the consultants selected specific techniques that would be used in each track. Briefly, the culture track would include a survey instrument—the Kilmann-Saxton Culture-Gap Survey—to find the several cultural norms that were holding the division back. This survey would help uncover the culture-gaps in each group and department in the division. The management skills track would include material on leadership style, conflict-handling style, communication style, motivation style, and personality types. Because the managers were formally trained in technical areas, they were somewhat deficient regarding basic on-the-job social and behavioral skills. It was felt that this human relations material had to be learned before the more difficult methods of problem management and assumptional analysis could be acquired.

The team-building track would begin by having one-on-one sessions with the identified troublemakers, of whom there were several (as is usually the case). Feedback sessions between the managers and their work groups would be held to improve two-way communication, information sharing, and, ultimately, decision making and action taking. The strategy-structure track would use a survey-based, computer-assisted technique—the MAPS Design Technology—to modify SFD's structure to better fit with its new strategic mission. Finally, the reward system track would use a participative process to adjust the mandated system of corporate Westinghouse; the unique circumstances of SFD would be reflected in the way employees were evaluated, rewarded, and counseled.

The consultants anticipated that the culture track would require several months of work before the management skills track could begin. The diagnosis had revealed large culture-gaps: Many norms seemed to favor the objectives and ways of the old R&D group rather than the cost-efficient and customer-oriented strategy of the new division. However, it was expected that once the culture began to shift and the managers had enhanced their human relations skills, both the team-building track and the strategy-structure track could be started simultaneously. The difficult issue of strategy was already decided, so efforts could focus directly on structure. After a few months for fine tuning the structures, the reward system could be designed and implemented. By this time, the culture and management skills tracks should have been finished, but they could be continued if needed.

Implementing the Tracks

It is one thing to plan and schedule the entire program of five tracks, but it is quite another to adjust and modify the program as it is implemented. Needless to say, the plan *never* takes place exactly as intended. There are always surprises. Human nature and human systems, being what they are, do not lend themselves to a predictable path. Besides, if people feel that they are being programmed in any way, it is not unlike them to purposely do something illogical, irrational, or unexpected just to show how free and independent they really are. Implementing the five tracks is just another example of dynamic complexity.

The key issue during implementation, therefore, is flexibility. It is important not to get too locked into any plan; this makes it very difficult to back off and change to a new one. The schedule of five tracks is helpful as a starting point, since without it there would be confusion and misguided efforts. As the schedule is implemented, however, the consultants must look for cues, take suggestions, and, in short, adapt.

Special requests are made for counseling sessions, feedback sessions for staff meetings, additional culture sessions, more management skills training, and so forth. In each case, the consultants and the managers must consider the request and respond according to their objectives and their sense of what will work. Sometimes requests are turned down, but the reasons are always presented and discussed. At other times, requests are acted upon—but in a fashion different from that first suggested. Often, it is the consultants themselves who initiate additional activity, adjusting to what they perceive is needed—to nudge this person or that group or to support any effort that turned out to be more difficult than first thought.

A shared expectation, which should develop as the program is initiated, is that the consultants have the freedom to schedule whatever activities are necessary to move the change effort forward. I have come across a number of organizations that initially failed to appreciate the importance of this option. I remember a few cases in which the managers expected the consultants to know exactly what activities would take place and when. This is reminiscent of the simple machine model of the world. In contrast, with a holographic view of the world, members and groups in the organization constitute *internal* stakeholders whose needs and demands are constantly changing; this perspective suggests why the implementation stage requires constant monitoring and flexible adjusting. Today's organization also needs the same approach relative to its *external* stakeholders. The former is merely a microcosm of the latter.

The most enjoyable part of the implementation stage is seeing changes and improvements take hold. Initially, everyone is a little leery of what to expect and unsure of whether the organization has the ability to change. As early successes are won, however, confidence develops, which inspires an even greater effort at improvement. This is not to suggest that the road is smooth and without obstacles; on a week-by-week basis, some things get a lot worse before they get better. In some cases, the organization expects the change to develop quickly and with little pain, regardless of what the managers or consultants have stated. When an event takes place that seems to reinforce the old ways or attitudes of the past, it is easy to be discouraged and feel that nothing has changed. If, instead of examining week-by-week fluctuations, one looks at month-by-month trends, the process shows a more definite pattern of improvement.

These fluctuations in perceived accomplishments and moods illustrate the importance of setting realistic expectations in the beginning and making sure that either a strong desire or an impatience for change does not raise member expectations to unattainable levels. Disappointment and frustration result when these expectations are out of line with reality, which subsequently affects both the individual's and the organization's confidence to continue. The managers and consultants have to nurture expectations very carefully during implementation.

After a number of months go by, it becomes more and more apparent that the membership has internalized the overt behaviors that have been observed. Each person does not have to apply new skills and enact new cultural norms in a conscious and deliberate manner; rather, the new ways are enacted quite automatically. The new skills and behaviors become more natural and easier. At a certain point (and this is very difficult to specify in advance), the "hump" is crossed and the old gives way to the new. The best way I can describe this transition is to say that the members and the managers could not return to the old ways even if they tried because the new ways are so obviously better and more useful for their personal satisfaction and for accomplishing the organization's mission. Strangely, it is even hard for these members to recall how different things were just six months or a few years ago. The past is really put aside in their behaviors, attitudes, and memories.

The implementation stage is complete when the consultants and managers both believe the organization can manage its problems on its own. During the last few months of implementation, the consultants become less involved in scheduling and implementing activities; the managers and the members now decide on their own what team building or skills training is needed and then proceed to fill the gap—sometimes with outside help, sometimes not. The organization thus moves into "independence." The membership has solved, and can continue to solve, the problems for which the program was initiated in the beginning.

In order to illustrate how the various tracks begin, continue, end, are reinstated, and all blend together, the SFD story is continued below in detail: This should help convey the evolving nature of an integrated program and the flexible, adaptive way in which it is implemented.

The five-track program for SFD, although carefully worked out, was altered by the second week of its contact with the managers. They were so eager to get started that they did not want to wait until late February or March to begin the management skills track. The consultants were asked if the first workshop for this track could begin by late January. Since our time permitted this and since we did not want to discourage this sort of enthusiasm, we agreed. The managers also wanted us to move up the strategy-structure track so that the strategic directions of SFD and the formally documented systems could be aligned before team building began. In this case, however, we recommended sticking to the schedule, since we felt that the openness, trust, and management skills necessary for undergoing such a vital decision process were not yet present. The managers seemed to appreciate this view, but it was clear that they were anxious to get started.

The culture track began in December 1982, when each member was asked to respond to the Kilmann-Saxton Culture-Gap Survey. The survey has twenty-eight norm pairs that sort into four types of culture-gaps (the difference between actual and desired norms): Task Support (sharing information and helping other groups), Task Innovation (being creative and doing new things), Social Relationships (socializing with one's work group), and Personal Freedom (exercising discretion). A total of 177 members in SFD responded (82 percent). The largest average gaps were for Task Support (4.5 out of a possible 7.0) and Task Innovation (3.5). The smallest average gaps were for Social Relationships (1.7) and Personal Freedom (0.5).

This culture-gap pattern was identical in every group and department in SFD, although the magnitude of the gaps varied from group to group. Essentially, there was a division-wide culture that was seen as blocking information sharing, group support, and efficiency in getting the day-to-day work done. Further, there was inadequate emphasis on innovation and creativity, which were needed for success in the future. However, members felt that they had appropriate opportunities to develop relationships on the job and the appropriate freedom to pursue their own interests.

Most of the change program in January 1983 was devoted to culture sessions for the approximately twenty work groups in SFD, with the managers meeting separately to ensure an open dialogue. Using the culture-gap results as background material, members were asked to develop a list of the specific norms that most stood in the way of their efforts. Next, they listed what the new norms should be. Not surprisingly, these lists were further detailed elaborations of the norms in Task Support and Task Innovation. Lastly, an action plan was developed by each group so that the new norms, not the old norms, guided member behavior. While some groups complained that the managers had to change first before any significant culture change could proceed, I did not accept such finger pointing. Rather, each group was to control its own destiny. If every group took this posture—that it would meet the other halfway—a successful change was likely.

At the end of January, the first two-day management skills workshop was held. All thirty-eight managers received basic behavioral science material on interpersonal, leadership, and small-group behavior. While the managers had received

some of this material before as part of various training programs, they had never discussed this material as a management
group with a collective commitment to transfer the learnings
back to the job. Moreover, the managers adopted several "buzz
words" and "trigger phrases" to remind one another of key
learnings after this workshop concluded.

In early February, I met one-on-one with a half dozen
identified troublemakers. During the interviews, certain names
kept coming up again and again—managers who, because of
their styles, were creating havoc for others. Some of these managers were ruling through fear and intimidation and by playing
favorites among the members. I summarized these perceptions
for each troublemaker, and we then discussed how these perceptions might have formed. Each session concluded with my
emphasizing that such disruptive behavior must stop. In each
case, I scheduled a follow-up meeting to keep a close watch on
these individuals.

Later in February, the consultants met a second time
with the twenty-plus groups in the culture track. Special attention was devoted to the various obstacles that attempted to
keep things the same. Additional guidelines and action plans
were developed to address several of these new barriers. Several
times we gave advice on how employees might approach their
managers with sticky problems—problems that never would
have been raised before.

In early March, managers began to request that the consultants gather specific feedback from their groups on how
things could be improved. The team-building track started quite
naturally. At least a dozen managers were willing to risk candid
feedback. After we met with each group, agreed-upon information was shared with the manager, who then met with his
group to discuss how these problems could be approached.
Eventually, it was no longer necessary for us to be present, since
the barriers were broken down. Managers could meet with their
groups and have open discussions about problems, group norms,
thorny issues, and previous "sore spots." The atmosphere became more one of trust and problem solving than of fear and
avoidance.

At this point, mid-March, an interesting series of events
unfolded. It was decided informally that the cafeteria would be
an ideal spot in which to test the new culture and the new spirit
of collaboration. Rather than sitting in work groups and cliques
as they had always done in the past, the members followed a
new norm: "Sit and eat in mixed groups. Go out of your way to
sit with someone new."

Within a few days, the seating arrangements in the cafeteria changed dramatically. The work groups and cliques split up. As people entered the cafeteria, the conversation among those already seated was: "I wonder where Joe will sit today. Look where he is going. I don't believe it. He is going to sit next to that manager!" The cafeteria became a setting for sharing ideas, information, and, of course, gossip. But it was an important beginning. One story went around that Sam sat with Frank, a member from another group, and learned more in one hour about what Frank's group was doing, its objectives, and its problems than he had in the whole previous year.

Or the time that a meeting was held up because Sally from another group had not arrived yet; before the change program, the group would have gone ahead and made a decision without her. Or the time that one group applauded another group's presentation because it included a strong statement about the competence and talent of the whole division. Or when the technicians were so enthusiastic about the prospects for change that they spent a whole weekend developing a work improvement plan on their own time. These and many other stories began taking the place of the stories about the division's problems.

At the end of March, all managers attended the second two-day management skills workshop. Before the main activities began, we asked the managers to discuss (1) the changes they had witnessed thus far, (2) what it felt like to go through this change program, and (3) what else we could do to help. The most significant response came from the second item: "This change program is painful!" The managers were under much pressure—from the consultants, from top management, from subordinates, from one another, and from their own desires to change. No one had expected to work so hard at being an effective manager and an agent of change. Some managers even lost sleep over it. "Did I use the right management style in the meeting today? Did I make my subordinates defensive again? How can I encourage them to trust me more with their problems and concerns?" It was becoming evident to all the managers why such an intense commitment to this change program was essential. Without this pressure and commitment, it would be so easy to return to the past.

The next part of the workshop was spent on reviewing the problem management process: sensing problems, defining problems, deriving solutions, implementing solutions, and evaluating outcomes. Also included was the method of "assumptional analysis," an elaborate technique that uncovers the underlying assumptions of any policy, plan, or decision. The managers were then given an eight-hour simulation of assumptional analysis applied to a strategic decision problem.

Most of April 1983 was spent collecting information for the strategy-structure track. In another management workshop, the strategic plan of the division was distributed to all managers. This plan had been developed over a two-year period by the top management staff. It described the background and business environment of the division, strategic conclusions, and possible strategies. Based on this document, the managers were asked to list the specific objectives that would have to be accomplished to achieve these strategies (objectives dictionary), and the specific tasks that would have to be performed in order to accomplish the objectives (task dictionary). Each manager was asked to review the first draft of these dictionaries with his group in the following weeks. Thereby, all employees were invited to add, delete or modify any objective or task.

In May, the finalized objectives and task dictionaries were formed into two questionnaires. Each member was asked to indicate (1) how much he could contribute to each listed objective, and (2) how much he should be involved in each listed task. This information was then prepared for the MAPS computer program—a technique used to discover the best structure for a firm's strategy.

Also in May, the first interteam workshop was held for several groups that had experienced considerable conflict concerning their respective work domains. The prior tracks had made sufficient progress for each group to share openly (1) their perceptions of the other groups' responsibilities, (2) the "gut image" they had of the other groups, and (3) their expectations of how the other groups saw them. The discussion that followed each group's presentation was enlightening and productive. Several participants in this interteam workshop commented: "Finally the different groups are talking directly with one another about the real problems. This would never have happened six months ago." And it had not. Following this one-day workshop, the groups met again—without the consultants— to continue their efforts to seek understanding and agreement about their respective jobs.

In early June, the third two-day management skills workshop was held for all the managers. Now it was time for the managers to apply their learnings to their most pressing and critical problem: developing a strategic survival plan. A number of recent developments had begun to threaten the survival of the division. For the past month, SFD had been expecting a final decision from corporate Westinghouse concerning its investment in the demonstration project. No formal announcement had been made, but, with the passage of time, the rumor mill projected the worst. At about the same time, the demonstration project had been put on hold, since work could not continue without the required funding. As uncertain, difficult, and depressing as the situation was, the managers decided that they should concentrate on this complex problem with their newly acquired skills of assumptional analysis. Specifically, what would be the best strategic move under these circumstances? Most of the workshop was spent on surfacing the critical assumptions underlying different approaches, debating these assumptions across diverse groups, and then arriving at a synthesis.

The work on the strategic survival plan continued after the workshop. By the middle of June, the groups had reached their synthesis: to actively seek a buyer for the division who would commit fully to the technology and invest what was necessary for commercialization. In more ways than one, the managers had learned the value of commitment! In addition, such comments as the following were heard: "If we hadn't gone through this process (assumptional analysis), we would have kept waiting around for Westinghouse to put their money behind a technology they don't understand and that doesn't fit with their strategic plan. When we finally debated the hell out of our assumptions, we could no longer ignore the realities."

The rest of June was spent analyzing all the information from member responses to the objectives and task dictionaries for the strategy-structure track. Also in June, the entire membership was asked to respond to the Kilmann-Saxton Culture-Gap Survey a second time, six months after the first administration. We were interested to see what improvements had taken place through the culture track and whether additional culture change was necessary.

Meanwhile, the formal decision by corporate Westinghouse on the fate of the division was finally available. On July 6, 1983, in an all-employee meeting, Bill Peace announced that Westinghouse had decided to sell the division. SFD was to search for a buyer. Ironically, this search had been initiated weeks earlier, in June, via the strategic survival plan. The managers and all the employees were not as surprised by this announcement as Westinghouse had anticipated. Through assumptional analysis and with open communication between managers and employees, the division was prepared for this. The mood was positive.

Later in July, the consultants reported the results of the MAPS analysis for the strategy-structure track. The computer program showed some strong similarities to the current organization chart, as well as some major differences. The differences concerned some new groups whose responsibility was to manage important tasks that had "fallen between the cracks" in the current structure. For example, a separate group was assigned the responsibility for setting priorities and managing changes in priorities within a "projects" department. Similarly, a new group was assigned the job of planning, documenting the technology, and managing patents. In addition, the MAPS analysis suggested two new management positions to help coordinate the critical interfaces between the technology and business aspects of the division. Otherwise, the groupings for personnel, controller, marketing, and engineering stayed largely the same.

In August, all attention became focused on searching for a buyer. The managers and consultants jointly decided that implementing the new structure and starting the reward system track should wait until a buyer was found. The new owner might have his own preferences for structure and reward systems. The change program was put on hold.

In the next months, top management and many members spent most of their time looking worldwide for a buyer. Several possibilities developed but fell through. It was not the best time to invest in alternative fuel sources, especially as the price of oil fell. Even the oil companies were struggling.

If SFD could not find a buyer, the division would be shut down by the end of 1983. As this time approached, SFD was able to convince Westinghouse to extend the cutoff date. However, in early January, termination notices were sent to all members in the division, effective February 1, 1984. SFD was living under a cloud of doom.

Then, in late January, a sudden breakthrough developed: Kellogg-Rust, Inc., expressed interest in buying a major interest in SFD. At the end of January, at the "eleventh hour," Westinghouse postponed the official shutdown for another month. As the Kellogg-Rust deal was developed in greater detail in February, Westinghouse again granted SFD a one-month extension. By early March, however, everything started falling into place. The deal would be finalized by the end of the month. The termination notices were canceled.

As SFD returned to its "normal" state of dynamic complexity in March, the consultants were called back to conduct another round of interviews—to catch up on all that had transpired in the interim. As the new owner's plans are made known, the remainder of the change program can be rescheduled and implemented.

Evaluating the Results

Usually this last stage of the program receives the least time and attention. My own experience is that the program "concludes" during the last formal efforts at implementation, as members take more and more responsibility for managing their problems. At this time, the consultants are seen less frequently on site and gradually disappear altogether. I think the major reason for concluding before the final evaluation stage is that most members, including top management, are fairly well convinced of the outcomes without needing a formal assessment. The members experience the effectiveness of their decision making and action taking in all work units. They feel very good about themselves, their organization, and their approach to problems.

What is the need, then, for a formal assessment beyond member perceptions and impressions? Formal assessments tend to confirm these informal evaluations and systematize the results for the whole organization. Perhaps the more vocal members are not a fair representation of the entire membership. It may be that the quieter members are more dissatisfied with the outcomes of the program than are their more vocal counterparts. Alternatively, it could be that the more vocal individuals are more negative about the change effort and the silent majority is very pleased. It is therefore important that a representative assessment be conducted to ensure a balanced evaluation.

Another reason for a systematic evaluation is to keep the idea and purpose of diagnosis alive and well within the organization. In fact, one could think of evaluation as a second round of the diagnosis. If the organization has been successful in solving its problems, then conducting another round of interviews across all levels and departments should result in a very different assessment. Ideally, if the program has been very successful and all members have internalized their learnings (as well as realigned the formally documented systems), the interviews should reveal no new problems. Any problems raised during the second round of interviews would be qualified with: "But, of course, we are already working on that problem and expect to solve it."

Evaluators, however, have been known to emphasize "bottom-line" results: return on investment, earnings per share, profit, sales, number of clients served, market share, budget increases, number of patents and new products, new contracts and orders, productivity gains, and many other performance measures. From the point of view of any stakeholder, one usually can suggest some "hard" outcome measures. Making a before-and-after comparison on any of these measures (before and after the change program) should provide a solid basis for assessing the impact of the program. If the change effort was successful, the differences in these measures should be evident—or so the argument goes.

While these hard, bottom-line measures certainly can be convincing, one must recognize their limitations. As mentioned in the last chapter during the discussion on the Barriers to Success model, improvements in the quality of decisions and actions do not translate to one-for-one increments in performance and morale. Normally, a whole series of decisions and actions is combined in complicated ways before their effects are noticed.

One should also not forget the time lag between decisions and actions on the one hand and performance on the other. Some of the bottom-line measures are not affected until months or years after a key decision has been made. For instance, improved decision making that results in new approaches to product development will not be felt in the organization's setting for years. If the before-and-after comparisons are made right after the change program has concluded, one cannot expect outside stakeholders to take note of any observable differences in outcomes. Ironically, if such before-and-after comparisons were to suggest significant improvements (or declines), they probably would be spurious or artifactual. Only if the bottom-line measurements are made over a period in which true effects can be expected can one take the results of such an evaluation seriously.

This brings us back to the metaphors of the world as a

simple machine versus the world as a complex hologram. If the simple machine view were an accurate representation of organizational phenomena, then the setting would be stable, predictable, certain, and easily measurable; the impact of the change effort on performance measures could be evaluated precisely and accurately. If, however, the complex hologram is a more accurate representation of organizational life, then external stakeholders can affect the organization at any time in dramatic and unpredictable ways. Here it is most precarious to try to specify the exact effects of a change program on various performance measures—especially since these vary according to each and every stakeholder. While the change effort was under way, a thousand other forces and events were having impact, any one of which could add to or subtract from the organization's own internal efforts. Boldly put, a single event produced by a single stakeholder can completely nullify the quality of decisions and actions the organization has learned to enact.

Accepting the holographic view and realizing the difficult measurement problems this view poses should not prevent any evaluation from being conducted. First, the diagnosis can be redone to see how well the identified problems were solved. Second, before-and-after surveys may help test the resolution of problems in one or more tracks. For example, a survey instrument that was used to pinpoint various culture-gaps (the difference between actual versus desired cultural norms) can be administered again to see what improvements in culture have occurred. Third, a number of morale surveys and attitude measures can be used to test the general spirit and satisfaction of the membership. While these evaluations are largely internal audits, they are helpful. If these diagnostic efforts and surveys reveal that significant problems still remain, it is unlikely that the "true" performance measures will signify success. But if these internal assessments are positive, it suggests that successful performance *may* follow if all other dynamics and forces favor the organization. This is not a simple machine approach and therefore is not a perfect methodology, but it is a useful approximation for today's organizations.

The SFD story illustrates how the program of five tracks

is managed under the same conditions of dynamic complexity the organization finds in its external setting. While the process of managing the five tracks is never smooth and predictable, it does take place. It also has a major impact on the life of the organization. Although SFD did not have much time or interest in formal evaluations (since it was preoccupied with survival), it is still instructive to examine some of the available indicators of organizational success.

Besides the very positive comments heard about the many changes that were taking place for SFD during the summer of 1983, a before-and-after assessment was available for the Kilmann-Saxton Culture-Gap Survey. This survey was taken first in December 1982 and then six months later, in June 1983. The culture-gap for Task Support, the most troublesome for the division, was virtually cut in half (from 4.5 down to 2.3 on a 7.0 scale). The gap for Task Innovation also decreased for the division as a whole, but not as dramatically (from 3.5 down to 2.4). Both the gaps for Social Relationships and Personal Freedom remained as insignificant as before (1.7 to 1.2 and 0.5 to 0.3, respectively). This division-wide pattern of culture change was almost identical in every department and work group in SFD, suggesting that the new culture was now behind the mission of the organization.

In November 1983, when the division still had not found a buyer and corporate Westinghouse was growing impatient as a result, the general manager, Bill Peace (1983, pp. 9-10), summarized the impact of the change program as follows: "Without the culture change, I don't think SFD would have survived the divestiture decision. As it is, we have a group of very capable and dedicated people who are working together to sell our business and who intend to build a very successful and profitable business for our new owner over the next ten years. . . . It's fair to say that all of us at SFD lived through a painful but enormously valuable process. We all learned a great deal in a personal, as well as in an organizational sense."

Conclusion

This chapter has described the practice behind the five tracks in the form of an action model. The five stages of planned change must be guided with care and commitment: (1) initiating the program, (2) diagnosing the problems, (3) scheduling the tracks, (4) implementing the tracks, and (5) evaluating the results. Ideally, these stages are conducted by managers, members, and consultants in a collaborative and participative manner. This ensures that all available talent and information is applied to creating and maintaining organizational success. At a minimum, the consultants should conduct an independent diagnosis of the organization's problems (regardless of what the managers may have discovered on their own), delicately guide the uncovering of cultural norms and assumptions, and manage the troublemakers and team-building sessions (which can become very sensitive and uncomfortable).

The next five chapters will present the five tracks in the proper sequence, including more specific action steps to guide the implementation of each track. However, while learning all these action steps, one must not forget the importance of managing all the other stages of planned change. If the whole program is not initiated properly with top management support, and if the problems of the organization are neither diagnosed correctly nor accepted by top management, the tracks cannot provide their potential benefits. Moreover, the five tracks must be implemented in an integrated manner, with flexibility and adaptability. Quick-fixing the five tracks would do the practice of management—and any organization—a great disservice.

CHAPTER FOUR

The
Culture
Track

Seeing the organization as a culture has wide ramifications, for it means shedding a humanistic light upon it, encouraging us to treat its members not as roles but as full human beings. . . . In a cultural approach, people are treated as multidimensional persons rather than as component parts of a mechanistic system.
—Allen and Kraft, 1982, p. 5

Culture . . . is a pattern of beliefs and expectations shared by the organization's members. These beliefs and expectations produce norms that powerfully shape the behavior of individuals and groups in the organization.
—Schwartz and Davis, 1981, p. 33

People in an organization frequently follow norms that have long since outlived their usefulness. . . .
—Allen and Dyer, 1980, p. 192

The likelihood that an organization will be effective in a dynamic and complex setting is not determined just by the skills of its leaders, nor will its adaptiveness be primarily determined by the strategy, structure, and reward systems that make up its visible features. Rather, the organization itself has an invisible quality—a certain style, a character, a way of doing things—that may be more powerful than the dictates of any one person or any formally documented system. To understand the essence or soul of the organization requires that we travel below the charts, rulebooks, machines, and buildings into the underground world of corporate cultures.

What exactly is culture? Nobody knows for sure, nor will there ever be a clear definition that meets with everyone's approval. The topic generates multiple meanings. William B. Renner (1981, p. 1), vice-chairman of the Aluminum Company of America, highlights the dilemma of defining culture:

Culture is different things to different people. For some, it's family, or religion. It's opera or Shakespeare, a few clay pots at a Roman dig. Every textbook offers a definition, but I like a simple one: culture is the shared values and behavior that knit a community together. It's the rules of the game; the unseen meaning between the lines in the rulebook that assures unity. All organizations have a culture of their own.

Most definitions of culture disagree only on *what* is shared among the members of an organization. Is it rules, norms, beliefs, expectations, values, philosophies, or all of these things? For most purposes, these intangibles are so interconnected that it makes little sense to argue about how each is similar to or different from the others. However, it is worthwhile to learn how these intangibles become shared among the members of any group, and why this creates such a powerful force that guides behavior. Thus, the most exciting thing about culture is discovering how it first captures and then directs the collective will of the membership.

Culture provides meaning, direction, and mobilization—a social energy that moves the corporation into action. One has to experience the energy that flows from shared commitments among group members to know it: the energy that emanates from mutual influence, "one for all and all for one," and "esprit de corps." Can management tap this source of energy for organizational success, or will the energy remain immobilized? Or, worse yet, will this social energy work against the mission of the organization?

I have encountered many organizations in which this social energy has barely been tapped. The energy has been diffused in all directions or even deactivated: It is not mobilized toward anything. Most members seem apathetic or depressed about their jobs. They no longer pressure one another to do well. Pronouncements by top managers that they will improve the situation fall on deaf ears. The members have heard these promises before. Nothing seems to matter. The soul of the organization is slowly dying.

In other cases, while the energy is alive and flourishing, it moves members in the wrong direction. The organization lives in an immense culture lag or culture-gap. The social energy pressures members to persist in behaviors that may have worked well in the past but that clearly are dysfunctional today. The gap between the outdated culture and what is needed for dynamic complexity gradually develops into a *culture rut*—a habitual way of behaving without asking any questions. There is no adaptation or change; only routine motions are enacted again and again, even though success is not forthcoming. Here the social energy not only works against the organization but is contrary to the private wishes of the members. Nobody wants to be ineffective and dissatisfied, but everyone pressures one another to comply with the unstated, below-the-surface, behind-the-scenes, invisible culture. This rut can go on for years, even though morale and performance suffer. Bad habits die hard.

Culture shock occurs when the sleeping organization awakes and finds that it has lost touch with its mission, its setting, and its assumptions. The new world has left the insulated company behind—a Rip Van Winkle story on a grand scale. Rather than experience this shock, the organization may decide not to wake up; its managers simply continue to believe the myth of erroneous extrapolation. Such organizations will be most susceptible to the whims of any stakeholder, old or new.

The first part of this chapter explores three interrelated

questions: (1) What are adaptive cultures (in contrast to dysfunctional cultures)? (2) How do cultures form—what brings
them into being? (3) How are cultures maintained—what forces
keep cultures intact? Understanding the answers to these questions is necessary for assessing and changing cultures. In these
discussions, we will see how cultural norms provide the leverage
points for creating and maintaining adaptive cultures more directly than any of the other manifestations of an organization's
way of doing things.

The second part of this chapter presents five steps for
managing the culture track: (1) surfacing actual norms, (2) articulating new directions, (3) establishing new norms, (4) identifying culture-gaps, and (5) closing culture-gaps. These five steps
show how the cultural norms of an organization can be brought
to the surface for examination and change. The organization
can gain control over its culture rather than vice versa. The
members can decide what new norms are needed for today's
complex problems and then can proceed to energize their work
groups toward the new directions they envision.

In this and the next four chapters, which cover the five
tracks to organizational success, all techniques will be organized
as "steps" in order to facilitate planned change. These steps are
a bit more specific and well defined than the "stages" discussed
previously. After the steps in each chapter are presented, we
will return once again to the SFD story.

What Are Adaptive Cultures?

Even if we accept the idea that the term *culture* will always be a bit vague and ill defined, unlike the more surface and
tangible aspects of organizations, it is still important to consider what makes a culture good or bad, adaptive or dysfunctional. Wallach (1983, p. 32) provides a summary of what cultures do for or against the organization; she also draws a sharp
contrast between the bureaucratic cultures that were functional in yesterday's world and the innovative cultures that are
adaptive today:

There are no good or bad cultures, per se. A culture is good—effective—if it reinforces the mission, purposes and strategies of the organization. It can be an asset or a liability. Strong cultural norms make an organization efficient. Everyone knows what's important and how things are done. To be effective, the culture must not only be efficient, but appropriate to the needs of the business, company, and the employees.

BUREAUCRATIC cultures are hierarchical and compartmentalized. There are clear lines of responsibility and authority. The work is organized and systematic; these cultures are usually based on control and power. The companies are stable, careful and, usually, mature. A high score on bureaucracy means the organization is power-oriented, cautious, established, solid, regulated, ordered, structured, procedural and hierarchical. . . . This culture is appropriate for a company with a large market share in a stable market. . . . American Telephone and Telegraph is an example of a bureaucratic culture. For 60 years the culture of AT&T reinforced norms and values supportive of a regulated monopoly. . . .

INNOVATIVE cultures are exciting and dynamic. Entrepreneurial and ambitious people thrive in these environments. They are creative places to work, filled with challenge and risk. The stimulation is often constant. An individual well-suited to an innovative company is driving, enterprising, challenging, stimulating, creative, results-oriented and risk taking. . . . Today's AT&T, no longer a monopoly, is moving toward an innovative environment. New communication technologies coupled with fierce competition make strong marketing and sales functions critical to organizational success.

Why does one organization have a very adaptive culture while another has a culture that lives in the past? Is one a case of good fortune and the other a result of bad luck? On the contrary, it seems that any organization can find itself with an outdated culture if its culture is not managed explicitly. I have found that, if left to itself, a culture does become dysfunctional. Human fear, insecurity, oversensitivity, dependency, and paranoia seem to take over unless a concerted effort at establishing an adaptive culture is undertaken. People have been hurt at one time or another in their lives, particularly in their childhoods. It is, therefore, rather easy to scare people into worrying about what pain or hurt will be inflicted in the future, even in a relatively nonthreatening situation. As a result, people cope by protecting themselves, by being cautious, by minimizing their risks, by going along with a culture that builds protective barriers around work units and around the whole organization. An adaptive culture, alternatively, requires a risk-taking, trusting, and proactive approach to organizational as well as individual life. Members must actively support one another's efforts to identify problems and adapt to solutions. The latter can be accomplished only by a very conscious, well-planned effort at managing culture. Consider what Roy L. Ash ("Conversation with Roy L. Ash," 1979, p. 53) has learned in his efforts to revitalize AM International, Inc., as chairman of the board and chief executive officer of the addressograph-multigraph company:

What we have discovered here, and I'm sure this is the case in many other companies, too, is that the older organizations become, the more they take on their own particular culture, their own personality. Organizations are just like people; their personality is shaped by their experiences over time. Most businesses, over time, tend to take on a bureaucratic culture. *Any large organization that goes through the same motions time after time after time tends to lose sight of the purpose for which it was created and instead emphasizes motions. . . .*
All these cultural attributes collect like barnacles on a ship and slow the organization down. These habits can become so ingrained in people that they can't change. They've fallen into a *culture rut.* Of course, some people, if they haven't been in an organization too long, can escape assimilation into its culture and can move on to another. But many long-term employees can't change. [Emphasis added.]

Taking a holographic view, culture also helps explain some of the self-defeating behaviors that have been observed in many organizations—behaviors that persist in spite of their many disruptive effects. These behaviors include doing the minimum to get by, purposely resisting or even sabotaging innovation, and being very negative in general about the organization's capacity to change. Worse yet, these behaviors may even include lying, cheating, stealing, and intimidating, harassing, and hurting others. While these behaviors may seem unthinkable, they do receive cultural support even though they cause difficult problems for the organization. They also significantly undermine, to say the least, both morale and performance.

In company after company and community after community, people are behaving in ways that make them ashamed, yet they explain their behavior in terms of "natural" tendencies and "the way things are." "You can't change human nature," some say, while others blame things on "city hall," or on "what people are really like," or on "our animal nature."

But there is more than either human or animal nature at work here. Social forces are transforming our groups. Cultural norms develop, teaching us what is expected, supported, and accepted by the people we live and work with. These norms exert powerful pressure, causing us to behave in ways that often run counter to our real wishes and goals.

As individuals we are almost all affected. How many of us, at one time or another, have joined a group or organization with the intention of working to change some of the things that seemed to be wrong with group behavior? And how many of us have found ourselves five or ten years later fully involved in the same behavior that we had once rejected? [Allen, 1980, pp. 31–32].

The most detrimental behavior in the long run, however, is continuing to see and act out what made the organization successful in the past rather than adapting to the dynamic complexity of today and tomorrow. The challenge facing AM International, Inc., is to get out of its culture rut, one created by falling into the trap of erroneous extrapolation. Ash ("Conversation with Roy L. Ash," 1979, p. 54) describes the predicament of his company quite candidly:

The common denominator of our problems at AM International has been the corporate culture. When a company has been in business for a long time and enjoyed a long history of success, such success reaffirms the validity of the way things have been done, of the corporate culture, in the minds of the company's managers and other employees. It's as though they were saying to themselves, "If we have been that successful, we must be doing something right." But it too often turns out that even when the company is no longer successful, employees persist in doing things the old way.

A *Business Week* article, "Emerson Electric . . ." (1983, p. 58), again underscores the cultural change needed by a company in order to break out of its old behavior patterns:

Emerson's very success in building a culture that focuses so thoroughly on year-by-year returns may hamper its quest to deliver the new technology its markets demand. A culture that was built on cost-cutting and total dedication to the bottom line must be made flexible enough to encourage the development of technologies and products whose payoff may be years down the road. . . .

But so deeply embedded is Emerson's old culture that some company officials still question whether top management will stick to its new policy if success does not come quickly.

In sum, any culture that encourages members to look the other way as key stakeholders in the organization's setting are changing or as internal stakeholders are acting out disruptive behavior is dysfunctional. This sort of culture is blinding both managers and employees to the severe problems all around them. Ultimately, if this continues, the organization will fall into a culture rut. Being in a rut will prevent any other needed changes from taking place. If we can learn how cultures first form and then are maintained, perhaps we can prevent them from becoming dysfunctional. With an integrated program of planned change, maybe we can transform a long-standing dysfunctional culture into an adaptive one.

How Do Cultures Form?

A culture seems to form rather quickly based on the organization's mission, its setting, and what is required for success: quality, efficiency, product reliability, customer service, innovation, hard work, and/or loyalty. Generally speaking, when the organization is born, a tremendous energy is released as members struggle to make it work. The culture captures everyone's drive and imagination. As the reward systems, policies, procedures, and rules governing work are formally documented, they have a more specific impact on shaping the initial culture—suggesting what behaviors and attitudes are important for success in each work unit.

Such situational forces in shaping culture, however, cannot compete with either the bold or even the more subtle actions of key individuals. For example, the founder of the firm—his objectives, his principles, his values, and especially his behavior—provides important clues as to what is really wanted from all members both now and in the future. Carrying on in the traditions of the founder, other top executives affect the culture of the company by their every example. Edson W. Spencer, chief executive officer and chairman of Honeywell, Inc., realizes what impact he has on the corporate culture ("Conversation...," 1983, p. 43).

Most of us, very humbly, don't wish to acknowledge that fact, but nonetheless the chief executive's tone, his integrity, his standards, his way of dealing with people, his focusing on things that are important or not important can have a profound impact on the rest of the organization. What I am saying is that the way the chief executive and senior managers of the company conduct themselves as individuals has a more profound impact on how other people in the company conduct *themselves* than anything else that happens.

Employees also take note of all critical incidents that stem from *any* management action—such as the time that so-and-so was reprimanded for doing a good job just because he was not asked to do it beforehand or the time that so-and-so was fired because he publicly disagreed with the company's position. Incidents such as these become the folklore that people remember, indicating what the corporation really wants, what really counts in getting ahead, or, alternatively, how to stay out of trouble—the unwritten rules of the game. Work groups adopt these lessons as norms on how to survive and make it, how to protect oneself from the system, and how to retaliate against the organization for its "sins of the past." Lewicki (1981, pp.

8-9) suggests how the double standard—managers asking for one type of behavior while rewarding another—motivates employees to develop the necessary rules to survive and prosper:

> From the employees' viewpoint, their organization's culture usually encompasses the answers to three questions: What does this organization expect from its employees? What kind of behavior does the organization reward? And what are the "dos and don'ts" of proper social conduct within the system? "What the organization expects" is usually management's public statement of employee priorities: quality vs. cost control in manufacturing the product, for example, or risk taking vs. restraint in pursuing new ventures, or service to current customers vs. development of new markets. "What the organization rewards" are those factors that are actually considered—when decisions about salary and promotion are being made. What an organization says it expects should be consistent with what it rewards—but that's not always so. If an organization says it wants to aggressively develop new businesses, then presumably it should reward those who are the most aggressive in new business development. However, if it consistently promotes those who have done the best job in nurturing current accounts and ignores the entrepreneurs, employees will soon get the message that an organizational double standard exists. Employee discontent about this duplicity will soon find its way into lunch table or cocktail circuit conversation, where the "dos and don'ts" of organizational life are shared, evaluated, and communicated to new members. "Don't listen to what management says," oldtimers will warn; "do what others have been rewarded for."

As a culture forms around a recognized need, the setting, and specific task requirements, it may be very functional at first. But, over time, the culture becomes a separate entity, independent of the initial reasons and incidents that formed it. The culture becomes distinct from the formal strategy, structure, and reward systems of the organization. As long as it is supportive of and in harmony with these formally documented systems, the culture remains in the background.

In a similar vein, culture becomes distinct from the membership and even the top managers. All members throughout the organization are taught to follow the cultural norms without questioning them. By the time employees have been around for

even a few years, they have already "learned the ropes." Even a
new top executive who vows that things will be different finds
out—often the hard way—how the culture is "bigger" and more
powerful than he is. Single-handed efforts by the executive to
counter the "invisible hand" are met with constant frustration.
For example, a top manager can call his subordinates into his
office individually and get verbal commitments for some new
policy or plan; however, when each person leaves the office and
again becomes part of the corporate culture, the manager finds
that the new plan is bitterly opposed.

Running up against the culture becomes even more apparent when management attempts to shift the strategy of the
firm or tries to adopt entirely new work methods: The culture
may not support the intended changes. Now the energy and the
separateness of the culture quickly become evident. The intangible culture is revealed when management cannot pinpoint the
source of apathy, resistance, or rebellion. Management is puz-
zled as to why the new work methods are not embraced automatically and enthusiastically by the members. To management,
it is obvious that these proposed changes are for the good of the
organization. Why can't everyone else see this?

Top management is also caught in the grip of the firm's
separate and distinct culture. Employees from below wonder
why managers play it so safe, why they refuse to approach
things differently, why they keep applying the same old management practices even though these simply do not work. Employees wonder why management is so blind to the world
around them. They wonder if management is "mean" or just
"stupid."

How Are Cultures Maintained?

The force controlling group behavior at every level in the
organization—a force that can brainwash members into believing
that what they are doing is automatically good for the company, their community, and their family—must be very powerful. That such dysfunctional and self-defeating behaviors can
persist for years again suggests some powerful force at work. Is

it magic or is it the psychology of what most people will do
to be a member of a group? We must understand the invisible
force if we wish to control it rather than let it control us. A
deeper knowledge of norms and how they are enforced is essential.

Social scientists speak of norms as the unwritten rules of
behavior (Moch and Seashore, 1981). In a company, for example, a norm might be: Don't disagree with your boss in public.
These norms are very crystallized when a strong consensus
exists among a group of people concerning what constitutes appropriate behavior. If a norm is violated—if someone behaves
differently from what the norm dictates—there are immediate
and strong pressures to get the offending party to change his
behavior. Consider, for example, an individual who persists in
presenting his reservations about the company's new product at
a group meeting—just after his boss has argued strongly for in-
vesting heavily in its advertising campaign. The individual is
stared at, frowned at, looked at with rolling eyes, as well as
given nonverbal messages to sit down and shut up. If these efforts do not silence the individual, he will hear about it later,
either from his coworkers or from his boss.

Every person's need to be accepted by a group—whether
family, friends, coworkers, or the neighborhood—gives a group
leverage to demand compliance to its norms. If people did not
care about acceptance at all, a group would have little hold,
other than formal sanctions, over individuals. The nonconformists and the mavericks who defy pressures to adhere to group
norms always do so at a considerable price.

A simple experiment conducted by Asch (1955) demonstrates just how powerfully the group can influence its deviants.
The experiment was presented to subjects as a study in perception. Three lines—A, B, and C—all of different lengths, were
shown on a single card. Subjects were asked to indicate which
of these three lines was identical in length to a fourth line, D,
shown on a second card. Seven persons sat in a row. One by
one they indicated their choices. While line D was in fact identical to line C, each of the first six persons, confederates of the
experimenter, said that line D was identical to A. The seventh

person was the unknowing subject. As each person gave the agreed-upon fraudulent response, this seventh subject became increasingly uneasy, anxious, and doubtful of his own perceptions. When it came time for the seventh person to respond, he agreed with the rest of the individuals almost 40 percent of the time. The error rate in choosing the wrong line without any other individuals present was less than 1 percent. This showed quite a difference in behavior!

In this experiment, which has been duplicated many times, there was no opportunity for the seven subjects to discuss the problem among themselves. If there had been such an opportunity, the effect would have been stronger. The six would have attempted to influence the seventh member. It is not easy being a deviant in a group when everyone else is against you. People need acceptance from others so much that they will deny their own perceptions when confronted with the group's norms of "objective" reality. Objective reality becomes a social reality.

Imagine just how easily such distorted perceptions of reality can be maintained when backed up by formal sanctions—pay, promotions, and other rewards. The group or the entire organization can reward its members so that they ignore not only the dynamic complexity created by external stakeholders but also the disruptive behaviors of troublemakers inside the organization. The members collectively believe that everything is fine, and they continue to reinforce this myth and reward one another for maintaining it. In essence, everyone agrees that the dysfunctional ways can continue without question. Any deviant who thinks otherwise is severely punished and eventually banished from the tribe.

Another experiment, this time a study in an industrial plant, sheds further light on the nature of cultural norms. Seashore (1954) studied the effect of group cohesiveness on work performance. Groups were found to differ as to whether their norms supported company goals—that is, whether the norms of the group encouraged high levels of production or favored low production and doing the minimum to get by. The study found that the best condition for the organization was having highly cohesive groups with norms that supported company goals. These groups did in fact achieve the highest levels of output. The worst condition was having highly cohesive groups with norms that were unsupportive of or even contrary to company goals. Here the groups used their social energy to keep output levels low. The uncohesive groups were intermediate in performance, regardless of their norms. In this case, individuals were left on their own to decide how much to produce, since the impact of any work group on their behavior was minimal.

Two important lessons can be learned from these classic studies. First, the impact of a group on its members is very powerful indeed: If the group is cohesive, if there is a strong sense of community and loyalty, there will be strong pressures on each member to adopt whatever the cultural norms specify. Second, if the cultural norms are supportive of the organization's mission, the efforts of members will continue to yield high performance. This demonstrates an adaptive culture for the organization. Alternatively, if the norms endorsed by a highly cohesive group oppose the corporate goals, then the culture will foster low performance and morale. This demonstrates a dysfunctional culture. It is better to have an uncohesive group with mediocre performance than to have a highly cohesive group with a counterculture. The latter will result in consistently low performance and headaches for everyone.

While the culture becomes specific through the development of norms, it manifests itself in other ways. For example, the stories told about critical events in the life of the organization imply to members what is valued and rewarded. These stories can take on the qualities of legends, as previous events are exaggerated in order to emphasize the corporation's traditions, its heroes, and its villains. Celebrated rites and rituals, whether conducted by management or by work groups, are additional ways of reinforcing desired behaviors and attitudes. Symbols in the form of a company logo, mascot, poster, song, or slogan remind members as well as the public of the meaning behind the organization's existence—perhaps the intended culture. Some organizations use these mechanisms extensively to indoctrinate new employees with their customs and traditions (Deal and Kennedy, 1982).

To control the culture by changing the stories, myths, symbols, and history itself, however, is undoubtedly a very difficult if not impossible task. The way to control the culture is by managing the norms. Even norms that dictate how one should behave, the opinions one should state, and one's facial expressions can be surfaced, discussed, and altered.

Norms are a universal phenomenon. They are necessary, tenacious, but also extremely malleable. Because they can change so quickly and easily, they present a tremendous opportunity to people interested in change. Any group, no matter its size, once it understands itself as a cultural entity, can plan its own norms, creating positive ones that will help it reach its goals and modifying or discarding the negative ones [Allen and Kraft, 1982, pp. 7-8].

Assessing and Changing Cultural Norms

Does the current culture (1) support the mission of the firm? (2) foster organizational success? (3) encourage an adaptive stance toward shifting stakeholders both inside and outside the organization? (4) motivate the membership to address complex and difficult problems? (5) enable members to take the time to address such problems?

A good way to gain control of an organization's culture is to ask members to write out what previously was unwritten. I have done this many times with a variety of organizations. I have found that members are willing and able to write out their norms under certain conditions: (1) No member will be identified for stating or suggesting a particular norm (individual confidentiality), and (2) no norm will be documented when one's superiors are present (candid openness). Further, the members must be able to trust that the norm list will not be used against them but will instead be used to benefit them as well as their organization. The consultants and managers who guide members to state norms, therefore, must generate trust and commitment throughout all five steps of the process.

Step One: Surfacing Actual Norms

The first step is for all group members (generally in a workshop setting) to list the actual norms that currently guide their behaviors and attitudes. This can be done for just one group or for many groups, departments, and divisions, depending on how many individuals can be included and managed in one setting. Sometimes it takes a little prodding and a few illustrations to get the process started, but once it begins members are quick to suggest many norms. In fact, they seem to delight in being able to articulate what previously was never stated in any document and rarely mentioned in any conversation.

In an organization whose culture is rooted deeply in the past, some of the norms people list are: Don't disagree with your boss; don't rock the boat; treat women as second-class citizens; put down your organization; don't enjoy your work; don't share information with other groups; treat subordinates as incompetent and lazy; cheat on your expense account; look busy even when you are not; don't reward employees on the basis of merit; laugh at those who suggest new ways of doing things; don't smile much; openly criticize company policies to outsiders; complain a lot; don't trust anyone who seems sincere. Ironically, the one norm that must be violated so that this list can be developed is: Don't make norms explicit!

Norms that often are listed that directly pertain to complex and difficult problems are: Don't be the bearer of bad news; don't tell your boss what he doesn't want to hear; don't think of things that are not likely to happen; don't spoil the party; don't be associated with an ugly event; see no evil, hear no evil, and speak no evil.

As these norms are listed for everyone to see, there is considerable laughter and amazement. The members become aware that they have been seducing one another into abiding by these counterproductive directives. But each individual did not make a conscious choice to behave this way; rather, as each individual entered the organization, each was taught what was expected behavior—often in quite subtle ways. The more cohesive the group, the more rapidly this learning takes place and the more strongly the sanctions are applied. In the extreme case, a highly cohesive group that has been around for a long time has members that look, act, think, and talk like one another.

It is the power that the group has over the individual—compliance with group norms in exchange for group membership—that makes the negative focus of the norms so critical and so potentially devastating. What makes matters worse is that individuals go along with group norms rather automatically without questioning the consequences either for themselves or for their organization. I have found that the decision process, if one can call it that, is quite unconscious. Individuals do not decide on a day-by-day basis to enact the dysfunctional norms. Rarely are the cultural norms discussed openly. They simply evolve.

In the projects in which I had managers and all employees of a company list their norms, it was surprising to discover the high proportion of negative norms that were cited. In a number of cases, more than 90 percent of the listed norms had mildly negative or even highly negative connotations. On the one hand, it may be that these members felt I was looking for the dysfunctions in their organizations rather than for the adaptive aspects. On the other hand, perhaps many organizations are plagued with a high proportion of negative norms from their bureaucratic cultures.

Step Two: Articulating New Directions

The next step is for all group members to discuss where the organization is headed and what type of behavior is necessary to move forward. Even when a corporation has a very dysfunctional culture from the past, members, as individuals, are aware of what changes are needed in order for the organization to survive and be adaptive in the future. Similarly, members are aware of what work environment they prefer for their own sanity and satisfaction.

A certain amount of planning and problem solving may have to occur before any new directions can be articulated. In work groups that have been in a culture rut, members are so absorbed with the negatives that they have not spent much time thinking about or discussing what they desire. Sometimes it is helpful to ask them to reflect upon their ideal organization: If they could design their own organization from scratch, what would it be like? This generally brings to light what could be different in the present organization and what should not be accepted just because it has been that way for a long time.

Step Three: Establishing New Norms

The third step is for all group members to develop a list of new norms for organizational success. For example, what new norms would encourage a more adaptive stance toward the organization's changing environment? Likewise, what new norms would allow groups to discuss difficult and uncomfortable issues that affect the long-term survival and success of the firm? What cultural norms would bring the difficult internal problems out into the open so that they could be resolved?

At this point, the members usually catch on to the impact that the unwritten rules have had on their behavior. They experience a sense of relief as a new way of life is considered. They realize that they no longer have to pressure one another to behave in dysfunctional ways. The members can create a new social order within their own work groups and within their own organization. Part of this sense of relief comes from recognizing that their dissatisfactions and ineffectiveness are not due to their being incompetent or bad individuals. It is much easier, psychologically, for members to blame the invisible force called *culture*—as long as they take responsibility for changing it.

In organizations needing to be more adaptive, flexible, and responsive to modern times, some of the norms that are often listed are: Treat everyone with respect and as a potential source of valuable insight and expertise; be willing to take on responsibility; initiate changes to improve performance; congratulate those who suggest new ideas and new ways of doing things; be cost-conscious so that the organization remains efficient relative to its competitors; speak with pride about your organization and work group; budget your time according to the importance of tasks for accomplishing objectives; don't criticize the organization in front of clients or customers; enjoy your work and show your enthusiasm for a job well done; be helpful and supportive of the other groups in the organization.

New norms that directly pertain to complex and difficult problems include: Bring uncomfortable issues out into the open; persist in drawing attention to problems even if others seem reluctant to consider the implications of what you are saying; listen to other members' viewpoints even if you disagree with them; encourage zany and bizarre perspectives to ensure that nothing has been overlooked; encourage everyone to speak up if there hasn't been a strong difference of opinion on a topic that should generate a heated debate.

Step Four: Identifying Culture-Gaps

The contrast between these desired norms (Step Three) and the actual norms (Step One) can be immense. My colleague, Mary Jane Saxton, and I refer to this contrast as a culture-gap. We have developed a measurement tool for detecting the gap between what the current culture is and what it should be: The Kilmann-Saxton Culture-Gap Survey (Kilmann and Saxton, 1983).

The survey was developed by first collecting more than four hundred norms from managers and employees in more than twenty-five different types of organizations. Many of these norms were also developed through projects that entailed assessing and changing cultural norms. The final set of twenty-eight norm pairs that appear on the survey were derived from statistical and clinical analysis of the most consistent norms that were operating in most of the organizations we studied. An example of a norm pair is: (A) Share information only when it benefits your own work group versus (B) Share information to help the organization make better decisions. Each employee chooses the (A) or (B) for each norm pair in two ways: first according to the pressures the work group puts on its members (actual norms) and second according to which norms should be operating in order to promote high performance and morale (desired norms).

The differences between the actual norms and the desired norms represent the culture-gaps. There are four types of culture-gaps, each made up of seven norm pairs:

1. Task Support—norms having to do with information sharing, helping other groups, and concern with efficiency, such as: "Support the work of other groups" versus "Put down the work of other groups."
2. Task Innovation—norms for being creative, being rewarded for creativity, and doing new things, such as: "Always try to improve" versus "Don't rock the boat."
3. Social Relationships—norms for socializing with one's work group and mixing friendships with business, such as: "Get to know the people in your work group" versus "Don't bother."
4. Personal Freedom—norms for self-expression, exercising discretion, and pleasing oneself, such as: "Live for yourself and your family" versus "Live for your job and career."

As shown in Figure 4, these four culture-gaps are defined by two independent distinctions: technical versus human and short term versus long term. The technical/human distinction contrasts norms that guide the technical aspects of work in organizations with norms that guide the social and personal aspects. This distinction has appeared as task orientation versus people orientation in virtually all discussions of behavior in organizations. The short-term/long-term distinction contrasts norms that focus on day-to-day concerns versus norms that more directly affect the future of the organization. The latter includes norms that emphasize work improvements (rather than just getting today's work done) and norms that define the relationship between the individual and the organization (rather than focusing on daily social interactions). This distinction has been discussed frequently as an operational versus a strategic focus.

A work group, a department, a division, or an entire organization can be surveyed with regard to its culture-gaps. By calculating the differences between the actual norms operating

Figure 4. The Four Culture-Gaps[SM].

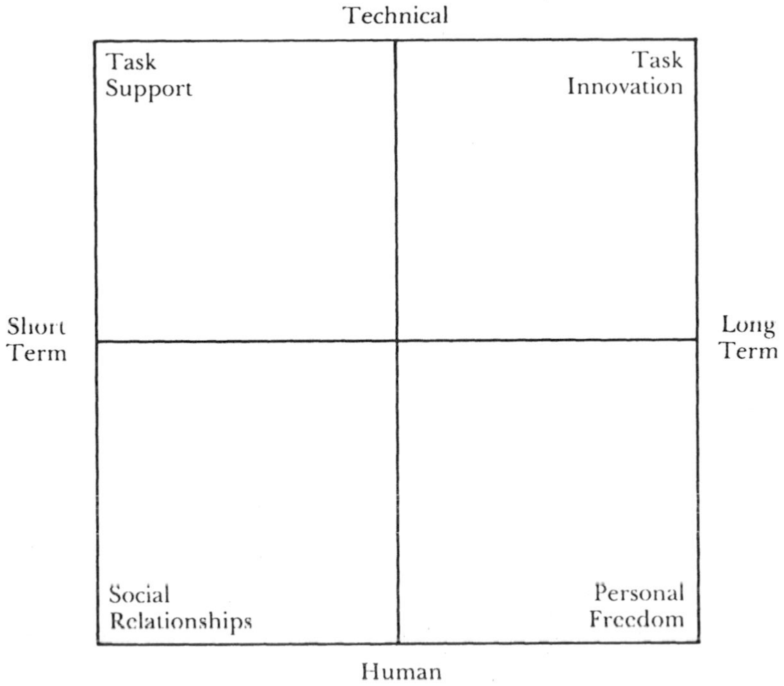

Technical

Task Support	Task Innovation
Social Relationships	Personal Freedom

Short Term (left) — Long Term (right)

Human

Source: Reprinted from the Kilmann-Saxton Culture-Gap Survey by permission of Organizational Design Consultants, Inc. Copyright © 1983.

versus the desired norms, the four culture-gap scores are obtained. The larger the gap, the greater the likelihood that the current norms are hindering both morale and performance. If the assessed culture-gaps are allowed to continue, work groups are likely to resist any attempt at change and improvement. Specifically, culture-gaps materialize as an unwillingness to adopt new work methods and innovations, as a lack of support for programs to improve quality and productivity, as lip service when changes in strategic directions are announced and, at the extreme, as efforts to maintain the status quo at all costs—even corporate efforts to improve member satisfaction and morale are met with either apathy or active resistance.

Figure 5 shows how culture-gaps are displayed as a profile for easy interpretation. Each work unit calculates its four

Figure 5. Culture-Gap^{SM} Profile.

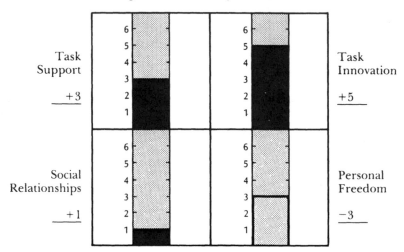

Source: Reprinted from the Kilmann-Saxton Culture-Gap Survey by permission of Organizational Design Consultants, Inc. Copyright © 1983.

average scores and then transfers these onto the appropriate bar graph, creating the profile. A positive culture-gap score is plotted as a filled bar (+1 to +7), a negative culture-gap score is plotted as an unfilled bar (–1 to –7), and a zero score is simply ignored. A positive culture-gap score means that organizational success would be improved by changing the actual norms to foster *more* Task Support, Task Innovation, or whatever is being considered. A negative culture-gap score means that *less* of that quality is desired for success.

As revealed by the sample culture-gap profile shown in Figure 5, the technical norms of the work group do not encourage the necessary information sharing and support for getting the day-to-day work done. More importantly, the actual norms do not encourage the necessary creative and innovative behavior that is required. However, the work group believes that the current norms that foster social interaction are essentially the same as what is desired. Regarding Personal Freedom, perhaps there is too much discretion in following rules and regulations; perhaps members support norms that favor their own needs at the expense of high performance on the job. Since three of the four culture-gaps reach a significant level (defined as three or more difference points), a broad-based problem is evident: The culture of the work group is holding back morale and performance in several ways.

Using the Kilmann-Saxton Culture-Gap Survey in numerous profit and nonprofit organizations has revealed distinctive patterns of culture-gaps. For example, in some of the high-technology firms, lack of cooperation and information sharing across groups has resulted in large culture-gaps in Task Support. In the automotive and steel industries, not rewarding creativity and innovation has resulted in large culture-gaps in Task Innovation. In some social service agencies in which work loads can vary greatly, large *negative* gaps in Social Relationships are found, indicating that too much time is spent socializing rather than looking to get the next job done. Lastly, in extremely bureaucratic organizations, such as some banks and government agencies, large gaps in Personal Freedom are evident. Here members feel overly confined and constrained, which affects their performance and morale.

The most general finding to date is the presence of large culture-gaps in Task Innovation. It seems that American industry is plagued by significant differences between actual and desired norms in this area. This is consistent with all the attention that has been given to the productivity problem in the United States. An industrial culture that pushes for short-term financial results is bound to foster norms against efforts at long-term work improvements, regardless of what the formal documents and publicity statements seem to advocate.

Do all members see the same culture-gaps? Apparently, this is not the case. The smallest culture-gaps are found at the top of the organization's hierarchy. Managers believe their own publicity; they say that they reward creativity and innovation but seem to forget that their actions speak louder than their words. In comparison with small culture-gaps at the executive level, culture-gaps are largest at the bottom of the hierarchy, where the gaps also reveal alienation and distrust. Here the work groups can explain what is meant by the norm: Don't trust management. In essence, work groups see management as being up to no good, getting caught up in fads to fool and manipulate employees, or thinking that the workers are too stupid to see what is behind management's latest whim.

This sort of grass-roots culture not only describes a culture rut but again suggests why the culture track must precede the four other tracks: Without a supportive culture, every action by top management will be discounted by the groups below—even top-down efforts to change the culture. I have seen cases in which executives have tried dramatic changes in their own behavior coupled with symbolic deeds and fiery speeches in order to dictate a new culture, but to no avail. Only when work group members encourage one another to be receptive to overtures by the other groups, as in a participative effort, can the whole change program be successful. For example, various work groups would include such new norms as: Give management another chance; assume good intentions. Managers and consultants, therefore, have to work especially hard to encourage the work groups, including the executive groups, to meet one another halfway.

Just as the *size* of culture-gaps can vary according to the shape of the organization pyramid, the *type* of culture-gaps can differ division by division in the same organization. Divisions have different histories, critical incidents, strategies, markets, and managers. However, a very centralized, single-product firm may have the same culture-gap profile in every group, department, and division. Wallach (1983, p. 33) vividly depicts how different cultural norms can exist within the same organization:

Organizational cultures are not monolithic. Although strong cultures will be pervasive throughout an organization, coloring each employee's reality of the company's "personality," many cultures exist within the corporate reality. We all work for the same company, but the norms will vary somewhat from division to division, location to location and functional area to functional area. Just as we are all Americans and share similar values, regional differences exist. Consider the stereotypical differences between a cowboy from Houston and a Brooks Brothers Bostonian. They look different, act different and their values are different. Relocate a New Englander to Southern California and what do you have? Culture shock! What might be totally appropriate behavior in one functional/ divisional/geographical piece of your company might be totally inappropriate in another.

The issue of company-wide versus division-specific cultures is clearest at the extreme—with a uniproduct domestic firm versus an international conglomerate. Consider the cultural dilemma of General Telephone and Electronics (GTE) (Lee, 1984, p. 31):

GTE is a conglomerate that includes operations as diverse as a light-bulb manufacturer and a high-tech microcircuit manufacturer, as well as telephone companies—each with it own cultural norms. In fact, it is such a diversified organization that another question enters the fray: Does it make sense to try to create some sort of "unified" GTE culture?

A special problem emerges when each division of a company has different cultural norms. Going from one division to another is like traveling from one foreign country to another. Communications and conflicts across divisions are more difficult to manage. The divisions have different jargons, values, work habits, and attitudes. As long as different divisions or different companies within the same corporation are mostly independent of one another, each can proceed with its own culture with little need to cross boundaries and work with other parts of the organization. Otherwise, if divisions have to work together frequently, the different cultures will get in the way of cooperative efforts.

A general rule that can resolve this dilemma is: Let each division develop the subculture that is conducive to its own high performance, but encourage each division to adopt those organization-wide norms that promote organizational success. The latter include norms that support cooperation and coordination among the divisions: Help other departments whenever possible; look at the problem from the other's point of view; remember that we all work for the same organization.

The Kilmann-Saxton Culture-Gap Survey recognizes that the divisions of the same organization may need different cultures and, in fact, displays the pattern of culture-gaps throughout the organization. Figure 6 shows an organizational culture-gap profile—a summary picture of the four culture-gaps for each identified work unit in the form of an organization chart. This profile is a convenient way to see if the organization has the same culture problems in every unit or if units have some very different profiles. It is critical to know this information before attempting to change the culture. One should not assume that a firm currently has or should have only one culture; it all depends on the nature of the work to be done and on just what behavior is required for success in each work unit. This important point is lost in a top-down approach, which generally assumes one culture for all.

Step Five: Closing Culture-Gaps

How can the culture-gaps be closed? How can an organization move its culture from the actual to the desired? Can a company be taken out of a culture rut and be put back on track for solving present and future problems? Will the organization survive this culture shock?

When the current culture is at least hopeful, it is almost miraculous what impact the survey results or the lists of desired norms have on the members of a work unit. As mentioned before, there is often a great sense of relief as people become aware that they can live according to different norms and that they have the power to change. Surprisingly, some change from the actual to the desired norms can take place just by listing the new set of norms. Members start "playing out" the new norms immediately after they are discussed.

When the current culture is cynical, depressed, and very much in a rut, however, the response to the survey results is quite different. Even when large gaps are shown or when a list-

Figure 6. Organizational Culture-Gap[SM] Profile.

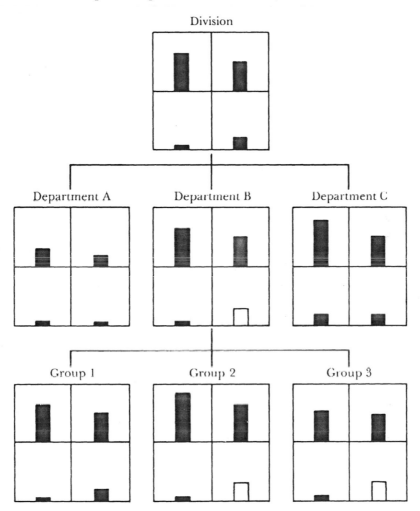

ing demonstrates the tremendous differences between actual and desired norms, the members seem apathetic and lifeless. Members respond by saying that their work units cannot change for the better until the level of management above them and the rest of the company change. Members believe that it is the external system that is keeping them down.

Curiously, when I do a culture-gap survey at the next-highest level, the very same arguments are heard again: "We have no power to change; we have to wait for the next level to let us change; *they* have the power!" It is shocking, after conducting the culture-gap survey for an entire organization, to present the results to the top management group only to find the same feelings of helplessness. Here top management is waiting for the economy to change. In actuality, it is the corporate culture that is saying: Don't take on responsibility; protect yourself at all costs; don't try to change until everyone else has changed; don't lead the way, follow; if you ignore the problem, maybe it will go away.

This is the perfect example of a company in a culture rut, where the shock of realizing the discrepancy between actual and desired norms is just too great to confront. Instead, the organization buries its head in the sand and hopes everything will be sorted out by itself. Even in the face of strong evidence of a serious problem, time and time again I have witnessed this form of organizational denial—a much more powerful and perhaps destructive force than any case of individual denial. The group's power to define reality clouds each person's better judgment. The bureaucratic culture "wins" again.

One large industrial organization asked me to present a three-day seminar to the top executive group (the chairman of the board and chief executive officer and the ten corporate officers) on the topic of corporate culture. I suggested that a representative survey of culture-gaps be conducted across all divisions in the company. In this way, I could report on the culture of that organization specifically, which could be expected to generate a more interesting and lively discussion than an abstract lecture. In a couple of weeks, the vice-president of human resources gave me his response: "No, we better not do this. I don't think the executive group really wants to know what is going on in the company. Besides, we can't take the chance of surprising them with your survey results." Who is protecting whom?

At another meeting with a major company on the same topic, I shared the above anecdote as an example of the industrial culture problem in America without, of course, mentioning any names. The response to my story was: "That must be our company you're talking about!" It was not the same company, but the message was still the same.

A major lesson to learn from changing corporate cultures, especially very dysfunctional and depressed cultures—those in a culture rut—is that people do not have to feel powerless and inept. If managers and members decide that taking on responsibility for change and feeling the power to change should be part of the new culture, then it can be done. Power and control are more a social reality than some objective, physical reality. Many times individuals and organizations have moved forward and achieved great success when everyone else "knew" it was impossible.

Merely listing and stating the new norms, however, is not enough to instill these throughout the organization. Also, norms cannot be altered by just requesting a norm change. Members have to develop agreements that the new norms will indeed replace the old norms and that this change will be monitored and sanctioned by the work groups. They must reinforce one another for enacting the new behaviors and attitudes and confront one another when the dysfunctional norms creep back into the work group. Consider the new norm: Congratulate those who suggest new ideas and new ways of doing things. If any member notices that a coworker frowns when some new product idea is suggested, the coworker should be given suitable stares and reminders of the new norms. He might even be confronted with some statement, such as: "I thought you were part of the team and had agreed to make the switch. What's your problem?"

In another major company undergoing a change program, I suggested that each new norm be written on an index card and given a number. Each member in a work group was then made responsible for monitoring several norms and bringing attention to behavior that did not conform. Eventually, this approach reached a point at which group members no longer cited the norms—only the numbers. Coworkers would state: "You just

committed a number twelve," or "You pulled a seven on me."
These members found it very effective to enforce their new
norms in this lighthearted manner, yet the point of adopting the
norms was made unequivocally. Of course, when "outsiders"
heard such interchanges they certainly were confused; but this
seemed to add to the group's cohesiveness, since the members
now had their own secret code.

Any organization that has determined the extent of its
culture-gaps using the aforementioned steps is then in a position
to chart the directions for a culture change. Conducting sessions
for each division, department, and work group, including the
ways in which the new norms will be monitored and enforced,
will begin the change process. However, any new culture will
gradually return to the old dysfunctional one if the four other
tracks are not implemented properly. For example, the management skills and team-building tracks will instill the right leadership styles in each work unit to support an adaptive culture.
With the strategy-structure track, the formally documented systems will be working with the informal, intangible work group
pressures to move the organization in the desired direction.
Also, the reward system track will design compensation systems
that monitor and reward behaviors that support the new norms.
The social energy of the members will be behind the organization—on a continuing basis.

An excellent example of a concerted effort at closing
culture-gaps is now taking place at Honeywell Information Systems (Lee, 1984, p. 31):

Honeywell's computer business was in need of change. "It was
bought from General Electric 25 years ago," explains Dotlich
[manager of corporate human resource development], "and was
never 'Honeywellized.' It was a poor performer and the employees were cynical and distrustful. Renier [president] wanted
to build a cultural effort that would produce trust, cooperation
and teamwork."

Honeywell's change efforts have included a communication program to emphasize teamwork and define values; a "cultural boot camp" which brought 25 top managers together for
six days to examine how to change the culture; participation in
Executive Challenge, an out-in-the-woods program that seeks to

build trust through teamwork activities; and training programs to let managers and employees at all levels know what kind of behavior is expected and rewarded.

Gaining control of the corporate culture is not only possible but necessary for the dynamic complexity that contemporary organizations now face. As changes in corporate directions are planned, a new culture may have to replace the old culture—in one or more divisions or for the whole organization. But just as old cultures can become out-of-date and dysfunctional, the same can happen with any new culture. Further changes in the organization's setting—and corresponding changes in strategy, structure, and reward systems—can make any culture less functional than before. An important part of managing the corporate culture, therefore, is to continue monitoring and assessing norms. If the culture is *not* managed explicitly, it may be just a matter of time before some stakeholder, internal or external, badly disrupts the organization. Ironically, it will not be the stakeholder, per se, but a bureaucratic culture that keeps the organization in the dark even when everything else has changed.

Manny Gerard [co-president of Warner Communications] was right about one thing—the importance of establishing a corporate culture. Doing that is more valuable than bringing out a hot new product or finding an exploitable market niche. In a competitive business, any particular advantage in a product or market position is likely to be transient. An established set of values can last a while, providing a base for cooperation and decision making. Unfortunately, you can't buy one—you've got to build your own [Hector, 1983, p. 52].

Return to the SFD Story

Even before the interviews were conducted during the diagnostic stage, the consultants felt that there could be some very dysfunctional norms operating in SFD. This impression was based on what had been presented by the top management staff. Consequently, as each interview took place, we asked the interviewee to list any specific norms that might be holding the division back. After we explained what a norm was and gave some examples, each person found it rather easy to make several norms explicit. Although most of the norms mentioned were simply variations of those already contained in the Kilmann-Saxton Culture-Gap Survey, twenty norms were unique. These norms, because of their specificity and language, expressed the particular culture of SFD which no standardized survey could fully document.

For purposes of illustration, ten of the twenty unique norm pairs are shown below. In each case, the (A) item was suggested by SFD members, while the (B) item was developed by the consultants as a "paired opposite." Members chose the (A) or (B) item in each norm pair in two ways: (1) Which one is the actual norm? (2) Which is the desired norm? Each norm pair also had a seven-point scale alongside it to record the strength of the choice for each member. This enabled a calculation to be made of the culture-gap.

1. (A) Show favoritism.
    (B) Treat employees equally.
2. (A) Don't respect management.
    (B) Management is worthy of respect.
3. (A) Be secretive and deceitful.
    (B) Be honest and open.
4. (A) Protect your own turf.
    (B) Do what is best for the division.
5. (A) Just give lip service to new programs.
    (B) Fully commit to and implement new programs.
6. (A) The group that controls the information makes the decision.
    (B) Leave decision making to the group that has the most expertise to solve the problem.
7. (A) Go along with pranks.
    (B) Discourage and prevent pranks, particularly when these could be harmful to someone.
8. (A) Protect your knowledge of the technology.
    (B) Document the technology.
9. (A) Don't trust anyone who is not in your clique.
    (B) Feel free to trust whomever you wish.
10. (A) Duplicate the work of other groups.
    (B) Don't duplicate the work of other groups.

These norm pairs portray some of the more troublesome behaviors that can be seen with a holographic view of the world. Thus, the whole culture is not just a matter of more or less Task Support, Task Innovation, Social Relationships, and Personal Freedom. The unique norms express favoritism, not respecting management, being secretive and deceitful, protecting one's turf, encouraging pranks that hurt others, and purposely duplicating the work of other groups.

What was staggering was that eighteen of the twenty unique norm pairs reached a difference score of +3.0 or more for the whole division (out of a possible 7.0), indicating a wave of significant culture-gaps. In most cases, therefore, the members chose the (A) item as the *actual* norm while they chose the (B) item as the *desired* norm. These results painted a rather gloomy picture of SFD's culture, suggesting that the term *culture rut* was descriptive of the situation. These results also showed the difficulty of closing the culture gaps—the four general gaps measured on the standardized survey plus the twenty unique ones assessed on the specially constructed form.

SFD embarked on the culture track in early December 1982, with work group sessions starting in January 1983. There were subsequent sessions in almost every month following January. All these sessions followed the steps outlined in this chapter. Special attention was devoted to making the culture-gaps explicit for each work unit, helping each chart its new cultural norms, and working to implement the new norms into the everyday life of SFD.

Conclusion

An adaptive culture sets the stage for all other organizational changes that need to be managed, as shown by the Barriers to Success model (Chapter Two). In contrast, a dysfunctional culture, breeding a lack of trust, confidence, and the sharing of information, would make it most difficult to proceed with the next four tracks.

Only with an adaptive culture will managers be willing to accept their skill deficiencies and to learn new approaches for addressing complex problems; they need an adaptive culture to recognize the many changes going on in the setting and, as a result, to uncover and update everyone's assumptions. With an adaptive culture, the membership can partake in team-building efforts to improve the quality of decision making and action taking on complex problems, where a collaborative effort is essential. Only with an adaptive culture will the membership be able to examine and then modify the formally documented systems—strategies, structures, and reward systems—representing very sensitive and close-to-home problems. With this new culture, the organization can expect significant improvements in morale and performance after all the change tracks have been implemented—so long as external stakeholders do not throw too many surprises.

CHAPTER FIVE

The
Management Skills
Track

Handwritten margin notes:
How Learn Skills? Responsibility
- Critical Thinker
- informated management
- Dec. making
- Ambiguity
How Promote?
- Leave?
- Peter Principle
- Good Skills?

Many of today's managers, though they may deny or not realize it, are members of a flourishing movement I call "the Panacean Conspiracy." These managers, typically promoted into management from such technical specialties as engineering, law, or finance, have little managerial know-how. Most don't have the time, interest, or awareness needed to learn their new craft, but they are anxious to produce immediately. What they are looking for, although they may profess to know better, are quick-fix solutions to dynamic, complex problems.

—Mayer, 1983, p. 23

Developing skills is the province of management training programs. There are many different types ranging from two-year MBA programs to one-day seminars on special topics. These programs are either conducted away from the work setting or held on site. They are composed of managers from different companies or designed for intact management teams from the same work unit or department. These programs attempt to aug-

125

ment technical, conceptual, analytical, administrative, social, and interpersonal skills.

The particular mix of skills required for successful performance depends on one's position in the management hierarchy. The importance of technical skills predominates at the bottom of the organizational pyramid, as supported by social, interpersonal, and motor skills (manual dexterity). At the top of the pyramid, administrative, conceptual, and analytical skills are most important for successful performance. Therefore, as members move up in the hierarchy, they will need skill development in these latter areas.

Many times I have observed the workings of the *Peter Principle*—the theory that managers rise to the highest level of their incompetence (Peter and Hull, 1969). Because of excellent performance at one level, employees are promoted to the next level. This process continues until poor performance results from the gap between the employee's current skills and the skills actually needed for the new job. The classic example is promoting an engineer to a management position because of his excellent technical skills and performance—only to find that he continues his efforts in the technical domain and ignores the management domain. Correcting this situation first requires an understanding of what the new management job entails. Then the right kind of classroom and on-the-job training must be provided so that the former engineer will develop the necessary management skills.

The basic theme of this chapter is that a qualitatively different set of skills is required for managing a complex hologram than for managing a simple machine. Conceptual, analytical, and administrative skills must be developed explicitly to handle dynamic complexity. In a nutshell, if managers are selected and trained to handle largely simple, well-structured, pre-defined problems—from the view of the world as a simple machine—the entire organization will reach its highest level of incompetence.

This chapter will provide the means for managing complex problems. First, the five steps of problem management are discussed. These steps recognize that today's managers must move beyond being just decision makers or problem solvers:

Dynamic complexity requires that managers first sense and define problems before they can select and implement solutions. Then, after the philosophical aspects of simple versus complex problems are examined, the second part of this chapter presents the six steps of assumptional analysis. These steps provide a systematic process for managing assumptions—the foundation of all arguments and conclusions. To make sure that any complex problem is managed correctly, the assumptions underlying the most extreme viewpoints are debated by different experts across different groups. It is through these extensive debates that a holographic world comes to life for all those who are prepared to manage it.

Problem Management — *Eliminate?*
What Causes problem

Most people in organizations experience and act upon problems, either implicitly or explicitly. While managers may differ in the ways they approach problems, one can define certain ideal steps that should be conducted whenever something is wrong and needs attention, regardless of approach. The five steps of problem management are sensing problems, defining problems, deriving solutions, implementing solutions, and evaluating outcomes. After these steps are conducted, the cycle repeats if any significant problem is still being sensed. These five steps of problem management, shown in Figure 7, parallel quite closely the five stages of planned change shown in Figure 2 (Chapter Three). In other words, just as consultants work with managers to define and solve *organizational* problems, managers must learn similar skills so that they can define and solve *technical/business* problems.

Problem management can be performed in a number of ways using any combination of individual and group arrangements. In most cases, the steps that are relatively simple can be assigned to one or a few individuals, while the more complex steps require interactions within and between several groups. The material on assumptional analysis presented later in this chapter will spell out how the intricate use of multiple groups must be applied in the most important and complex steps of

Figure 7. The Five Steps of Problem Management.

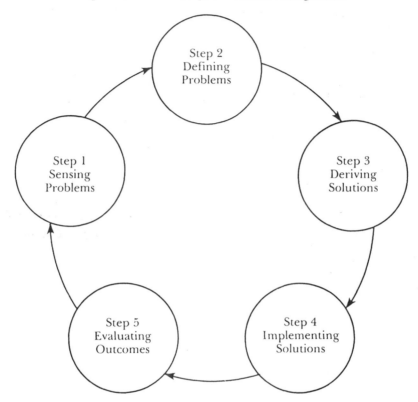

problem management. In this section, however, each step is discussed without reference to how it is performed.

Step One: Sensing Problems

The process starts when one or more individuals in the organization sense that something is wrong or that some problem exists. A problem is defined as a gap between what is (current or actual performance) and what could or should be (expected or desired performance). Once this gap breaks some threshold, a problem is sensed. For example, the expected turnover rate in a company may be 15 percent per year. However, if the turnover rate becomes as high as 40 percent, individuals may well perceive that something is wrong, since this rate significantly exceeds their acceptable range.

Any number of indicators, both formal and informal, for any stakeholder, either internal or external, can be used to sense whether a problem exists: increased cost of providing services, smaller appropriation of resources, decrease in clientele, smaller market share, more companies providing the same products or services, declining public image, decreased earnings per share, low morale, high turnover or absenteeism, or increase in consumer complaints. Aside from these "hard" measures, any of the manifestations of a culture rut discussed in the previous chapter also may signal a significant problem—such as general apathy, resistance, anxiety, frustration, or disruptive behavior. Once any or several of these indicators break some threshold of what is considered acceptable, members in the organization usually sense that some problem exists.

Typically, someone with power and influence senses that something is fundamentally wrong with the way the organization is responding to its problems. This awareness may be precipitated by changes in technology, competition, government regulations, and other environmental forces. On the other hand, a key executive may simply be dissatisfied with organizational processes and behavior as manifested by poor performance, low morale, and other symptoms.

At this stage, the "problem" may not be articulated or truly identified. Many organizations have embarked upon problem solving and, in the course of events, have found that they were dealing with symptoms and not the causes [Marchione and English, 1982, pp. 53-54].

Sanderson (1982, p. 60) refers to problem recognition as an important managerial skill for sensing today's complex problems. His description of the sensing process again demonstrates how the world is a complex hologram rather than a simple machine:

This points to a much neglected area of decision making and problem solving—problem recognition. Being aware that you have a problem, recognizing problems when they appear, or identifying situations as potential problems is an important managerial skill. Finely tuned antennae are often required, for problems don't necessarily make themselves immediately apparent. They may lie in wait for a long time, and even when they do appear, their symptoms could be subtle, elusive, or disguised.

Not sensing or recognizing problems might also occur when goals and expectations are so low that everything seems fine even though the organization is slowly decaying. Managers may be denying problems or may be afraid to set high standards because they are constrained by numerous barriers to success. In general, ignoring a trivial problem is one thing, but an *intense* denial by several managers is usually a signal that an important problem is being avoided.

Denying the existence of a problem is referred to as a *sensing error*: the likelihood that a problem exists but is not recognized. The other side of the sensing error is when the organization believes that there is a problem when in fact there is not. Here the organization may be overly sensitive to minor fluctuations in various indicators and, thereby, it tends to initiate problem management efforts prematurely and unnecessarily. The worst that can happen in this case, however, is that time and resources are wasted when everything is really within an acceptable range. In such a situation, perhaps the organization should raise its threshold levels. But I do think it is better to err by being too sensitive to problems than to ignore the really important problems.

Step Two: Defining Problems

Once it is sensed that a problem exists, the next step is to discover just what the problem is. For example, is the organization's high turnover rate the result of interpersonal conflicts, a culture rut, low job commitment, few promotion opportunities, competitive job offers from other firms, a change in expected salaries, a lack of clarity in job descriptions, or outdated, boring tasks? Any or several of these problem definitions could be the reason behind the high turnover rate. Essentially, the problem definition is viewed as the *cause,* in contrast to the *symptom,* for an indicator breaking a threshold level. Symptoms are defined as the changes that occur in any stakeholder (changes in buying behavior, decreases in market share, declining morale), while the definition of the problem is the reason these changes took place (a change in a competitor's strategy, the introduction of a new product, a change in the compensation system). The objective of this step, therefore, is to work backward from what registered on any indicator to try to determine the "whys" that caused it.

A *defining error* can be described as the likelihood of addressing the wrong problem instead of the right problem or of working on a trivial problem rather than the most important problem given the organization's mission and its setting. How do managers define problems? More often than not, individuals assume that their view of the world (their specialty) defines the essence of the problem. This selective perception is natural for anyone who has received extensive training in any skill area. Professionals wear blinders in order to become specialists: A finance person sees a financial world; a marketing person sees a marketing world; a social scientist sees a world of human interaction. This biasing effect is reinforced by one's department as the culture puts pressure on members to see problems a particular way.

Any problem definition arrived at in an implicit manner can result in a defining error. For example, a problem implicitly defined as not being able to recruit the best engineers may be defined more accurately as losing experienced engineers because of few promotion opportunities. Similarly, a problem implicitly defined as a weak advertising campaign may be better defined as having an outdated product line. Strangely enough, a particular definition of the problem is often assumed because that is the way it always has been addressed, even if the problem never disappears or is resolved. Consider the executive who always defines a low performance problem as a need for tighter controls over his middle managers. Every time something goes wrong, he "tightens the screws," but to no avail. Perhaps the middle managers need more freedom to perform, not less, or it may be that low performance results from any of a dozen other causes, but alternatives are just not considered. As Sanderson (1982, p. 59) states:

> Solving the wrong problem is costly in all senses of the word. In today's world, time is too short and resources are too scarce to gamble with the large investments that long projects demand.

Step Three: Deriving Solutions

The next step is generating solutions to the already defined problem and then selecting the "best" of them. Most discussions on decision theory, management decision making, and statistical analysis concentrate on this step. Usually one constructs a "decision tree," with the problem as the stump of the tree and the alternatives as branches. Alongside each alternative branch are associated costs, benefits, and probabilities of leading to the desired outcome. Sometimes several action steps follow beyond each first-level alternative, which results in branches leading off from other branches. Then a cost-benefit analysis is calculated for each series of branches so that the decision maker can choose a single—or integrated—solution.

A *solving error*—the likelihood of accepting one alternative when another is in fact better—can be made regarding the choice among two or more solutions to a problem. This error, of course, assumes that a defining error has not been committed. If a defining error *has* been committed, then worrying about a solving error is misplaced precision. It is far better to select a weak solution to the right problem than to choose the best solution to the wrong problem. Solving errors concern the choice among the branches of a given decision tree; defining errors concern whether the right decision tree was chosen in the first place when compared to all other decision trees.

Perhaps an anecdote will help illustrate the fundamental differences between defining problems and deriving solutions and their associated errors:

The story takes place in the marketing department of a large industrial organization, where virtually all the middle managers were complaining that they did not have the necessary information to make quality decisions about introducing new products. Sensing that an important problem existed, a senior executive contacted the information systems group in the company. Not surprisingly, this technically oriented group offered three alternative computerized systems to solve the problem. While the alternative systems differed according to size and flexibility, each was very expensive and required some training for the user.

As the executive was deciding among these alternative systems, he happened to share his problem with a psychologist who worked for the corporate planning staff. The psychologist suggested that the problem might be more human than technical—that the managers were complaining about their lack of information as a way of discounting their responsibility for making very risky decisions involving huge sums of money. Defining the problem in these terms, he offered two alternative solutions: modify the reward system to emphasize overall long-term results rather than single mistakes in new product introductions or require groups of managers to sign off on these decisions rather than separate individuals, as was the case at the time.

Although the executive was intrigued by these latter suggestions, he decided to go ahead with one of the computerized systems, since it promised more, better, and quicker information; after all, this is what his managers had complained about. However, even though it took less than six months to install the chosen system, the managers showed little enthusiasm. While somewhat disappointed with this response, the executive assumed that this would change as soon as the system was utilized.

It never was to be. Even a year after the system was in operation, very few managers were using it. In fact, less than 50 percent of them had bothered to attend any of the training sessions. From what the executive could see, his managers continued to make their decisions just as they had before; but now they complained that R&D was not providing quality products for them to promote, which made the introduction of these new products even more difficult to arrange.

Fed up with the continued complaining, the executive was now willing to try one of the suggestions offered by the psychologist almost two years ago. He decided to institute a new procedure for signing off on large promotional expenses using group decision making (five to ten managers). The results were astonishing. Within a short time, the managers became much more enthusiastic about the prospects for the new products coming out of R&D. As a group, they also developed more creative ways to promote these products—such as designing a consumer panel in their own community.

With this change in attitude and approach, the executive began pushing his managers to use the very expensive computer system that had been installed. The managers responded: "Why would we want to use a system that cranks out reams of statistical calculations when we can collect the necessary information much more easily by questioning the relevant sample on our consumer panel?"

This anecdote illustrates how various problem definitions not only address the same situation differently but result in vastly different solutions. Choosing the "technical" definition (the need for more information) versus the "human" definition (denying decision responsibility) is an example of a defining error (in choosing a wrong decision tree). Once a problem definition is chosen, the choice of alternative solutions is an example of a solving error (in choosing a wrong branch on a decision tree—reward system changes rather than changes in decision procedures). Thus, minimizing the defining error puts you in the right ball park; minimizing the solving error gets you to root for the right team.

Step Four: Implementing Solutions

It is one thing to derive what appears to be the best solution and quite another to implement it effectively in the organization. There are many examples of excellent solutions that were implemented poorly, at the wrong time, or by the wrong people. Implementation should not be taken for granted: One should not assume that a good solution will automatically be accepted and find its way into the mainstream of organizational life. There is resistance to change in any organization—members may perceive costs and psychological losses as outweighing the benefits of the proposed change. Thus, in addition to the technical and economic aspects of implementing solutions, there are psychological and cultural aspects as well.

Not anticipating obstacles, resistance, and forces operating to keep things the same results in an *implementing error*:

the likelihood of not implementing a solution properly. No matter how well the other steps in the process have been conducted and to what extent the other errors have been minimized, committing an implementing error will nullify the total effort at problem management.

In the example of the marketing department, an implementing error occurred when the executive selected the solution of installing a computer system but did not ask the middle managers about their preferences regarding its design. In addition, the managers may have had some anxieties about learning a computerized way of processing information. Certainly the assumption behind installing the system was that the managers would be motivated to use the computer system. Ignoring the intricate technical features and the many psychological factors that affected the use of the solution resulted in an implementing error.

Step Five: Evaluating Outcomes

Did the implemented solution actually solve the problem? If the indicators are no longer beyond threshold levels, the organization may assume that the problem has been managed properly —at least the organization does not need to be further concerned about the problem at this time. It is possible, however, that the initial problem may have stirred up new problems, and these might motivate the organization to continue the problem management cycle. Alternatively, if the initial problem is still sensed after the organization has gone through all five steps, it is likely that one or more steps were performed incorrectly and that one or more errors were committed. After a full study of each possible error has been made, the steps should be performed again. Going through the cycle once or a few times should resolve the initial problem and help manage recurring problems.

Distinguishing Simple and Complex Problems

Knowing the difference between a simple and a complex problem is helpful in deciding how to conduct each step of problem management. If the problem is simple, one person can travel through each step with little need to search out additional expertise or to collect information from others. With a simple problem, it is unnecessary to spend much time on defining the problem and implementing the solution. The simple problem consists of one decision tree, and its impact on the organization is quite predictable. Complex problems, however, require considerably more time and effort in all steps of problem management, particularly in defining problems and implementing solutions. Because of the limited mental capacity of individuals, it is unlikely that one person can be an expert in many different subjects. This is why other individuals and groups have to be brought into the steps of problem management—to see problems from every possible angle.

Because this issue of simple versus complex problems is so fundamental, it is worthwhile to review the underlying philosophy of these two types of problems before outlining the steps of assumptional analysis.

Churchman (1971) presents a number of approaches for "knowing" derived from the philosophy of science. Each approach assumes certain things about the nature of problems as well as about the particular way to guarantee that "truth" has been obtained. In essence, philosophy asks: How do we know when something is true? How can we be sure that we know something at all? While these questions may seem merely speculative and only suited for those studying philosophy, it turns out that understanding the importance of these questions and their answers is quite useful for managing dynamic complexity. For present purposes, it is sufficient to concentrate on two such "knowing" or inquiring systems (IS): the Lockean IS and the Hegelian IS.

The Lockean IS generally assumes the existence of simple problems for which a group of experts can uncover the true definition or solution via agreement and consensus. For example, if a group of experts were given some problem to solve or asked to state some opinion or make a prediction, the one solution, opinion, or prediction on which they could agree would become the truth. The Lockean IS can be shown on a graph as a normal distribution (a bell-shaped curve) in which the extreme positions are eliminated simply because agreement cannot be reached on these "minority" views. However, support for the middle of the distribution can be achieved, since the majority of experts holds that view. Thus the Lockean IS tends to gravitate toward the mean (average) and stay away from the endpoints. An example of the Lockean IS is the Delphi approach to planning, in which those holding minority views are asked to revise their judgments because they differ from those of the majority. Another example is the method for scoring a diving competition, in which the high and low scores by expert judges are thrown out and the remainder are averaged to derive the "true" performance of a person on a particular dive.

The Hegelian IS portrays a very different approach to knowing truth and the best definition or solution to any problem. This approach assumes that problems are complex and, therefore, that any one person is not likely to have all the expertise and information needed to define or solve it. Rather, each person with a different area of expertise might be able to address, at best, only a piece of the whole problem. According to the Hegelian IS, wisdom is not in the majority but resides in minority viewpoints—as integrated or synthesized. In fact, any majority view would be suspect and would be regarded as *common ignorance* on the problem. Therefore, the Hegelian IS can be represented as a normal distribution that deemphasizes or even rejects the middle and concentrates on the extremes.

Truth for the Hegelian IS is revealed through the dialectical debate. Experts representing opposite positions debate their differences. During these debates, underlying beliefs are exposed and challenged, and thereby each extreme position is scrutinized and dissected. It is through these debates that the truth is expected to emerge for any complex problem. But the final conclusion reached with the Hegelian IS need not be any of the initial positions that were debated. It is the debate that enhances understanding so that the best problem definition among all alternatives can be chosen or some synthesis can be derived. Furthermore, the dialectical debate is not the same as the "straw man" approach, in which one alternative is set up as the "devil's advocate" only to be disarmed so that the original position is chosen. In the Hegelian IS, each extreme position is real and equal. The debate, therefore, is intense and balanced, not one-sided.

The Lockean IS and the Hegelian IS are quite different and in fact almost opposite to one another, as diagrammed in Figure 8. Here the relevant portion of each IS is shown on a normal distribution of problem definitions or proposed solutions. This diagram also suggests how both inquiring systems

Figure 8. Two Inquiring Systems.

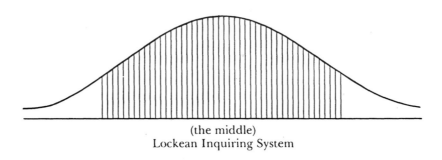

(the middle)
Lockean Inquiring System

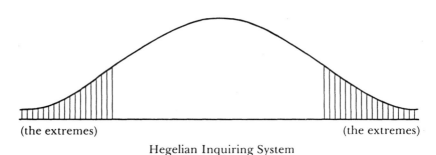

(the extremes)   (the extremes)

Hegelian Inquiring System

 = Points of focus

together present the "full picture." In essence, each system presupposes the other and must deal with the other in some form. For example, before the Lockean IS suppresses disagreement and extreme positions, it must recognize them. Consensus may be the final outcome, but surely some debate will have taken place along the way. The Lockean IS does not like to acknowledge this and tends to minimize conflict as such. Alternatively, the Hegelian IS has to achieve some agreement regarding which extreme positions to debate and for how long and which synthesis to represent as the choice of the experts. The Hegelian approach, in its emphasis on differences, tends to suppress or make light of the role consensus plays in its method.

The difference between the two "knowing" systems is a critical matter of emphasis. Both come to agreement in the end, but the Hegelian IS first creates debates to *diverge* from the initial positions before it moves toward a synthesis (emphasizing the former over the latter). The Lockean IS tries to *converge* directly to the final choice by ignoring and downplaying any differences that occur. Figure 9 shows these two inquiring systems as each begins, proceeds, and then ends with a conclusion.

To understand the differences between the Lockean IS and the Hegelian IS is to understand the essential differences between viewing the world as a simple machine and viewing the world as a complex hologram. In the former it would be a waste of time, energy, and resources for the organization to design numerous groups (different areas of expertise and information) to solve a simple problem (requiring a very narrow range of expertise). This is inefficient. However, it would be ineffective and perhaps disastrous to approach a complex problem with a single kind of expertise. The following sections present assumptional analysis as a method that makes the Hegelian IS work for problem management.

Assumptional Analysis

Assumptions are the foundation for all decisions and actions (Mason and Mitroff, 1981). Whenever someone concludes that something is the best thing to do, his arguments are sound

Figure 9. Diverging and Converging Aspects of the Two Inquiring Systems.

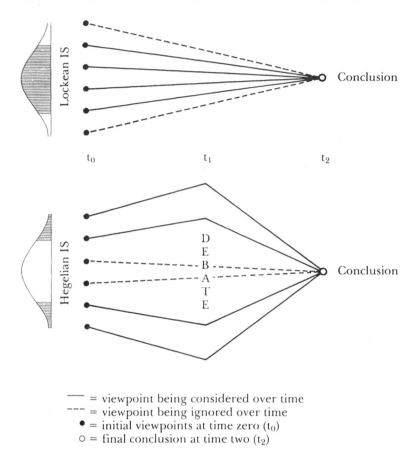

—— = viewpoint being considered over time
--- = viewpoint being ignored over time
● = initial viewpoints at time zero (t_0)
○ = final conclusion at time two (t_2)

only if their underlying assumptions are true. Here we will define the term *conclusion* as anything argued for, such as a plan, policy, problem definition, or course of action.

Most often, individuals assume—unquestioningly believe—that things automatically will be the same in the future as they were in the past, that everyone is basically the same and wants the same things, that people make decisions in a totally rational manner, that the organization is designed with effectiveness in mind, that the consumer easily can discern the value of the organization's product, and so on. In other words, people accept very basic and sometimes simplistic assumptions just because these assumptions have never been exposed for questioning. Yet so much of what individuals may argue for—such as continuing to provide the exact same products to consumers, designing certain advertising campaigns, or proposing budget increases to offer more services—may be based on inaccurate or outdated assumptions. In fact, one could reverse each of the "typical" assumptions just stated (forming counterassumptions) and realize that these "atypical" assumptions also are plausible but lead to vastly different conclusions!

A striking example of assumptions driving all decisions and actions is provided by the automobile industry. O'Toole shows how a set of ten core assumptions guided the success of the American automobile manufacturing companies during a fifty-year period. When these firms failed to update their assumptions to be in tune with today's world, those very same assumptions were responsible for the companies' near demise. Examining the assumptions of a "fictitious" automobile company called Monolithic Motors (M.M.), O'Toole (1983, p. 4) presents the case as follows:

The guiding principles that led to M.M.'s early success were crystallized into operating assumptions for all subsequent generations of managers. . . . All the guiding assumptions were based on the pioneering policies that had made M.M. one of the most successful industrial organizations in the world. By repeating what had made it successful in the past, the company became even more successful. In turn, this reinforced the legitimacy of the operating assumptions. These assumptions then became unchallengeable—and unchallenged. Why challenge an idea with eternal validity? Only a fool would knock success.

Here we see that erroneous extrapolation causes companies to fall not only into culture ruts but into "assumption ruts." O'Toole (1983, p. 4) discusses ten unchallenged assumptions that took Monolithic Motors into the 1970s:

1. M.M. is in the business of making money, not cars.
2. Success comes not from technological leadership but from

having the resources to quickly adopt innovations success-
fully introduced by others.

3. Cars are primarily status symbols. Styling is therefore
more important than quality to buyers who are, after all,
going to trade up every other year.

4. The American car market is isolated from the rest of the
world. Foreign competitors will never gain more than 15%
of the domestic market.

5. Energy will always be cheap and abundant.

6. Workers do not have an important impact on productivity
or product quality.

7. The consumer movement does not represent the concerns
of a significant portion [of] the American public.

8. The government is the enemy. It must be fought tooth
and nail every inch of the way.

9. Strict, centralized financial controls are the secret to good
administration.

10. Managers should be developed from the inside.

As we all know by now, the world changed drastically in the
1970s. Dynamic complexity caused these ten assumptions to
become outdated—in fact wrong. Almost overnight, the very
existence of one of the largest industrial organizations was
threatened as never before (O'Toole, 1983, p. 5):

Gasoline became expensive; the auto market became in-
ternationalized; the rising cost of (and time required for) re-
tooling made it necessary to be a leader rather than a follower
in the introduction of new technology; consumer values changed
from styling to quality; the size of families shrank; people could
no longer afford to trade their cars in every few years; worker
values and attitudes changed; successful government relations
required cooperation rather than an adversarial relationship;
the few "kooks" in California who bought Volkswagens and
read Consumer Reports [became] an important segment of the
auto buying public. . . . By 1980 the environment had changed
so thoroughly that the brilliant assumptions created by the
company's founders to meet the exigencies of the environment
of the 1920s were inappropriate in the radically altered environment fifty years later.

Monolithic Motors is just a thinly disguised name for
General Motors (GM); there is no further need to persist in the

cover. Some analysts have argued that one of the worst th
that could have happened to GM happened recently: It announced a net income of more than $1 billion for the second
quarter of 1983. "[Its] earnings for the year will probably be
the best since 1978" (Burck, 1983, p. 94). What is so bad about
this? GM's short-term success may reinforce the old-time management beliefs that nothing really has changed and, therefore,
that GM should return to the proven ways and assumptions of
the past. The need for change in the 1970s was just a temporary
fluctuation. Surely, the ways that made GM such a giant in the
past will be the direct line to organizational success in the
future.

The changes GM is attempting are greater in scale and
scope than those of the 1970s—indeed greater than anything the
company has undertaken since the days of Alfred P. Sloan, Jr.
and perhaps unprecedented for any organization of GM's size
and complexity. At the same time, many of GM's 45,000 managers have yet to get the message. One GM executive glumly
mused last fall that from what he could see, no more than half
the company's managers had really grasped the need to change
old ways of operating. Overconfidence dies hard, particularly in
an organization as conservative as GM. And of course it dies all
the harder when sales and profits are moving up [Burck, 1983,
p. 100].

Every time General Motors or any other firm in the automobile industry addresses an important problem, which set or
subset of assumptions will be the foundation for all arguments
and conclusions? Most likely the assumptions that made the organization successful in the past will continue to guide all decisions and actions. Will unstated and unexamined assumptions
cloud the issue of how to define and then solve problems in today's world? Of course they will! Complicating matters further,
perhaps certain new assumptions will have to be made about
new stakeholders that did not even exist ten or twenty years
ago. Without making all assumptions explicit and thereby seeing whether proposed solutions (conclusions) are likely to be
true or false, any company will be driven by unknown and unstated forces. This will not lead to organizational success.

Assumptional analysis is the way to thoroughly and systematically examine the essence of the most complex problems facing the organization. By applying this method, managers and their organizations will address dynamic complexity in the best way possible. The six steps of assumptional analysis are (1) forming initial conclusions, (2) designing groups around conclusions, (3) performing group assumptional analysis, (4) performing intergroup assumptional analysis, (5) resolving and synthesizing assumptions, and (6) deriving the synthesized conclusion.

These steps involve various combinations of within-group and between-group activity. Consistently putting similar experts within the same group results in reaching the best Lockean conclusions possible by discovering the common wisdom that is present in each group. Deliberately forming different groups of experts and requiring them to argue their differences across group boundaries results in the most intense and probing Hegelian debates. Using Lockean IS within groups and Hegelian IS between groups works much better than attempting to perform all of assumptional analysis within one group. Since every group has a tendency to suppress its deviants, it is difficult to have a true dialectic within a single group; the majority seems to prevail in most if not all cases. It is very unusual to have two or more equal views argued in one group. However, having the debate occur across groups takes advantage of the natural tendency for team competition. In fact, it is relatively easy to give equal weight to each viewpoint simply by building a group around it. Even if there are different numbers of individuals in each group, a team is a team.

Step One: Forming Initial Conclusions

Assumptional analysis begins with a minimum of two very different conclusions. Often, a number of competing conclusions are available and have been articulated in the past. Sometimes only one or two different conclusions have been voiced and it may be necessary to formulate additional viewpoints. In either case, drawing on a wide and diverse set of individuals will ensure that very different viewpoints are available for a complex, ill-defined problem. While in theory it would be nice to have every possible viewpoint represented, generally this is not feasible. As long as sufficient diversity is present (for example, ten to fifty individuals representing several different conclusions), the process can begin.

Consider GM's problem of deriving a strategic plan for the twenty-first century. What are some alternatives? (1) Continue producing cars that the engineers and the marketers want to sell to the public. (2) Emphasize economy cars exclusively in order to compete with foreign competition. (3) Return to producing big, fancy cars. (4) Shift more heavily into other modes of transportation. (5) Diversify into altogether new markets that will help balance out the periodic swings of the automobile industry. While these alternatives as stated are somewhat extreme—as a choice of one or the other—this helps bring out differences rather than similarities. The former is the basis for the dialectical debate on assumptions that follows. However, the "final" conclusion can be any integrated combination of the earlier viewpoints—or something entirely new.

Step Two: Designing Groups Around Conclusions

Once all the individuals have been assembled, a small group is formed around each of the initial conclusions. These conclusions are referred to as *initial* because they will surely undergo change as their underlying assumptions are exposed and challenged. Initial conclusions are just a way to start the process—a way of getting at the tried-and-true assumptions. Later, the initial conclusions will appear naive (and perhaps foolish) once the asumptions have been examined.

Take the case of General Motors. In order to formulate a new strategic plan based on all the wisdom available, perhaps fifty people throughout the corporate structure would be asked to participate. These individuals would be drawn from each division in the organization and thus would represent different functional areas and specialties: engineering, marketing, public relations, legal counsel, finance, new product development, manufacturing, human resources, and so on. Just to make sure that the corporate culture has not overly narrowed the organization's perspective, perhaps outside experts in a number of areas also would be included.

These individuals, once gathered together, would look over the initial list of conclusions and self-select into a group. In addition to the five initial conclusions that were listed (keep things the same, move toward economy cars, move toward big cars, shift to other modes of transportation, and diversify into other industries), a provocative sixth viewpoint might be added: Go out of business! While many members might consider this unacceptable, such an initial conclusion generally fosters a very strong debate on some fundamentally different assumptions about the organization's capacity to change. The possibility of going out of business would put pressure on all the other groups to fully document their cases.

Step Three: Performing Group Assumptional Analysis

When the different small groups have been composed, each group works in a separate room and, for the time being, is not concerned about the other groups. For convenience, these conclusion groups will be referred to hereafter as *C-groups*.

Generating assumptions for any conclusion can be accomplished by first listing all the potential stakeholders who may affect or be affected by the conclusion and who therefore have a stake in what happens. Individuals in an organization implicitly make assumptions about what the various stakeholders want, believe, expect, and value, how they make decisions or engage in actions themselves, and what outcomes from stakeholder decisions and actions they expect to materialize. The primary reason for identifying stakeholders is not to list people and groups for its own sake but to generate assumptions. In particular, the objective is not to miss any relevant individual or group, whether internal or external to the organization. First developing a comprehensive list of stakeholders is expected to minimize the chance of missing any potential set of assumptions.

For each stakeholder, a list of assumptions is developed to state what would have to be true about any and all aspects of the stakeholder in order to provide maximum support for the conclusion. Each assumption is stated in a form intended to maximize this support, no matter how obvious or, alternatively, how ridiculous the assumption may seem. The "truth" of each assumption will be investigated later. For the moment, assumptions are stated about any property or characteristic of each stakeholder that may have a bearing on the validity of the conclusion. Assumptions *are* properties of stakeholders.

For example, continuing with the case of GM, each C-group would list all stakeholders, internal and external, relevant to its conclusion. The group arguing for keeping things the same might include the following stakeholders: the economy, the government, foreign competition, the consumer, consumer advocate groups, domestic competitors, stockholders, top management, and the rest of the members of GM. Then the group would list five to ten assumptions for each stakeholder that would have to be true in order to most strongly support keeping things the same. Most of these assumptions would be quite similar to the ten core assumptions of GM listed earlier: Foreign competition will remain stable; the consumer groups are weak; domestic competitors will not provide technologically improved autos; the membership will continue to be satisfied to work on the same cars in the same way; the energy crisis is a thing of the past.

Another C-group in the GM case, however, may suggest some new stakeholders and, as a result, some new assumptions. Specifically, the group whose conclusion is to shift into other modes of transportation would list these stakeholders: the airline industry, the railroad industry, the inner-city rapid transportation industry, new fuel sources, R&D efforts at new technological breakthroughs, and the communications industry (as a substitute for transportation). How these industries can enter into GM's setting must be discussed. Then assumptions of the dynamics and effects of these new stakeholders must be made explicit. In contrast, an internal stakeholder—all GM members—

would require a different assumption to support the strategic shift. Essentially, this C-group would have to assume that the members want to change, are willing to learn new skills, and are prepared to have their jobs reclassified as GM shifts all its structures along with its strategy.

Are all assumptions of equal importance? It seems that there are always several tangential assumptions that, even if one or more are false, do not prevent one from still arguing strongly for the same conclusion. However, there may be one or more assumptions that, if they indeed turn out to be false, would greatly undermine one's entire argument. In this case, one can no longer argue for the conclusion when the fallacy of such a central assumption has been revealed.

Taking the case of GM, the group arguing for returning to producing big, fancy cars will not be affected much by assumptions concerning *how* foreign auto makers will sell their cars in the United States. However, this group's argument is heavily affected by assumptions concerning what consumers want and the availability of gasoline. If research surveys suggest that American consumers now prefer high-quality, fuel-efficient autos because they anticipate another energy crisis in the 1990s, this C-group will find it impossible to make a convincing argument for its initial conclusion.

Are all assumptions equally plausible? It seems that some assumptions are more certain (or uncertain) than others. A *fact* is an assumption that is believed to be true with a very high certainty (perhaps 100 percent). For example, it is considered by many to be a fact that the United States government will not nationalize the automobile industry in the next ten years—or at least it is an assumption that is highly certain. Alternatively, an assumption has great uncertainty when no one in the organization can predict or control its eventual outcome. Assuming that no competitor will introduce a major technological breakthrough in the auto industry in the next ten years is highly uncertain.

Figure 10 shows a matrix on which any assumption can be plotted according to its importance to the initial conclusion

Figure 10. Assumption Matrix.

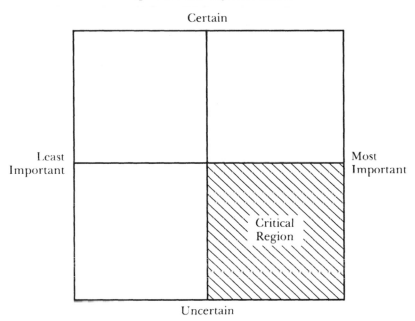

as well as according to its uncertainty. Is the assumption, relatively speaking, most important to arguing for one's conclusion or is it least important? Is the assumption, as stated, fairly certain to be true, or is its truth uncertain? Combining these two dimensions for judging assumptions results in four categories: (1) certain, least important, (2) certain, most important, (3) uncertain, least important, (4) uncertain, most important.

The first category (certain and least important assumptions) represents trivia—highly certain facts that have little significance in the issue at hand. The second category (certain and most important assumptions) represents important facts; but since we know these to be true, these assumptions do not reveal anything new. The third category (uncertain and least important assumptions) shows what is not fully known to be true, but it does so about matters that really are not central to the arguments being presented. The fourth category (uncertain and most important assumptions) highlights the whole reason for going through this analysis, the whole point of investigating assumptions. Essentially, this fourth category displays assumptions that are most important to the group's argument—if the group is wrong about these assumptions, its argument will be destroyed—yet there is considerable uncertainty as to the truth or falsity of these assumptions. In fact, maximum uncertainty suggests a 50/50 proposition. The assumptions, as stated, are just as likely to be false as they are to be true.

The fourth category is referred to as the "critical region" for each C-group. This is where the debates undoubtedly will focus; this is where the ultimate strength of any argument rests. Too often, this critical region not only is ignored but is purposely repressed. Individuals and groups arguing strongly for their positions do not want to expose their "Achilles' heel": Others would see the weakness and softness of their arguments. Stated boldly, building one's argument on assumptions that sort into the critical region is like building one's house on a foundation of quicksand.

One main reason for engaging in a dialectical approach, in contrast to using only one group or individual, is that every group is likely to ignore those stakeholders and assumptions that do not allow it to provide the strongest support for its case. Each group finds it convenient to overlook the assumptions that might weaken its case or at least to minimize the effect of wrong assumptions by sorting these into the less important cells of the matrix. Clearly, if only one group were involved in the entire process, the final results would be very biased and misleading. However, the biases of the other groups compensate for the bias of any one group. These biases can be expected to be different to the extent that each group was composed differently at the start. Therefore, what one group takes as a given (or conveniently chooses to ignore) the other groups consider an unwarranted assumption. Stated even more strongly, these biases are the hallmark of the dialectical approach; they are always operating, if only implicitly. Making these biases explicit, especially in an extreme form, not only makes them open for examination but forces a confrontation of biases.

Each C-group is given felt pens and easel pads and asked to plot each of its assumptions into the appropriate cells of the matrix. Often each group develops a code to identify the stakeholder that is associated with each assumption. In the case of General Motors, the C-group arguing for shifting into other modes of transportation would sort these assumptions into the critical region: What makes for success in one form of transportation leads to success in another (transportation is transportation); the abilities and skills of GM personnel are transferable to solving other types of transportation problems; the stockholders will support such a strategic shift; other auto firms will not follow this strategic shift; shifting to different forms of transportation will provide more growth and profit opportunities than will be provided by remaining predominantly in the automobile industry; automobiles will represent a small proportion of transportation in America in the decades ahead.

Step Four: Performing Intergroup
Assumptional Analysis

After each C-group has prepared its matrix, the participants move into a community room for an intergroup challenge of assumptions. Each C-group is placed on the "hot seat" as the other groups have the opportunity, one by one, to question and challenge the focal group's assumption matrix. Sometimes concessions are made during the debate as one or more groups realize that they cannot "get away with" one or more assumptions that, upon inspection, do not seem very credible. As a result, many assumptions are modified and others are created.

After an active debate has taken place on any or all assumptions, the time has come for each C-group to return to its own room and list the remaining issues that have not been resolved. These issues represent the differences that one or more groups cannot "live with" or cannot quite accept. Often these issues are the absolute core of the problem—the most critical assumptions that fall into the two most important regions of the matrix. However, there may be considerable disagreement as to the wording of these assumptions, whether a particular assumption is to be viewed as true or false, and how uncertain these assumptions really are.

In the case of establishing GM's strategic plan for the twenty-first century, it is difficult to predict what the ultimate areas of disagreement would be. This is precisely why such an elaborate method for surfacing and debating assumptions is so necessary for any complex problem. The greatest danger is to analyze assumptions using only one or a few persons. The biases of the limited view would go unchallenged, or the group pressures toward creating a social reality would convince these participants that they had captured the essence of the problem. Nothing could be farther from the truth.

Step Five: Resolving and Synthesizing Assumptions

The next step is to resolve the issues that still divide the C-groups so that a complete synthesis of assumptions can be formulated. This resolution cannot be accomplished by any of the C-groups, because they are too close to their own biases. Instead, a new group—a synthesis group—is formed by drawing together representatives from each of the original C-groups. For convenience, these synthesis groups will be referred to hereafter as *S-groups*.

It may not be easy for members of an S-group to switch from the earlier emphasis on disagreements (Hegelian IS) to the new emphasis on agreement (Lockean IS)—see Figure 9. Among other things, there is an inherent tendency for members to be loyal to their earlier group and to try to influence other members in the S-group toward this bias. Holding on to former group loyalties would result in "splitting the differences" or compromising behavior: "I'll give in on that one if you give in on this one." This trading behavior does not foster a creative synthesis.

A simple method can be used to overcome the obstacles created by prior group loyalties when these arise in a single S-group. The trick is to form several S-groups, where each group contains representatives from each former C-group. At first, this approach of multiple S-groups may seem awkward or cumbersome, but in actuality it tends to minimize earlier group loyalties by shifting competition among the C-groups to competition among the S-groups. Specifically, all S-groups are given the instruction: "Let's see which group can come up with the best synthesis—the synthesis that (by vote, perhaps) is deemed most acceptable to all participants in this process." Members in the synthesis groups forget or simply put aside their earlier loyalties, since the rules of the game have now been changed.

Not surprisingly, the various syntheses that emerge from this multigroup process are not all that different from each other. In contrast to the composition of the C-groups, the various S-groups have a very similar pattern of membership. Every S-group is composed of the exact same representation of the former C-groups, but with different people. Each of the S-groups uses the same expertise and information, although some differences in group process can be expected.

Step Six: Deriving the Synthesized Conclusion

Whether one or more S-groups partake in this last step, the product that emerges is a synthesized, agreed-on assumption matrix. Where the C-groups may have differed substantially with regard to assumptions and the sorting of these onto separate matrices, the S-groups seek to resolve these differences in a creative way, making use of all available knowledge and expertise.

As the S-groups focus on what was sorted into the critical region of the matrix, it often is desirable to collect additional data on the actual "truth" of these assumptions (from any source available, including scientific research). This additional information may move the assumptions into the certain region, although the assumptions may have to be stated differently as a result of the new information. The advantage of moving assumptions out of the critical region is that one can then argue both for the conclusion and for subsequent action with more confidence. Conclusions do not have to be founded on flimsy assumptions.

For example, the S-groups in the hypothetical GM case might recognize that several critical assumptions concern the wants and desires of the consumer. One C-group may have assumed that consumers want economy and quality, another C-group may have assumed that consumers want styling and comfort, and still another may have assumed that consumers are switching to other forms of transportation. Since all these assumptions fall into the uncertain and most important cell in the matrix, it is essential to know the "truth." The strength of all the arguments and their corresponding conclusions rests on deciding what is an accurate reading of the consumers. Perhaps some extensive market research studies can be undertaken to learn the validity of each assumption.

Nevertheless, decisions must be made and actions must be taken with some amount of uncertainty. No matter how much research is conducted, all assumptions will never fall into the two upper (certain) cells of the matrix—this is the nature of dynamic complexity. An assumption that was once true can become false (and vice versa) just as the relative certainty and importance of the assumption can change at any time. Assumptions are as dynamic as any stakeholder, since assumptions *are* the properties of stakeholders. Such a holographic view suggests that assumptional analysis needs to be an ongoing process of stating conclusions, examining assumptions, collecting new information, restating conclusions, reexamining assumptions, and so forth. This amounts to keeping the firm's "assumption bank" —which may be as important as any of its financial banks—up to date. This is what monitoring assumptions is all about.

The synthesized matrix, adjusted for any new information, now becomes the foundation for deriving (deducing) the "final" conclusion. In other words, what conclusion would receive the strongest possible support from the synthesized assumptions? What conclusion follows directly and logically from all the assumptions as stated, particularly the assumptions in the most important cells of the matrix? Prior experience with this method suggests that, in most cases, the conclusion derived from the synthesized set of assumptions is really new. It is not, typically, a restatement of one of the earlier, initial conclusions. When assumptional analysis is conducted as intended, the final conclusion is not something that anyone could or did anticipate at the outset. It is like magic when a new conclusion emerges that was never even contemplated before. This kind of "magic" does not happen when the Lockean method is applied to simple problems because of the closed, mechanical nature of the approach; any final conclusion results from picking the best of the initial bunch. Only with a holographic view is there considerable room for discovering entirely new conclusions. Dynamic complexity becomes the basis for creativity.

In the hypothetical case of GM going through all six steps of assumptional analysis, it is fun to speculate what the final conclusion would be (as long as one realizes that speculation is no substitute for the actual process). When the realities of today's marketplace have been reflected in all of GM's operating and management assumptions, the following strategic plan for the twenty-first century might be appropriate.

First, GM would establish an automobile industrialization curve for every nation. This curve would show the decades when the highest growth potential for the sale of automobiles could be anticipated. This curve would show that the United States has already passed this period; for developing nations, such as Mexico, the growth in automobile usage is just beginning. GM then would concentrate its auto designing, manufacturing, and marketing efforts for these new markets, as its assumptions warrant.

Second, once the industrialization curve passed the high growth potential for automobiles in any nation, GM would supply alternative forms of transportation. This plan would require a major shift in resources, culture, structures, and skills (all aspects of the Barriers to Success model) during the next fifty years. When the high-growth segments for autos were no longer plentiful, GM would be involved primarily in the other forms of transportation and perhaps heavily involved in service. Lastly, since "transportation" seems to be qualitatively different from "communication," GM would not enter this latter industry. Firms such as IBM and AT&T would probably continue to excel in moving information instead of people.

A *Business Week* article, "Detroit's Merry-Go-Round" (1983, p. 72), emphasizes the importance of auto makers man-

aging their assumptions—perhaps even more than their products:

> U.S. auto makers realize that concentrating on plants,
> equipment, and product will not be enough to solve all their
> problems. A more important and more difficult metamorpho-
> sis, industry leaders say, must take place within their own
> managements. They must create a philosophy that questions
> almost every traditional operating and management assump-
> tion. . . .
>   Deming estimates that it will take Detroit a staggering
> 30 years to complete its management makeover. . . . That goal
> amounts to a revolution in thinking for the auto industry.

Return to the SFD Story

Most of the material in the three management skills workshops for all thirty-eight managers in SFD concentrated on
problem management and assumptional analysis. However, the
first workshop did provide some basic material involving social
and interpersonal skills. Since most of the managers had received
a technical background in engineering, they were not as sensitive as they might have been to their behavioral impact on others, particularly on their subordinates. Their technical view of
the world did not always include the human side.

It is interesting to note that all these managers had attended numerous workshops in the past that had covered a wide
range of material in the social science area. Not much of what
they had learned in these off-site workshops, however, had
transferred back to their jobs. This is a very typical result. It
seems that whatever is learned is suppressed by the culture once
the manager returns. I have seen cases in which managers have
tried very hard to implement what they learned, only to be met
with: "I'm glad to see you back on the job. Now stop using all
those fancy terms and those silly ploys, and get back to work."
I call this the three-day washout effect. According to Main
(1982, p. 235):

> Executives who have attended almost any sort of manage-
> ment training usually recall the experience warmly. Of course,

no one is likely to come back from Aspen and admit
just wasted two weeks. But if asked to specify exac
company has benefitted from a course or seminar h
the executive may have trouble coming up with an answei. ⌣_
the record, he will often admit that the course he took was boring, irrelevant, or misleadingly marketed. Short seminars get the
most criticism. The academically rigorous and well-organized
courses lasting two weeks or more at the better-known business
schools are generally higher rated. Clients seem particularly
pleased with courses specially designed by consulting firms for
the entire top management of a particular corporation.

Since the purpose of management training is to transfer
the learnings back to the job, I no longer rely on off-site training programs. Rather, management workshops are held on site
and attended by the managers who work together on a daily
basis. In this way, the new material, insights, and methods are
more likely to be applied during work. In addition, at the beginning of each workshop the managers are asked how things are
going and how well they are using the material. At the end of
each workshop, they are asked to develop action plans on how
the material will be applied to their jobs. Building these discussions into each workshop tends to reinforce the desire to move
learnings back and forth between the "classroom" and the "real
world."

Another important aspect of the workshops is the ongoing
nature of these sessions. Three workshops were conducted for
SFD over a period of six months; the consultants had a full two
days of contact each time. This repetition was important, as a
single workshop, no matter how long, needs to be followed up
if the learnings are going to be transferred to the work place.
After a couple of months, it is easy to fall back into the same
old style and approach. But just as this was beginning to happen, the managers of SFD had their next two-day workshop. In
fact, after all three workshops were held, the managers requested that the consultants meet with them more frequently
(once per month) for a shorter duration (one half to one day)
so that the material would work for them continually.

All the material covered in the three management workshops can be classified as methods to manage *people* better and

methods to manage *problems* better. Since the use of people and solving complex problems go hand in hand, it is apparent that one set of methods cannot be learned without the other. New conceptual, analytical, and administrative skills to define and solve complex problems must be supported by new social and interpersonal skills.

While it is difficult to summarize all that the SFD managers learned (the process involved more than fifty hours of each manager's time during the six-month period), perhaps the following "process rules" will convey the spirit behind this kind of management training. These rules were developed so that the managers would apply what they learned every time they got together for any discussion or meeting. They were to remind one another of these rules if any violation occurred. I will first present the twelve rules for people management and then the twelve rules for problem management:

Twelve Rules for People Management

1. Treat people as equals; don't act superior and godlike to others.
2. Be genuine and spontaneous; don't be manipulative and sneaky.
3. Be empathic and feeling; don't be cold, impersonal, and uncaring.
4. Be exploratory and open-minded; don't be so certain and dogmatic.
5. Be descriptive and specific; don't be evaluative and vague —you will make people defensive.
6. Foster a problem management culture; don't try to control or blame others—they will get even more defensive.
7. Assume good intentions; don't assume that people are being devious or deceptive.
8. Remember that you have blind sides; don't assume that your intentions are automatically understood.
9. Listen carefully to what others say; don't assume that your reality is the only reality—perceptions are reality.
10. Give everyone the opportunity to participate; don't dominate the meeting—don't keep talking on and on.
11. Be receptive, open, and responsive to others; don't let stereotypes and the past run your life.
12. Stop and examine the people management process at

every meeting; don't assume it takes care
doesn't.

Twelve Rules for Problem Management

1. Plan before doing; don't attack a complex probl
ly and foolishly.
2. Subdivide a complex problem into parts; don't lose sight
of the forest because of all the trees.
3. Make assumptions explicit; don't let quicksand be the
foundation for your arguments.
4. Test assumptions; don't assume that everyone sees the
problem your way.
5. Debate assumptions and positions before any consensus is
reached; don't be afraid of productive conflict.
6. Define the problem before solving it; don't implement a
quick fix to the wrong problem.
7. Collaborate on complex problems; don't stifle any available information—it may come back to haunt you.
8. Look to the deviant when the problem is complex; don't
assume the majority is correct—it has common ignorance.
9. Foster trust and candor in gathering information; don't
develop a CYA atmosphere.
10. Consult/join on complex, important problems; don't force
your simple solution on others, expecting them to accept
it.
11. Tell/sell on simple, unimportant problems; don't bother
others—they have more important things to do.
12. Stop and examine the problem management process at
every meeting; don't assume it takes care of itself—it
doesn't.

If all group meetings requiring decisions and actions on
complex problems could be managed with the spirit of these
rules, the members would increase the likelihood of effective
performance and morale. SFD has relied on these rules to make
sure that its managers practice what they learned. This also
demonstrates how the management skills track can support the
other changes taking place. Enacting these "rules" becomes ingrained in the corporate culture. Now the culture will pressure
all members to address important and complex problems with
the latest management skills. That is just what adaptive cultures
must do.

Conclusion

As managers are learning the skills of problem management and the methods for assumptional analysis, they become more and more eager to apply these to real problems and not just to workshop exercises. After the culture track has made significant headway, taking on the real world becomes feasible. The team-building track can now help the membership define and solve its business/technical problems.

As managers apply their new skills in each work unit, their long-standing, recurring problems take on a very different light. The managers now recognize the various errors that have been made in the past: sensing errors, defining errors, solving errors, and implementing errors. They also realize that only by bringing assumptions out into the open for a thorough and systematic examination will they get to the very heart of their problems. Gracefully, but deliberately, the managers move below the surface into their new holographic world.

CHAPTER SIX

The
Team-Building
Track

Over the past fifteen years, the role of the manager has changed significantly in many organizations. The strong manager capable of almost single-handedly turning around an organization or department, while still a folk hero in the eyes of many, has given way to the recent demands of increasingly complex systems for managers who are able to pull together people of diverse backgrounds, personalities, training, and experience and weld them into an effective working group.

This modern manager has shifted from dealing with problems on a one-on-one basis to solving more problems collectively, involving everyone that has a contribution to make in either solving a problem or implementing actions. In this context, the manager is a coach, a facilitator, a developer, a team builder. Many managers have not been trained in these new collaborative skills and this deficiency has given rise to the organization consultant, both external and internal, whose job it is to work with managers in developing a strong, viable, working team.

—Dyer, 1977, p. xi

Groups are the building blocks of organizations. They enable individuals to transcend their own limitations of both body and mind in order to define and solve the problems of nature and civilization. While groups create settings in which interpersonal and social needs can be met, their greatest contribution is in moving beyond individual efforts into the realm of large-scale endeavors. Thus, groups and the linking of groups into organizations stand as the greatest "invention" of all time. Without these group and intergroup arrangements, other great inventions neither could have been created nor would have been brought to the marketplace.

Group efforts, however, are not automatically effective. They require more than the best of individual efforts and abilities: Effective groups require a whole additional set of energies and skills. The discussion on culture emphasized how the group must pressure its members toward more effective behaviors and attitudes. The discussion on management skills highlighted how the learnings from workshops must be transferred to the everyday life of the work group. Now we will see how the team-building track completes what these other change tracks started. Team building mobilizes both the culture and the management skills of each work group to achieve high-quality decisions and actions.

Most people have found themselves in either very effective or very ineffective groups more often than in simply average-performing groups. I have found this distribution to be quite prevalent and can explain it only as a result of members' high expectations of group behavior. This may generalize from the high, perhaps unrealistic, expectations people have of their families. When one is young, parents are supposed to be perfect, good, and pure. We seem to expect the same of our groups later in life. Certainly, this dynamic helps explain the powerful hold that groups have over their members. Groups can get members to engage in acts, for good or evil, that they would never contemplate as individuals.

This chapter outlines how to establish and maintain effective *teams* rather than working to achieve the organization's mission through loose collections of individuals (nominal groups with little or no synergy) or cliques (powerful groups that can block productive efforts with their countercultures). In order to achieve high-quality decisions and actions, all the expertise and information in each group must be utilized in efficient and creative ways. If all group efforts become instances of effective team and interteam behavior, high morale and performance for the whole organization should result—assuming proper organizational design (to be discussed in the next two chapters) and a benign organizational setting.

The material for this chapter is organized into three main approaches: individual counseling, team building, and interteam building. The first approach, individual counseling, considers how to manage the very uncomfortable and difficult problems created by troublemakers—individuals whose behavior severely disrupts the performance and morale of groups throughout the organization. The second approach, team building, considers ways to make each group an effective team. The third approach, interteam building, recognizes that organizations consist of interlocking groups, not independent units. Therefore, attention is given to addressing problems that cut across many groups and require a multigroup effort. These three approaches are conducted in sequence: The troublemakers must be managed before groups can be developed into fully functioning teams; similarly, each group must be functioning well before the more compli cated intergroup problems can be tackled.

Since understanding and managing troublemakers explores the depths of the human psyche, this approach represents a marked departure from the traditional view of the world as purely rational and orderly. In fact, only by understanding the psyche—how it forms and how it protects itself—can we appreciate why the troublemakers cannot learn much from the change program. Learning is just not their style. Because of the confronting manner in which the troublemakers are controlled, this process should be guided by consultants until the managers and members can learn to do this themselves. Similarly, both team- and interteam-building techniques require consultants in the early steps of the process to ensure open feedback and candid discussions.

Individual Counseling

Just how badly can people behave? What happens when their deepest animal instincts and their most aggressive fantasies go unchecked? What behaviors are possible when the culture and the system of organization do not curtail mankind's darkest sides? Building on accounts given by Colin Turnbull—an anthropologist with the American Museum of Natural History—Allen (1980, pp. 27-28) vividly depicts the epitome of bizarre and horrendous behavior by a tribe known as the Ik:

It is hard to imagine a group of people more selfish and ruthlessly cruel than the Ik, a small tribe of nomadic hunters who were living out their lives in a remote region of East Africa in the early 1960s. They were not only unkind, but heartless; not only stingy, but maliciously grasping; not only dishonest, but cunningly deceitful. They were selfish and ruthlessly cruel beyond the imagination. They pushed their children out of the home at three years of age to fend for themselves—and then stole food from them. They stole from the elderly, the weak, the blind. The strongest men grabbed the limited food supply for themselves. When they found game in the fields, they ate it on the spot instead of taking some home to their starving families. They even ate it raw, for fear the smoke might attract others and force them to share. It was common for a brother to take food from the hand of a sick brother, to turn a sick family member out of the house to die. Even the last of the ritual priests was abandoned by his son and sent out to his death. Old people were frequently left alone in their huts to die. Sometimes they were pushed off the sides of the mountain to the amusement of other tribesmen, and once, when a blind woman fell off a cliff and landed on her back like a tortoise, helpless with all four limbs flailing the air, the others went into peals of laughter and left her struggling. The killing of a child by a leopard was seen as a cause for celebration—it meant that there was edible game nearby. The people went out, found the leopard, ate both it and the child on the spot.

Allen (1980, p. 28) recognizes that the behavior of the Ik is not restricted to East Africa but can be witnessed in any organization or society, no matter how "civilized" it appears to be:

With very little effort of the imagination, we can discover the Ik in the office, in the classroom, in the committee and boardroom, everywhere demonstrating just how badly it is possible for people to behave. There is the pusher, the grabber, the stealer, the nonsharer, the one who abandons, the one who laughs at others' struggles, the one who hides his riches for fear that they will be taken from him, and the one who risks the lives of others to add to his own wealth.

Especially with a holographic view of the world, it is critical to distinguish between *troublemakers* (destructive individuals) and *objectors* (well-intentioned deviants). These two different types should never be confused. Objectors, according to Ewing (1983), are mentally healthy individuals who just happen to disagree with some decision or action by those holding—or controlling—the majority view. By definition, objectors express the minority view and, therefore, are also referred to as complainers, dissenters, whistle blowers, mavericks, and nonconformists. The previous material on managing complex problems emphasized the importance of listening to the deviants, since they are the ones who have the specialized knowledge for their piece of the whole problem. Overruling these objectors may smooth the process of managing simple problems but will soon result in numerous errors in problem management when the issues are complex.

In contrast, troublemakers are *not* well-intentioned individuals who simply express disagreement with company policy. Rather, troublemakers enact rather unhealthy and even destructive forms of behavior, as displayed by the Ik: lying, cheating, stealing, harassing, intimidating, and purposely hurting other people. These behaviors kill the organization's spirit and performance. We need to use every ounce of energy to manage the critical problems imposed by the external stakeholders, not to divert energy to unnecessary problems created by any internal stakeholders. Yet, when troublemakers are allowed to act out their destructive tendencies on others, as supported by a dysfunctional culture, it is very difficult to have an open and meaningful discussion on complex problems. The troublemakers prevent *both* majority and minority views from being voiced, let alone heard.

Troublemakers come in many varieties. Bramson (1981), in his book *Coping with Difficult People,* profiles some of these characters as Sherman tanks, snipers, exploders, and bulldozers. It does not take much imagination to picture these types in action or to identify people we know who fit these types almost to a T. These troublemakers create special barriers to organizational success.

In a recent article in *Psychology Today* titled "The Intolerable Boss," Lombardo and McCall (1984, p. 45) show how some bosses—described variously as snakes-in-the-grass, Attilas, heel grinders, egotists, dodgers, and detail drones—torment their subordinates:

> He was a living snake and a pathological liar. His decisions were based on whoever talked to him last. He was a little dictator. . . . If anyone else tried to make a decision, he took it as a personal insult.
> Does this sound like anyone you know—your current boss, perhaps, or one you've endured in the past? Most people have met up with at least one impossible boss—someone who fully deserved unflattering characterizations like the ones above.

In a recent *Business Week* article, "Following a Tough Act at Commodore" (1984, p. 30), former Commodore president Jack Tramiel's management style is acknowledged as having had many disruptive effects, despite his hard-driven success:

> For all his business brilliance, however, Tramiel's dominant personality led to constant management turnover. The 55-year-old survivor of a World War II German concentration camp "ran Commodore like a dictatorship," says Alan H. Friedman, a former finance director at Commodore who left last April after two years. According to Ralph D. Seligman, a director and an attorney based in Nassau, the Bahamas, where Commodore has its corporate headquarters, "all sorts of heads have rolled at Commodore" because of Tramiel's nature.

It would take too much space to provide a full account of each type of troublemaker and the psychodynamics that make these people the way they are. Suffice it to say that underlying each type is an insecure and troubled person, one who copes with his inner conflicts and negative self-image by projecting these onto other people. For some types of troublemakers, there is a dire need to control everything that goes on. No matter how much power and authority such a person may have, it still is not enough: The need is insatiable. For other types who have grown up in an atmosphere of suspicion, insufficient love, and constant disappointment, there is an overwhelming mistrust of others in everything they do. Other troublemakers are aggressive and hostile toward their coworkers as a way of getting back at people (mainly parents and "significant others") who inflicted such pain and suffering on them in the past. The same connections between how one was treated in years past and how one copes with the world today are evident with all the troublemakers (Fenichel, 1972).

Not everyone who has ever suffered in childhood, however, becomes a troublemaker. Most people learn along the way and thereby break the unconscious tendency to act out on others what was acted out on them. But this requires a certain threshold of ego strength (so the individual can look inside at himself) and a willingness to take some responsibility for one's life and its consequences (so the individual will be motivated to learn and change). However, if an individual has been badly shattered or abused in childhood (physically or psychologically), has never felt good about himself as a person (because he was taught to see himself as bad and guilty—how else can a child explain the abuse?), and has never acquired a sense of responsibility for his actions (the possible shame and guilt of doing one more thing wrong would be too much to bear), then becoming a troublemaker is a likely outcome.

If we understand these psychodynamics, it is no surprise that troublemakers are not likely to learn from a management skills track, from reading self-awareness books, or from observing how others seem to examine themselves and change for the better. I used to believe that a management skills workshop could reach these troublemakers and that they would change their ways as a result of their learnings, but this rarely happens.

More often than not, these individuals attest to the great value of the material for all the other managers who desperately need to change. The troublemakers do not see that they themselves need to question their behavior and learn new management skills. The troublemakers are too troubled to look inside, see what is there, and change it. They spend most of their energy surviving, defending, protecting, and living out their problems on others. There is a stark intensity in this life-and-death struggle with the world. And make no mistake about it, troubled persons are very much at war—they have little or no inner peace.

The more aggressive troublemakers are found in management positions throughout the hierarchy. As long as their intense drive to succeed—or rather to control and ravage their environment—has not resulted in more negative than positive outcomes, they do succeed. It is hard to discourage employees or managers who have intelligence and ability and who are willing to work twenty hours a day if that is what it takes to succeed. These driven troublemakers, however, are to be distinguished from well-functioning "high achievers." The latter do not "step on people" and enact other harmful and disruptive behaviors on their way to the top. The troublemakers who succeed generally have extracted a high price from those around them—including family and friends—and have hurt many others along the way.

A change program encourages all members to look at themselves and to expose their culture and their assumptions. Team building focuses attention on bringing awareness and learning right into the everyday life of intact work groups. How are the troublemakers likely to feel and react to these intrusions into their war zones? How are they likely to interpret these efforts at learning and change?

A troublemaker very well may interpret any change program as an act of war, as an invasion of his territory, as a real threat to the maintenance of his ego. Troublemakers, therefore, strongly resist the first suggestion of bringing in outside consultants (who are not under their control) and try to undermine, if not sabotage, the whole change program. To the extent that these troublemakers hold important positions of authority, they cause both the consultants and the organization severe headaches. If a troublemaker happens to be the top executive of the organization, it is unlikely that the change program will be successful. In all probability the consultants will be brought in for ulterior motives—for political and self-serving reasons. In such a case, the program will succeed only if the consultants discover this problem early on and do not initiate the program until the right conditions are present.

Often, the organization's troublemakers come to the attention of the consultants during the diagnostic stage. While the interviews are being conducted, certain names are mentioned again and again. Stories are told of very mean and hostile acts that have hurt other people or even the organization as a whole. While stories often are exaggerated, distorted by many years of repetition, one must be careful not to discount these stories when told by many interviewees. In some cases, the stories are so intense and alarming that even if 10 percent of them were true one would have to take such information seriously.

The consultants also become aware of troublemakers during the culture track and the management skills track. Since troublemakers are neither sensitive to feedback nor aware of how their behavior affects those around them, they create trouble right in front of the consultants. This is shown by acting out defensiveness-producing behavior, such as making many negative comments that are not germane to the topic of conversation, showing anger and hostility in verbal and nonverbal ways, and discouraging others from taking the discussions seriously. Also, as the culture track and the management skills track proceed, several members may speak to the consultants about the difficulty they experience in applying new learnings back on the job. Their own managers ridicule them and even threaten them with negative performance reviews if they persist in going to the various sessions.

Why do the organization and its managers allow such behavior to go on? First, as mentioned above, the troublemakers often are very hard workers who succeed despite their disruptive behavior. Second, it is very uncomfortable for most "normal" people to deal with troublemakers. Normal people may have their internal conflicts under control but, nevertheless, these intrapsychic dynamics exist in all persons to some degree. Perhaps there is always the fear of acting out the unconscious and aggressive thoughts that pop up from time to time in all of us. This latent fear might discourage "normal" people from thinking about or confronting abnormal behavior. Perhaps it is easier (safer) to ignore (deny) the severity of what is observed in the organization. Essentially, people look the other way and hope that the problem, such as an alcoholic coworker, is not really there. Such difficult problems can be suppressed by the culture as well: see no evil, hear no evil, and speak no evil.

The counseling process for managing the troublemakers consists of four steps: (1) listing the troublemakers, (2) conducting the first feedback session, (3) conducting follow-up sessions, and (4) concluding the sessions. The objective of these steps is not to provide therapy for the troublemakers but to help them get their disruptive behavior under control. It is especially important to make sure that others are not intimidated by the troublemakers. If members wish to learn and change, let them. This freedom should be the reigning spirit of the entire program.

Step One: Listing the Troublemakers

Combining the names of troublemakers who were mentioned repeatedly during the diagnostic interviews with any additional troublemakers mentioned in comments or observed during the earlier tracks suggests a list of troublemakers. This list can range from a few people to as many as twenty-five for a large organization; *every* organization has at least one such individual. However, it is important not to overreact when a particular story is told or when an incident is observed. Sometimes, two people just do not get along. This does not mean that one or the other is causing disruptions for many others. The trouble may be restricted solely to the two individuals.

As professional as the consultant tries to be with such a sensitive topic, word usually travels around that the consultants are developing a "list." Regardless of how the counseling sessions are introduced to the organization, there may be gross distortions concerning their objective. This follows from the very uncomfortable nature of confronting some difficult people. These individuals are good at stirring up trouble anyway, and the advent of the counseling sessions can provide another opportunity for them to act out their tendencies. The consultants should be very sensitive to the possible meanings attributed to these sessions by being very direct in communicating their objectives and intentions.

Developing the list of troublemakers is more difficult than it may seem. When there has been widespread intimidation on the part of one or more managers, victimized members may be afraid to come forth and reveal injustices. Sometimes they are convinced that if the troublemaker even suspects that others have revealed his name and have reported certain incidents, he will harass them even more. It is not uncommon for members to fear that this troublemaker can and will fire them for revealing anything to the consultants. Whether this is all due to fear or has some basis in reality is not clear. But it does cause members to hold back information on who is making trouble for others.

In those organizations in which a number of individuals have expressed fear about reprisals or terminations of jobs, I discuss the general nature of this predicament with the top executives of the organization. I propose that a thorough investigation be conducted if any surprise termination, unusual switch in job assignments, or extremely negative performance appraisal occurs. This policy and the reasons behind it are then communicated to all managers. The point is to bring this topic out into the open once and for all. I insist that we cannot take the chance that members will be hurt in any way by their efforts at change and improvement and their willingness to confront some very difficult problems.

Top management often is surprised that I would even have this discussion with them. They cannot believe that anything like this could happen in their organization. This sort of thing could only happen in someone *else's* organization. I emphasize to them that I simply want to make sure that this is the case. Top management may have been looking the other way as troublemakers played on the fears and doubts of the membership, but the organization should not do this anymore—the cost is too high. As everyone in the organization is put on alert, everyone becomes much more conscious of this troublemaking phenomenon. Some begin to wonder why it has been ignored all along. How did their organization get into such a rut?

Step Two: Conducting the First Feedback Session

Each listed troublemaker is scheduled for a separate feedback session with one of the consultants. During this session, the consultant first summarizes why the individual was asked to attend. The consultant shares the reported incidents and impressions (while protecting the confidentiality of the source), emphasizing that these might be totally distorted and inaccurate. Any one incident can be explained away quite easily. But as a total package, as a pattern, is there any plausibility to any of this? How can the identified person account for the "troublemaker" perception others have of him? How could this have happened?

Often, the person is totally shocked at being identified as a troublemaker and disturbed by the comments that have been made. In the best cases, the person responds very positively and suggests how the incidents developed and how the perceptions must have formed. The individual proceeds to outline how he plans to correct the perceptions, as well as his behavior. Here the individual recognizes the problem and wants to solve it. In most cases, however, the initial response is more defensive and hostile and becomes a replay of all the stories and incidents that were reported. The consultant uses his judgment in deciding whether to point out that the person's response seems to confirm what has just been described. When there is extreme defensiveness, there is little likelihood that the individual will even hear the message—he works hard at protecting himself, as always. But a message has been given, and the individual has been put on the alert. The consultant concludes the meeting by encouraging the individual to think about what was discussed and indicating that there will be follow-up meetings to see how "things are going."

Some troublemakers will go through a process of acting as if their behavior has changed, hoping that the consultants will leave shortly and that everything will go back to "normal." At the same time, the rest of the membership hopes that the consultants will stay around so that the troublemakers will not go back to their old behaviors. If the whole change program is successful, the troublemakers may escape the consultants, but they will not escape all the other managers and members in the organization. These others will pick up where the consultants left off. Any disruptive behaviors of the past will be confronted quite dramatically—the new culture will make certain of it.

It is important to appreciate why top management support and the power of the hierarchy must be behind such a confronting approach. Without this support, the troublemakers will not show up for their counseling sessions and will ignore all the related discussions. Without this support, members will not confront the troublemakers for fear of reprisals. However, if both the members and the troublemakers are told in no uncertain terms that disruptive behavior will not be tolerated, the message will be received.

Step Three: Conducting Follow-Up Sessions

As the consultants observe behavior during the other tracks or as new information comes to their attention from members throughout the organization, decisions are made as to whether to schedule additional counseling sessions. For those troublemakers who responded positively and immediately changed their behavior, there is no need for further sessions. However, for those who responded defensively during the first session, one can expect the same disruptive behavior to continue. Essentially, because these individuals are not in control of their inner dynamics and because they have difficulty hearing and responding to feedback, follow-up sessions are required.

The consultant schedules another round of sessions to review what has transpired. Often the exact same discussions are held again. The troublemaker insists that he has changed his behavior—why can no one else see this? He claims that he is a victim of circumstance, of a series of misunderstandings. If only others knew how much he cares about them and about the organization, surely they would understand. He just does not see how his motives and behaviors can be so misconstrued. Perhaps other members are simply jealous of his energy, intelligence, and accomplishments.

During these sessions, the consultants see creativity at work. The troublemakers can turn, twist, rationalize, distort, and justify almost anything. These individuals, because of their wartime tactics, have learned to define and create reality so that it matches the image they have of themselves. If the facts do not fit their needs, they change the facts. They come up with a new reality to explain the value and worth of their net contributions. The most vivid example of these distortions is illustrated by the troublemaker's insistence that he likes and cares for certain individuals—who just happen to be the very same ones who have been hurt by the troublemaker time and time again. Often these mentioned individuals are the ones who reported the troublemaker to the consultants in the first place. Such is the power of psychological compensation!

To reiterate, the purpose of the counseling sessions is to stop the troublemakers from disrupting others—to stop the behavior. If this is successful, then it becomes another matter if the troublemakers want to gain a better understanding of themselves and to remove their struggles from within. However, any therapy must be voluntary and should be conducted outside the organization by professionals other than the consultants.

Step Four: Concluding the Sessions

For the troublemakers who do not respond positively to their first feedback session, there may be as many as four to six sessions over a period of several months. It is hoped that each individual will learn to squelch his disruptive tendencies before they cause trouble. At the same time, as the rest of the organization benefits from the earlier tracks, other members become much more assertive about confronting disruptive behavior. Although in the past the troublemakers had been able to get away with their shenanigans, now they find that members speak up and stop them cold. Furthermore, if members feel intimidated and scared of what might happen, they are more likely to discuss it with another manager than with the consultants. In the past, they might not have discussed it with anyone.

In essence, feedback loops are all over the place. Everything is more visible and under close watch. What was unconscious and habitual before is now very transparent. People cannot get away with what went on before. The members gain more and more control over their organization. They put a check on the troublemakers themselves.

Team Building

As the troublemakers are being managed and controlled, attention shifts to improving the functioning of each intact work unit. During the management skills track, managers realize that they can benefit by receiving feedback from their own work groups. As they learn new insights about their social, interpersonal, analytical, conceptual, and administrative skills, they begin to wonder about their effectiveness. Simply asking these questions and initiating such discussions with the consultants suggests sufficient ego strength to receive feedback and learn. It is much easier to engage in group development when the impetus for learning comes from the manager himself and not from the consultant.

Dyer (1977, p. 57) describes several indicators that lead members, managers, or consultants to believe that a work group might require some team-building activities:

1. Domination by the leader.
2. Warring cliques or subgroups.
3. Unequal participation and uneven use of group resources.
4. Rigid or dysfunctional group norms and procedures.
5. A climate of defensiveness.
6. Uncreative alternatives to problems.

7.   Restricted communications.
8.   Avoidance of differences or potential conflicts.

Such conditions would reduce the team's ability to work together in collective problem-solving situations. The role of the consultant would be to help the group become aware of its processes and begin to develop greater group skills. Specifically, after becoming aware of a process problem, the group needs to establish a procedure, guideline, or plan of action to reduce the negative condition.

The five steps for team building are (1) entry into the work group, (2) diagnosing group problems, (3) deriving solutions and developing action plans, (4) implementing the action plans, and (5) monitoring and evaluating the results.

Step One: Entry into the Work Group

There are several different ways to enter a work group for the purpose of data collection and diagnosis. One approach is for the consultant to meet with the work group—without the manager. A second approach is for both consultant and manager to be present at the first team-building session. A third approach is for the manager to conduct the first step of team building, without the consultant present, after the manager has received some guidance from the consultant on how to proceed.

The particular approach taken depends on the trust level in the group and on whether the members will be willing to share group problems with their manager. Often, however, the manager may be the last one to know if his group can be open about its deepest problems. If the manager goes ahead and conducts the first session by himself, he may find that the trust is insufficient for members to share their problems openly. The manager may ask for open and honest feedback about himself and about any group issues but may be met with silence or superficial comments suggesting that everything is fine. If this happens, the manager may be left feeling a little foolish or thinking that the whole thing was a waste of time. I much prefer for the initial effort at team building to be successful—even if only slightly—so that both the manager and the members are encouraged to continue. Besides, the goal of team building—to have the work unit handle its own problem management—can be accomplished over time; it does not all have to happen in the first session.

It is not infrequent to find that the biggest problem that interferes with a working unit functioning effectively as a team is the boss or manager. If the boss is unaware of this, the situation becomes especially difficult, since unit members are often unwilling to confront the boss with the disruptive consequences of his or her own managerial behavior. If this issue is avoided during the team-building session, all other actions will probably be seen as mere window dressing, for the main issue has been carefully sidestepped [Dyer, 1977, pp. 125-126].

The conservative approach is clearly for the consultants to test the waters first—to find out if the members are ready for an open dialogue with their manager. If they are, it does not take much effort to bring the manager in for the next meeting. Alternatively, if the members mistrust their manager and fear reprisals if real and honest feedback takes place, some preliminary work needs to be done. The group should meet on its own to discuss safe issues first and more delicate issues a little later. As trust develops, the manager can enter the process.

Step Two: Diagnosing Group Problems

The work group develops answers to the following questions. Sometimes it is useful to have each member answer these questions individually before a group discussion takes place:

1. What are the group's objectives?
2. Is the group accomplishing these objectives?
3. What does the group do particularly well in performing its tasks?
4. What obstacles prevent the group from performing its tasks?
5. Are group members spending the right amount of time on the right tasks with the right objectives in mind?
6. Do group members feel that their time is not spent in the most productive way? How is their time being diverted?

7.   Do members feel that all their expertise and experience are being utilized? How could their talent be used more productively?
8.   Are all issues brought out so that any problem can be addressed with full information and member expertise? How are some issues being avoided?
9.   Do problems get solved or do they constantly reappear? Why do group solutions get lost during implementation?
10. Are members satisfied with the quality of decision making? What is the source of their dissatisfaction?

There always will be some special issues, depending on the objectives and tasks of the group, but these general questions highlight some important aspects of work group functioning.

Either the consultant or the manager summarizes the core individual and group responses on a flip pad for everyone to see. Copies of this can be made later so that everyone can have a record of what was discussed. Sometimes it is helpful to divide the responses into two categories, making use of Lewin's (1951) force field analysis—still one of the most basic tools for problem diagnosis. Specifically, comments are divided into *driving* forces and *restraining* forces. The former describe what is moving the group forward and the latter describe what is holding it back. The group's "equilibrium" can be altered by either enhancing the driving forces (doing even better what the group already does well) or removing the restraining forces (eliminating the blocks)—channels and barriers, respectively.

As the important questions about work group performance and morale are answered and then categorized, information that penetrates the inner workings of the group becomes available. Sometimes the restraining and driving forces are categorized further into a model of work group problems, not unlike the Barriers to Success model that is used to sort all the organization's problems (Chapter Two). In any event, it is now necessary to define the most important problems facing the work unit so that a new equilibrium that promises higher performance and morale can be established.

The definition of the critical problems can be formulated by the appropriate methods of problem management. If any of the data that were sorted into the driving and restraining forces (or any other classification scheme for problem identification) suggest a simple problem, consensus can be used to resolve any differences (Lockean IS). For example, the group's need for clarification and documentation of work procedures could be handled easily in this way. Alternatively, if the data suggest a complex problem, a more elaborate method should be used. For instance, establishing why the group's support services are not used more extensively throughout the organization entails numerous and contradictory perspectives. Is it because of the quality of the service, the way the service is advertised, the alternative services provided by other groups, or the declining need for the service? Perhaps a modified assumptional analysis can be done by forming several subgroups to debate and then synthesize the underlying assumptions of each problem definition (Hegelian IS). This would enable the work group to define its problems with the least chance for committing a defining error prior to deriving and implementing a solution.

It is also possible that the data collection and diagnosis suggest problems that not only are complex but have ramifications beyond the group's boundaries. Even conducting assumptional analysis within the group would be insufficient. The full range of expertise and information needed to define the problem would not be contained in the analysis, since it resides in other groups in the organization. The problems that fit this type would be postponed until the interteam-building efforts could be undertaken. The work group, for now, does the best job it can in defining both the simple and complex problems that fall under its jurisdiction.

In cases in which the consultant has met with the work group without the manager present, the same diagnostic questions are discussed and the same methods are used to categorize the key issues. The only difference is that at the end of the meeting the consultant discusses with the group how the data can be presented to the manager. Sometimes the group suggests that the consultant summarize the data for the manager—as long as individual names are not connected with any of the responses. At other times, the group allows the consultant to share most of the data and discussions, specifying any parts to be kept private. The nicest outcome is when the group realizes on its own that it *can* meet face-to-face with the manager. Fears often are relieved when the members discover their commitment to the data and feel confident enough to stand up to the manager. Members feel the strength of their group, not unlike the strength of their work group culture. In these cases, the first meeting ends with the members looking forward to having their manager present for the next meeting. At that time, all the discussions can be reviewed to include the manager's viewpoints. Subsequently, the manager is included in all team-building sessions.

Step Three: Deriving Solutions and Developing Action Plans

Usually a very active discussion unfolds when the members are asked to consider what can be done to solve their group's problems—to derive solutions that address either the driving or restraining forces. Some of this exuberance stems from the promise of managing their own problems, whereas in the past the members were controlled by their habit of not examining how their group functioned. The only topics that were discussed previously were task and business issues, not group process and socioemotional issues.

Since deriving solutions is considered a simple task once the problem has been defined, consensus can be used to select one or more solutions to implement. Perhaps a cost/benefit analysis can be performed to aid in choosing solutions. Developing action plans for implementing solutions, however, constitutes a more complex problem. Special care should be taken to ensure that the work group understands the context of implementation. It might be useful to apply a modified assumptional analysis to uncover the various assumptions being made concerning the availability of resources, how other groups will react to the contemplated changes, how top management will respond—in short, any assumptions about any relevant internal or external stakeholder. Where possible, once the important/uncertain assumptions have been uncovered, more information should be collected before any action is taken. For example, *will* top management provide the necessary resources to implement the action plans? Knowing such information would help move any uncertain assumptions toward more certainty. The group would then be implementing its solutions based on the most accurate knowledge of the organization's culture, politics, human nature, and all relevant stakeholders.

Step Four: Implementing the Action Plans

A useful approach is to form several subgroups of two to four members each to take responsibility for implementing one or more of the action plans. For example, a group of fifteen members may take the five plans and assign them to five subgroups. Either the manager or a member can coordinate this distribution of assignments. This approach helps foster ownership of the whole team-building effort. There also may be a need to coordinate follow-up meetings at which intermediate results can be shared and discussed. A procedure might be designed whereby each subgroup reports back to the entire group on a frequent basis so that everyone knows what the other subgroups are doing and has an opportunity to offer suggestions, advice, and feedback.

As implementation proceeds, the initial plans will need to be modified as more is learned about the critical assumptions made about each relevant stakeholder. The subgroups, as well as the work group, may find it necessary to brainstorm about new ways to implement their plans. Enough time should be devoted to each work group meeting so that the topic of group functioning is not ignored but is given as much attention as any of the technical and business problems the group must solve.

Step Five: Monitoring and Evaluating the Results

The last formal step of team building is assessing the outcomes of all the prior steps to see if the identified problems have been resolved. It should be apparent by now that team building *is* problem management applied to a single part of the whole organization. As a result, the five steps of team building parallel quite closely the five steps of problem management, just as the steps of problem management correspond to the five stages of planned change. The issue is always discovering what is wrong, doing something about it, and then finding out if the solution worked—and, if it did not work, trying again. Similarly, the errors of problem management (sensing errors, defining errors, solving errors, and implementing errors) are equally relevant to team building throughout its five steps. If any of these errors is detected during an evaluation of what went wrong, certain steps in team building should be adjusted as the cycle of problem management continues.

Interteam Building

Since team building works on single parts of the organization, one at a time, interteam building is necessary because the parts of an organization do not make up a mechanical system. Rather, the parts are highly interdependent, which makes for an open system, if not a complex hologram. Even if each work group were independent in a task sense, each group would have to be physically isolated from the others to be independent in a socioemotional sense. Members from one group observe and interact with members of other groups. They compare, compete, help, and hurt one another. The objective of interteam building is to promote the most functional relationships among groups.

The troublemakers must be managed before any significant progress can occur with team building; similarly, sufficient progress with each team-building effort is necessary before an interteam effort can begin. It is very difficult to work out the problems that divide two or more groups if the groups themselves are unable to discuss their own behavior. Unless team building has already been successful, interteam building will result in finger pointing, scapegoating, and disruptive behavior. Just as troublemakers tend to project their internal conflicts onto others, emotionally torn groups project their mistrust and suspicions onto other groups in the organization. Groups thus become cliques fighting over the same issues that troublemakers fight over, except that a group is a much more powerful force than any one individual!

The five steps of interteam building are (1) entry into the other groups, (2) diagnosing intergroup problems, (3) deriving solutions and developing action plans, (4) implementing the action plans, and (5) monitoring and evaluating the results.

Step One: Entry into the Other Groups

Once team-building efforts have improved the functioning of several work groups, it is quite apparent how various intergroup problems are holding the groups back. Any group may not be able to begin its tasks until it receives certain inputs from another group (information, materials, designs, resources), and the value of the group's contributions may be affected by how well its output is actually utilized by some other group (intermediate services or products). These important task flows may be hindered by one or more intergroup barriers:

1. Unit members avoid or withdraw from interactions with people from the other unit when they should be spending more working time together.
2. The mutual product or end result desired by both units is delayed, diminished, blocked, or altered to the dissatisfaction of one or both parties.
3. Needed services between units are not asked for.
4. Services between units are not performed to the satisfaction of those in the units.
5. Feelings of resentment or antagonism occur as a result of unit interactions.
6. People feel frustrated, rejected, or misunderstood by those in the other unit with whom they must work.
7. More time is spent in either avoiding or circumventing interaction with the other unit, or internally complaining about the other unit, than in working through mutual problems [Dyer, 1977, p. 118].

Often these intergroup problems are listed when the separate groups begin their data collection and diagnosis during team-building sessions. As solutions and action plans are being developed, each group delays the discussion of these problems until its internal functioning has improved. But as soon as each group has "its own house in order," it is time to consider these intergroup problems further. The first step is for one group to approach another with an invitation to explore intergroup problems, assuming that this other group also is ready to move beyond its own borders. The invitation proposes that the two or more groups meet for one or two days to begin the process.

Step Two: Diagnosing Intergroup Problems

Each group meets in a separate room to prepare a different list for every other group attending the session. The members in each group list (1) their perceptions of the other group's objectives, tasks, and responsibilities, (2) the "gut image" they have of the other group, and (3) their expectations of how the other group sees them. If there are four groups attending the workshop, each group prepares three such lists, one for each of the other groups (Blake, Mouton, and Sloma, 1965).

The first item on the list is task related, the second item is feeling and culture related, and the third item gets at the possible distortions in self-image operating within each work group. When all the lists have been completed (usually in two to four hours, depending on the number of groups involved), the groups all meet back in the community room. One by one, each group presents its lists to the other groups. All groups are encouraged to take extensive notes on what is presented.

The groups then meet back in their separate rooms, where the members review their notes, analyze what they have discovered, and develop a plan for what they wish to discuss with the other groups. Several revelations emerge during this discussion. Group members become aware, often for the first time, of the vastly different perceptions that exist concerning the work domain of every group. Presumably, each group is guided by some formally documented charter, but this charter may be very much out of date. Depending on the past chain of events and critical incidents that have occurred among the groups, work responsibilities have been established informally, often implicitly, and therefore are prone to selective perceptions and other distortions—depending on which group is questioned. This may seem obvious to the casual observer. To the groups, however, the conscious recognition of these differences becomes a significant revelation.

A second major discovery is made when each group learns of its image within the other groups. I have found that the sharing of "gut images" is often very powerful. While group members can rationalize different perceptions of work domains rather easily, it is much more difficult to justify how they are seen as empire builders, know-it-alls, kamikazes, disrupters, beggars, sinners, misers, or tightwads. Such images convey a strong emotional message that cannot be justified rationally. Rather, each group must come to terms with the whole style in which it has related to the other groups in the organization. Does its image help or hurt its own objectives, let alone the objectives of the whole organization?

The third kind of revelation concerns the last item on the list that was prepared by all the groups. A comparison can be made between each group's explicit expectations of how it would be seen and how it actually was seen by the others. This comparison can be rather startling. For example, one group may have expected other groups to see it as productive, hardworking, and helpful to others. In fact, the other groups see the focal group as working hard only on the fun projects and being willing to help only certain "favored" groups—and then only when this is to its immediate advantage. Here the group has to examine why it might have made such poor predictions in judging its public image. Perhaps the group has been carrying around a glorified vision of itself based more on how it wants to be seen than on how it really works with other groups. Such a discrepancy may have affected its contributions to the whole organization.

Since both the culture track and the management skills track have made significant progress (otherwise, the current track would not have been initiated), one can expect minimum defensiveness among all the participants as these data are generated, collected, and diagnosed. It is refreshing to see how each group gets right down to the issues and says: "Were we off base! No wonder we've had problems communicating with the other groups. And here we thought they simply couldn't appreciate how much we have been doing for them."

All groups then meet back in a community room to discuss these findings in an open forum. Many new insights emerge from such exchanges. Even if a number of issues and problems do not get resolved in this setting, at least everything is brought out into the open. After a few hours, the members summarize the key issues that still divide the groups. These are the problems that get in the way of effective task performance and morale.

If the problems appear to be very complex—such as establishing new group charters and mission statements—it may be useful to conduct assumptional analysis. Since all group members are present in this session, the necessary diversity in expertise and information also should be present. If not, additional persons can be asked to join the session. Initial conclusions defining the nature of the problems can serve to organize a number of subgroups for assumptional analysis. For example, a subgroup might be formed around each of these perspectives: Continue to see each group as an island; shift to emphasizing intergroup cooperation and shared resources; disband all the groups and form entirely new ones.

Step Three: Deriving Solutions and
Developing Action Plans

Either in the same workshop or in a subsequent meeting, a community discussion is held to derive solutions and formulate action plans to resolve the problems that were identified. If the problem of implementing these plans appears to be complex, the methods of assumptional analysis again come in handy. Since the focus is on *inter*team building, however, subgroups that form around "initial" action plans should consist of members from several different work groups. It is most important to see that the very problems that were *created* by current group boundaries do not get in the way of *solving* the problems.

Step Four: Implementing the Action Plans

When the action plans have been formulated, a community meeting of all the involved groups should be arranged. After a sharing of the plans has taken place, discussion moves to the implementation phase. Just as with the team-building effort, consideration must be given to the feasibility of these action plans and to the time and resources necessary to carry them out. It might be best to implement first those plans that promise some short-term results or that will make it easier for the other plans to be successful. Much as with the scheduling of the five tracks, a timetable should be developed in order to coordinate all plans into action.

The more members participate in the implementation of the plans, the more likely it is that these plans will succeed. It may be necessary to hold some follow-up meetings in which all the groups in attendance can discuss how well implementation is going, what obstacles have arisen, and what to do about them. Since many separate groups are involved, special attention must be given to the scheduling of these intergroup meetings. The objective is to balance the effort of resolving *intra*group problems with *inter*group problems according to the relative importance of the problems—not the relative convenience in scheduling meetings.

Step Five: Monitoring and Evaluating the Results

If the action plans and the methods of implementing them match the identified problems and the unique circumstances of the organization, and if sufficient time and energy have been devoted to these intergroup activities, considerable progress should have been made. Naturally, a number of errors in defining problems and in deriving and implementing solutions may have occurred. The interteam-building program must be prepared to cycle through these problem management steps several times. As long as some successes are experienced and the managers across these groups remain committed to this effort, interteam building becomes an ongoing part of identifying and managing the organization's problems. The managers have learned another way to take the methods of problem management and apply them to the particular case of group and intergroup problems.

Littlejohn (1982, pp. 23-24, 28) provides a fitting summary of the benefits derived from most team-building efforts:

> Employees tend to develop a caring and sharing attitude. Mutual trust and support are fostered. Consequently, conflicts within the team can more easily be dealt with openly and constructively. Prior to introduction of the team concept, sensitive issues often lie hidden and are not discussed. After teams are formed, however, a healthy, constructive atmosphere for conflict resolution develops.
>
> Team members become better problem solvers, thanks to greater communication and mutual team support. Creativity and innovation can be expected to permeate the team interaction. As the team develops and grows, it becomes more cooperative and reflects greater coordination. Ultimately, productivity is significantly increased through the team's synergism. A collective strength is formed that is far superior to the sum of individual strengths, enabling the individual within a team to grow and produce. . . .
>
> Team management is not magic nor a panacea for all management ills. However, it is a better way to manage. It is a common-sense approach of letting people improve their performance by improving the process they use.

Return to the SFD Story

SFD had its share of troublemakers, just like any other organization. These individuals were identified repeatedly during the diagnostic interviews as causing considerable bad feelings and hardships for those around them. It also was suggested by several interviewees that these troublemakers would do whatever it took to undermine the change program. Many stories were told of how they had responded when other projects had challenged their little empires.

In virtually every case, the identified troublemaker acted out some of the same behaviors at the management skills workshops. While I was cautious not to prejudge any of these individuals, I could not help noticing the strong and disruptive impact these members had on the rest of the managers. In some cases, I was surprised myself that these individuals were given the leeway to be so discourteous and disruptive toward others. The organization had become accustomed to these behaviors, despite their dysfunctional effects.

I scheduled meetings with about half-a-dozen trouble-makers in February 1983. I purposely waited until after the first management skills workshop had been held, for two reasons: First, I wanted to observe these individuals in action myself. This would allow me to experience these individuals' behaviors firsthand rather than having to rely on second- and third-hand reports exclusively. Second, I wanted these individuals to be familiar with the concepts of ego strength, communication style, and leadership style. I expected that having a common language would enable me to present the feedback to them more effectively. Both of these reasons again suggest why the team building track must follow the culture and management skills tracks.

The results of the first scheduled counseling sessions were mixed. Some individuals were absolutely shocked by the feedback they received but seemed grateful to learn about this now rather than later. Other individuals were equally shocked but responded in a highly defensive manner, sometimes in a very rude manner as well. It was these latter individuals who eventually were scheduled for numerous follow-up sessions until their behavior patterns were under control or until the membership became willing to provide the control that the consultants first had to muster on their own.

As mentioned in Chapter Three, at least a dozen managers contacted me right after the first management skills workshop, wanting to begin the team-building track. The managers who first made these requests turned out to have some of the most effective groups in SFD. They had the ego strength to test their own perceptions and to work on their group problems even more than before. As word got around as to who had requested the team-building activity, more managers also volunteered. Some of these latter managers had more troubled groups but were ready to learn now that others were team building and surviving the ordeal. As this snowball began rolling, participating in team building became the "in" thing to do. As long as managers did not feel intimidated into doing this before they were ready to begin, I felt that this healthy competition was fine.

After a few months, many of the internal troubles of the work groups cleared up. These changes were helped by the second management skills workshop, which was held in March, and by the continued culture sessions for each work group, which were conducted almost every month. In some cases, it was difficult to say whether a particular session was being held for purposes of implementing the new culture or for continuing with team building. But it really did not matter, since all these sessions involved improving the work group. The point was to collect data, define problems, derive solutions, implement solutions, and then find out what happened. This cycle of problem management was instituted numerous times in each work group, regardless of which issues arose.

Attention then shifted to examining several barriers that were blocking the performance of several interdependent groups. Some of these groups had developed the reputation of being powerful cliques that existed just to maintain their own empires, to control resources, and to vie for even more power. The managers of several of these cliques, as might be expected, were some of the identified troublemakers with whom I had met several times in the counseling sessions. Needless to say, designing an interteam-building workshop for these groups was a challenge—a very necessary challenge because of the central role these groups played in SFD.

In early May 1983, members from three groups met to identify and begin resolving their difficulties. The interteam workshop took place in an eight-hour period and followed the steps outlined earlier. While the initial atmosphere was tense, as soon as each group shared the gut images it had of the other groups, the atmosphere changed. Tenseness gave way to laughter —nervous laughter at first but more enjoyable laughter a bit later. It seemed that a shared attitude emerged, a culture if you will, that guided the mood of the day. This workshop culture, not unlike the organization-wide culture change in process, encouraged all participants across the three groups not to take everything as a life-and-death matter but to realize that this was just one day in the life of the organization. Members began to sit back, relax, and look at the whole situation—and not just according to their own group's vantage point. The cliques gave way to a team perspective.

This first day of interteam building for the three troublesome groups was very successful. In fact, it was the first time that these groups had ever gotten together to discuss the issues that divided them rather than to replay all their previous battles and the stereotyped images they had of each other. Many discrepancies and misperceptions were revealed as comparisons were made with regard to work responsibilities, gut images, and expectations of other groups' perceptions. The day concluded with documenting all the key points that were discussed. In the following week, everyone involved received a copy of this material. Additional meetings were scheduled to continue the effort to define problems, develop action plans, and implement changes for effective interteam functioning.

Conclusion

When the three portions of the team-building track (individual counseling, team building, and interteam building) have had their impact on the organization, the overall quality of decision making and action taking will be improved. The learnings from the management skills track will be ingrained in the way all complex problems are addressed in each group (process problems and technical/business problems). The culture will have changed to support information sharing, assertiveness in stating new positions and perspectives, and cooperation among all work units. The latter will help define and solve problems that cut across group boundaries. These problems are of the organization and not just of the group.

Even if all these change tracks are entirely successful, the formally documented systems will not yet have been questioned or changed. Only the informal agreements, understandings, and cultural norms will have been modified. Now it is time to get the visible and tangible features of the organization moving in the right direction. The membership is now ready to address the very difficult and close-to-home problems of strategy, structure, and reward systems. We must make sure that each group is working on the right tasks according to the right objectives and is rewarded properly for doing so.

CHAPTER SEVEN

The
Strategy-Structure
Track

The structure of an organization is no longer viewed as a rigid definition of hierarchical levels and interrelationships among different groups. Managers use the organizational design process as a fundamental tool for implementing and communicating the strategic direction selected for the firm.

—Hax and Majluf, 1983, p. 72

Many organizations are reshaping and reorganizing departments to find ways of accomplishing work more effectively. The frequency with which reorganizations occur appears to be accelerating; economic and technological change have made it essential, if companies are to survive in a tough environment. Making a transition from one organizational structure to another can be a period of intense creativity and progress or it can be one of disruption, anxiety, and low productivity. The ease with which a transition can be made depends to a great extent on management.

—Kaplan and Kaplan, 1984, p. 15

Human beings are not entirely rational, nor are they very objective, when contemplating decisions and actions. They have inherent limitations in mental capacity (only a few variables can be understood and analyzed at one time), memory (time erases the clarity and recall of events), and objectivity (psychological needs bias the interpretation of both current and past events). If these characteristics did not exist, human beings could remember everything and every person would see things in the same way. Under these conditions, there would be no need to document strategies, organization charts, incentive plans, work procedures, or job descriptions. Once such agreements were established, they would prevail exactly as intended—for all persons, for all time, in all their complexity.

It is because these particular limitations *do* exist that formally documented systems are required in every organization. When documents are at their best, they are convenient and necessary guides to all decisions that should not be left to memory, subjective interpretation, and simplistic analysis. If there were no documents at all, members would spend excessive time reestablishing previous "agreements" whenever conflicts arose; this time would be diverted from the primary work of the organization. When documents are at their worst, they steer behavior in the wrong direction. Members assume that because a document indicates exactly what to do, it must be the right thing under any circumstance. The deadliest document is one that is very difficult, if not impossible, to change.

The first part of this chapter presents the theories and methods for documenting strategy and structure. Strategy sets the direction for the firm; structure formally aligns the human and technical resources to move the organization in the intended direction. If strategy and structure are not established properly, especially at the highest levels in the organization, it makes little difference how well particular work procedures and incentive plans have been designed at the lower levels. The organization will be off track.

Determining strategy—perhaps the most complex problem facing the organization—requires assumptional analysis. Since this method has been covered in some depth already, relatively greater attention will be given to the structure side of the strategy-structure track. Designing structure requires an understanding of the different types of "task flows" that occur within and between subunit boundaries. Because of the sheer number of task flows to consider in designing any organization, restructuring is often treated in a piecemeal or superficial manner. Only with a computer-assisted method—the MAPS Design Technology—can restructuring be done thoroughly and systematically.

Of special interest is the way strategy and structure affect performance. While member morale can be affected by the frustrations of working in a structure that constrains the necessary task flows, performance can be affected dramatically by an inappropriate structure of departmental boundaries and by outdated work procedures. Defining *effectiveness* as getting the right job done according to each stakeholder's own criteria and defining *efficiency* as completing the job with little wasted effort will enhance our understanding of performance.

The second part of this chapter shows how to organize for "complex surprises." Even if the formally documented systems are guiding the organization properly, these cannot anticipate all new events. The world as a complex hologram just does not allow it. Rather than reorganize every time any new problem unfolds, a unique supplement to the operational structure can be offered: *the collateral structure.* This very adaptive, temporary structure is designed for addressing dynamic complexity. Only when the operational structure is noticeably out of line with the firm's strategic mission will the collateral structure be used to design a new organization chart. Together, the two structures combine to form the Problem Management Organization (PMO). As a total package, the PMO will help make the organization *efficient* in the short run with the operational structure and *effective* in the long run with the collateral structure. The PMO is the best "two-punch" combination for aligning strategy and structure in today's world.

Redesigning any organization's divisions and departments can be a very unsettling experience for members. Disbanding old groups and forming new ones dramatically alters the distribution of power, friendships, and traditions in the organization. If the earlier tracks have not been managed properly, members will fight—overtly and covertly—to hold on to their fiefdoms, cohorts, and "security blankets." The promise of higher morale and performance will not be enough to motivate acceptance of a structural shift. Only if the firm has an adaptive culture, only if its managers at all levels have learned the skills for managing dynamic complexity, and only if the troublemakers have been controlled will the whole membership choose to realign its strategy and structure for the future.

Making Strategic Choices

The stated mission or purpose of the organization defines the products or services that are offered to consumers at large. In the case of a not-for-profit organization, the mission is to solve one or more problems, such as disease or poverty. Generally, the mission is deciding on what is worthwhile to do and desiring to do it well: to survive, to be profitable, or to have a large clientele. The mission statement communicates the essential reason behind the organization's existence in the most general way. It does not get down to specifics.

A statement of strategy pinpoints the directions of the firm much more finely than does a general statement of mission. Strategy is choosing particular approaches to financing, producing, and marketing the firm's product or service—*how* it plans to accomplish the mission. Specifically, how will the organization finance its operations? Should its existing production facilities be upgraded to provide lower costs, or should more of the same plants be built? Should R&D work to improve the existing product lines or concentrate on developing entirely new ones? Should marketing efforts be aimed at a low-priced, high-volume product or a high-priced, low-volume product?

These questions are all matters of strategic choice once the mission has been set. Which combination of choices to select is perhaps the most complex, far-reaching problem any organization can face. Just one mistake in an assumption about one stakeholder could spell doom for the organization. For example, making an assumption that the federal government will not interfere with exporting a particular industrial product could be disastrous to a firm if certain lobbying groups forced government policy against such an export. If the firm's major business consisted of this export, the organization's wrong assumption behind this strategic choice would lead to its downfall.

How should strategic choices be made? In the 1970s, a number of quick-fix procedures were used to quantify and systematize the choices. These methods were expected to make the strategic plan more objective and rational. Once the strategy was established, senior executives, with their staffs of similarly minded consultants, tried to sell it to the rest of the membership—in a top-down manner. It is a shame that formulating and implementing strategy is not a simple problem with simple solutions for a simple machine.

The past decade has seen widespread adoption of such strategy analysis methods as portfolio classification models and PIMS [Profit Impact of Marketing Strategies] analyses of profitability determinants. Users were attracted by the logic and relevance of these methods to perplexing questions of strategic direction and resource allocation. . . .

The picture is changing with healthy skepticism or even complete disillusionment likely to prevail in the face of unrealized expectations. Critics fault the methods for abdicating management imagination to quantitative factors and thereby suppressing creative alternatives, depersonalizing the resource allocation process, and prescribing strategies which are simplistic, doctrinaire, and possibly misleading. Even former advocates of the methods are counseling caution in their use in the face of changed circumstances [Day, 1983, p. 51].

Kiechel (1982, p. 34), one of the oft-cited critics, colorfully reports on the demise of strategic panaceas:

We're going to miss corporate strategy, that sweet collection of surefire concepts—matrices, experience curves—that promised an easy win. Oh, it'll still be around here and there, showing its by now slightly grimy face in this corner and that, but things won't be as they were. Who can forget the excitement he felt when he first heard its siren song: *There are a few simple rules—understand them, make them your own, and you too can be a winner.*

All that's over now. . . . What went wrong? Where did the dream fail?

Lamb (1983, pp. 68-69) suggests several reasons for the dismay about strategy felt in many corporate circles today. In an article titled "Is the Attack on Strategy Valid?", he summarizes his observations:

Many cases of strategic failure have resulted from a "cookie cutter" approach to strategic planning, either by an outside strategy consulting firm or by corporate management itself. Applying some supposedly all-purpose or universal restructuring strategy to whole ranges of entirely different types of companies in entirely different industries with entirely different corporate cultures, product mixes, and competitive markets is virtually destined to result in a list of business strategy failures. . . .

The split among strategic design, implementation, and control has partly resulted from "hit-and-run" strategy consultants who prepare a strategic plan and then do not stay around to see it implemented, evaluated, and fully integrated into management practice. Often, corporate management does not choose to have outside consultants stay on to implement plans. In the final analysis, management must make the strategic plan its own, and structure its own process and schedule for implementation and control.

Consistent with Lamb's analysis, Day (1983, p. 52) emphasizes the critical role participative management plays in the planning process. At the same time, he recognizes the hidden complexities involved in making strategic choices:

There is a truism in planning circles that the process of strategic planning is more important than the plan. An effective process has broad management participation that encourages a shared understanding of strategic issues and alternatives. The payoff is subsequent commitment by these managers to the implementation of strategic decisions. Strategy analysis methods can improve this payoff by providing a common language and a logical structure that can be used to:

- Isolate areas where critical information is lacking;
- Communicate judgments and assumptions about strategic issues;
- Facilitate the generation of alternatives to be given detailed consideration; and
- Identify trade-offs involved in undertaking various strategic alternatives.

Day's philosophy of the strategic planning process is captured in the steps of assumptional analysis in three ways: (1) utilizing wide-scale participation by managers and members throughout the organization, (2) requiring an intensive examination and debate of the most important assumptions underlying different alternative strategies, and (3) encouraging a creative synthesis for the firm's strategic choices. If an organization uses assumptional analysis for only one type of problem, that problem should be *making strategic choices*. It should be quite apparent that the mission and strategy statements set all other decisions in motion.

Designing Organizational Structures

Once the strategic choices have been made, the next problem is how to organize (for the first time) or realign (for the nth time) the firm's resources in order to achieve its mission. Types of resources include financial, technical, material, informational, and human. Because of the limitations of human beings, all the resources of a firm must be subdivided into manageable portions. To move these resources into action, the strategic choices also must be broken down into subsets of more specific objectives and tasks. Each subset of objectives and tasks is assigned a portion of resources. Thereby, a division, department, or work group is born.

Stated more formally, I define *organization structure* as (1) objectives to be pursued, (2) tasks to be performed, (3) the arrangement of objectives and tasks into work units, and (4) the management hierarchy that coordinates the work units into a functioning whole. Making this structure operational requires that people and all other necessary resources be assigned to each work unit in order to perform the tasks with the relevant objectives in mind. Beyond this, various *job structures* (such as policies, job descriptions, work procedures, rules, and regulations) are designed to ensure that the organization functions as intended. Lastly, the reward system (described in Chapter Eight) is documented so that all members are motivated and rewarded for accomplishing their objectives. If all the documentation is done correctly, from the general mission statement down to specific job descriptions, the organization should be on track (assuming that the right culture, management skills, and team behavior are in place).

Figure 11 illustrates an organization's internal structure in the context of its external setting. The topmost circle shows the full set of objectives, tasks, and people (including all other resources) that would be assigned to the president or whoever has chief responsibility for all that transpires. The next level breaks this total set of objectives, tasks, and people into divisions, defined as the broadest decomposition of the whole into its parts. Each of these divisions is responsible only for its assigned subset of objectives, tasks, and people. At the next level, each of the divisions, in turn, is divided into smaller, more specialized work units, each with an even more focused subset of objectives, tasks, and people. These may be departments or sections. Depending on the size of the organization, this decomposition continues until the work group level is reached—a group of people that does not need to be subdivided any further. The linkages that emerge from this level-by-level decomposition become the management hierarchy. Its purpose is to coordinate the work that flows across subunit boundaries.

For the sake of convenience, the term *subunit* will refer to a decomposition of the whole into its parts that usually implies a division but that also can be taken as a department or work group, depending on the focus. If the division level is designed incorrectly, however, the subsequent structure of each division into departments and then of the departments into work groups will be designed incorrectly as well. The structural errors at the higher levels are carried through automatically to the lower levels.

Perhaps the greatest challenge in designing organiza-

Figure 11. Organization Structure.

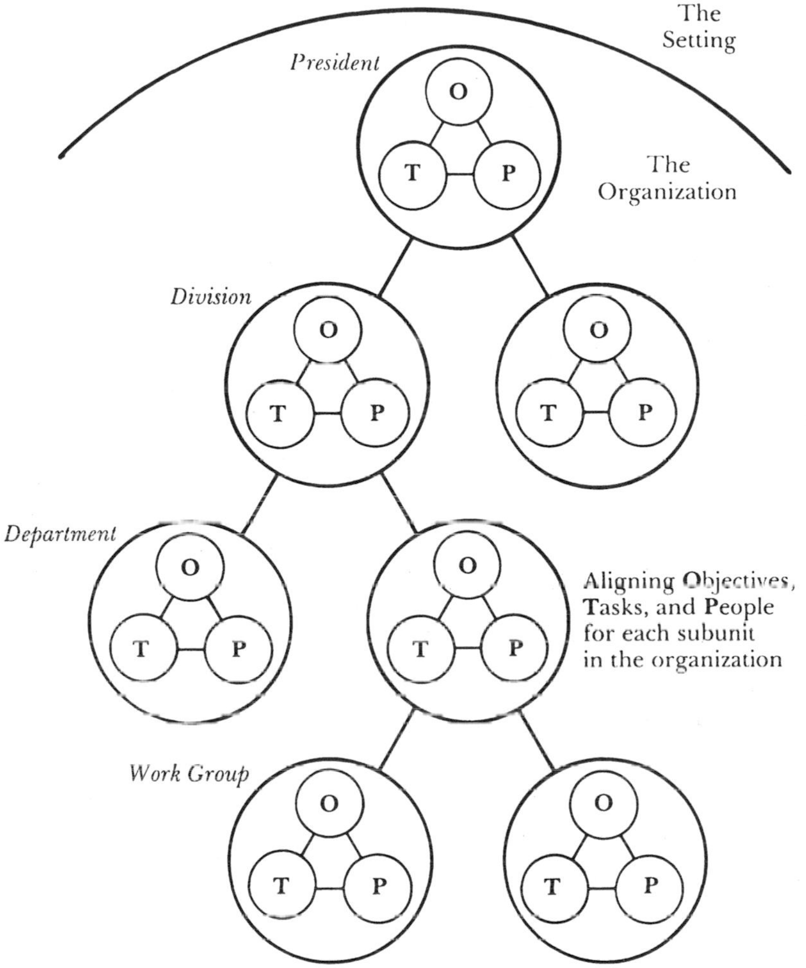

tional structures occurs during periods of rapid change—especially growth. Colvin (1982, pp. 91, 92) describes how Digital Equipment Corporation (DEC) was structured, subdividing the whole into its parts, in order to manage growth in the 1970s.

In business, as in nature, there seems to be a law that things slow down as they grow toward the elephantine. Now 25 years old and with annual revenues of $3.2 billion, Digital

Equipment Corp., the Maynard, Massachusetts, maker of mini-computers, continues blithely to ignore the law, to the increasing astonishment of investors and competitors. DEC's revenues have grown at an average annual rate of 36% over the last decade. Restrained by recession, they'll probably rise a mere 25% this fiscal year [1982], which ends July 3. What's more, DEC has achieved this staggering expansion without ever acquiring another company. . . .

Of course, yesterday's low-cost producer is often today's dinosaur. Once a company starts counting its sales in the billions a pervasive sluggishness can settle over operations, engulfing them in a bureaucratic morass. DEC has avoided much of that by organizing itself into 18 business units, each with considerable autonomy. A big reason DEC can keep growing, says Stephen Dube, a security analyst with Dean Witter Reynolds, is that "it's not one big business—it's 18 small ones." The same principle applies within departments. "Large groups are always less efficient than small ones," says Bell [DEC's engineering vice-president]. To keep his engineering staff of 5,000 from becoming inefficient as it grows, he tries to subdivide it into small teams. The ideal size: 30.

Forming Subunit Boundaries

A critical question to address is: What criteria should be used in designing subunit boundaries at each level in the hierarchy? The guiding assumption is that the way all the objectives, tasks, and people are organized into subunits might make a critical difference in performance and morale. Thompson's (1967) notion of task flows—how the performance of one task is dependent on the results of another—is exceedingly helpful.

Thompson defined three types of task flows: pooled, sequential, and reciprocal. *Pooled* flows occur when two or more tasks can be performed independently of one another and the results from different individual efforts can be added together, at any time, to produce useful output. *Sequential* flows occur when one task must be completed prior to beginning another task, as a particular sequence of individual efforts, before any useful output is produced. *Reciprocal* flows occur when a frequent input/output exchange must take place among individuals performing several tasks in order to produce useful output. Figure 12 diagrams the three types, showing pooled flows as dotted

Figure 12. Identifying Task Flows.

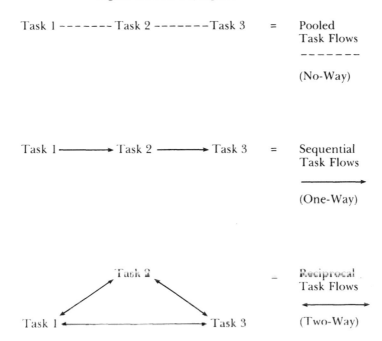

Task 1 ------- Task 2 ------- Task 3   =   Pooled
                                                 Task Flows

                                                 (No-Way)

Task 1 ———————→ Task 2 ———————→ Task 3   =   Sequential
                                                 Task Flows

                                                 ———————→

                                                 (One-Way)

                    Task 2   _   Reciprocal
                                                 Task Flows

                                                 ◄————————►

Task 1 ◄————————————————► Task 3   (Two-Way)

lines, sequential flows as single arrows, and reciprocal flows as double arrows.

Thompson suggested that each type varies in the cost of managing (coordinating) the task flows. Pooled flows are the least costly to manage simply because the outputs of different tasks can be combined quite easily by rules and procedures. Sequential flows are more costly to manage than pooled flows, since a certain amount of planning and scheduling is required to ensure the proper sequence of task performance. Reciprocal flows are the most costly to manage, as "mutual adjustment" and frequent monitoring of input/output exchanges are required above and beyond schedules, plans, rules, and procedures.

Thompson argued that subunits should be designed to include the more costly task flows *within* as opposed to *between* subunit boundaries. Ideally, all tasks that are reciprocally and sequentially linked would be placed within the same subunit, whereas tasks that are pooled could be left to fall between the

cracks. In all real, complex organizations, more tasks are interdependent than independent. Therefore, subdividing objectives
and tasks into manageable subunits means that some important
task flows will cross subunit boundaries. The design criterion,
then, is to separate all the objectives and tasks into a hierarchy
of subunits from the division to the work group level where, as
much as possible, reciprocally and sequentially linked tasks are
placed in the same rather than different subunits.

Figure 13 illustrates this design criterion by portraying
first the ideal case and then the worst case. The ideal case has

Figure 13. Forming Subunit Boundaries.

Correct Boundaries

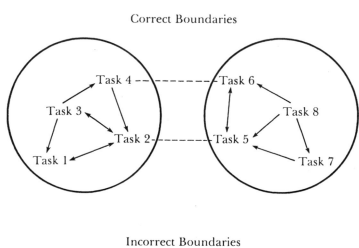

Incorrect Boundaries

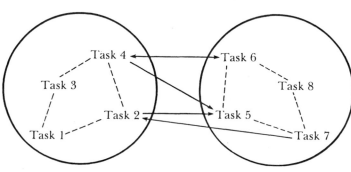

only pooled flows (dotted lines) between subunits. The worst case has reciprocal flows (double arrows) and sequential flows (single arrows) between subunits. The closer an organization's subunit boundaries are to the ideal, the lower are the costs of managing all the work.

Perhaps it would be worthwhile to elaborate on just why additional costs are incurred when tasks are coordinated between rather than within subunit boundaries. While Thompson spoke of the relative costs of rules and procedures versus schedules and plans versus mutual adjustments, one can also consider the impact of group loyalties and reward systems.

Briefly, whenever a boundary is drawn around a small number of people, a group or team emerges, which provides a strong psychological bond among its members; a "we" versus "they" attitude tends to reinforce the strength of the subunit boundary. The culture of each work unit also pressures each member to be loyal to the tribe and not to other work groups. Since members are usually in physical proximity to one another, the dictates and pressures of their work group are more powerful than any documents that "require" cooperation among all groups and loyalty to the whole organization. The latter may be just an amorphous mass, hardly competitive in loyalty with one's own peers and work group.

In addition, most organizations design their performance appraisal systems so that subunit managers control the distribution and withholding of rewards. For example, subunit managers often have primary input (if not sole authority) in hiring and firing decisions, wage and salary increases, and promotion decisions. Such authority over important rewards to members tends to reinforce members' loyalty and adherence to their subunit's objectives more than to the organization's and certainly more than to some other subunit's objectives.

One of the biggest frustrations for a manager is to be held responsible for a subunit's performance without having the authority to allocate members' time (and other resources) to all the necessary tasks. These necessary tasks, because of reciprocal and sequential task flows, are located in other subunits. The manager in this case has to either "beg, borrow, or steal" so that other subunits complete their work on time or adjust what they are doing so that his subunit can complete *its* job on time. The manager does not have any formal authority to request how the other managers allocate their members' time and efforts. I have seen cases in which as much as 80 percent of members' time was spent going back and forth across subunit boundaries and only 20 percent was spent on tasks that were strictly within the jurisdiction of the subunit. The members spent more time negotiating, pleading, and fighting with other subunits than they did performing their own assigned tasks.

When any particular firm is first established, perhaps its subunits are properly designed to contain all the critical task flows. But as its external setting changes and the firm grows, its task flows are altered and may no longer be contained within the same subunit boundaries. Top management often responds to this structural problem by creating new middle-management and staff positions to coordinate the new cross-boundary task flows. Over time, a rather extensive management hierarchy evolves, resembling a light bulb more than a pyramid, as managers coordinate managers who coordinate other managers and so on. If these same task flows were placed within new subunit boundaries, the need for many middle managers would be reduced substantially. What is a difficult task flow problem for managers between subunits becomes an easy matter for peer pressure, group loyalty, and consensus within subunits.

DEC has recently become aware of task flow problems that were created by new products, new competition, and its stupendous growth. For example, the dramatic changes in the computer industry in the early 1980s significantly altered the task flows between DEC's subunits. The formally documented systems could no longer manage the new streams of complex problems brought on by shifting stakeholders. An article titled "A New Strategy for No. 2 in Computers" (1983, pp. 66, 68) describes the new strategic and structural problems for DEC:

Now revolution is sweeping the computer industry again. Personal computers and office automation systems are putting computer power directly onto the desks of managers and executives. But this time, instead of leading the trend, Olsen [DEC's founder and president] has found himself having to play catch-up. "DEC for a period of time seemed to lose strategic direction —which markets it would go after and what its targets were," says Aaron C. Goldberg, a researcher at International Data Corp. in Framingham, Mass. . . .

DEC's previous power structure was built around 18 separate product-line groups that concentrated on selling to specific industries, such as engineering, education, and commercial OEM's [original equipment manufacturers]. . . . Eventually, the product-line groups became headquarters-bound fiefdoms that grew more and more protective of their own interests and lost sight of the company's long-range goals. Strategic planning mechanisms broke down because the narrowly focused groups were not anticipating new market demands that fell beyond their immediate purview. . . .

The DEC bureaucracy not only stymied product planning but also gummed up operations and hindered the sales force. Salespeople had no flexibility to bid competitively on contracts because prices could not be changed without the approval of the product groups. Worse, the product-line groups began fighting among themselves for limited central engineering and manufacturing resources. If a group wanted to develop a new product, it had to build a consensus among some of the four central departments and the product groups. The process got so complex that it soon became difficult for DEC to move decisively.

In all likelihood, simply adding on new managers and staffs to coordinate these troublesome cross-boundary task flows will not provide a lasting or efficient solution. DEC will need to reexamine and change the design of all affected subunits before its responsiveness to the marketplace can be improved.

Linking Performance to Subunit Boundaries

It is useful to view performance as having two components: effectiveness and efficiency. *Effectiveness* is getting the right job done according to each stakeholder's own criteria. *Efficiency* is completing the job with little wasted effort or use of

unnecessary resources. In the extreme, effectiveness means maximizing the chances for long-term survival while efficiency
means maximizing short-term productivity. Naturally, if an organization is diverting resources away from its mission on a day-
to-day basis, long-term survival will be endangered. On the other
hand, being efficient does not guarantee long-term success, since
the demand for the firm's products or services may change. Unless the firm responds by changing its strategic choices and
restructuring its resources, efficiency is irrelevant. Both effectiveness (strategic relevance to all stakeholders) and efficiency
(structural alignment throughout the organization) are essential
for high performance.

I will elaborate on the efficiency component, since it is
most germane to the focus on structure in this chapter. Specifically, efficiency can be defined as the proper allotment of members' time (hence, cost) to working on the right tasks for accomplishing the right objectives. In other words, one can consider
the amount of time spent on tasks as a way of seeing how well
all resources—financial, technical, material, informational, and
human—have been used efficiently toward accomplishing the
organization's objectives.

What would be considered inefficient? Members would
(1) spend time on the wrong tasks—those that do not help
achieve objectives, (2) not spend enough time on the right tasks
—those that do lead to these objectives, (3) be unable to work
on the right tasks because they had been assigned to some other
subunit, and (4) not be given the opportunity to suggest what
new tasks need to be performed so that objectives could be
achieved. It should be apparent that efficiency can be improved
by shifting the time spent on the wrong tasks—or the wrong
time spent on the right tasks—to the right time on the right
tasks. Here, "rightness" is defined as the particular allocation
of resources to tasks that will achieve the organization's objectives, its strategy and, ultimately, its mission. This proper allocation of resources is possible only if strategy and structure are
aligned properly throughout the organization.

Figure 14 shows how three important interfaces comprise
this strategy-structure relationship. The *strategic interface* asks

Figure 14. Strategy and Structure.

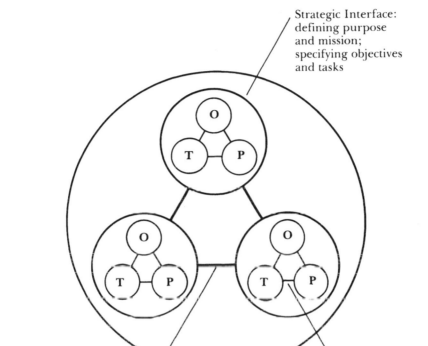

Strategic Interface:
defining purpose
and mission;
specifying objectives
and tasks

Structural Interface:
designing subunits to
minimize important
task flows across
boundaries

Job Interface:
reallocating time
of people on tasks
from actual to
desired

whether the mission and the strategic choices (1) are realistic
and appropriate—given the setting (external stakeholders), the
capabilities within the organization (internal stakeholders),
and the available resources, and (2) have been operationalized
accurately into objectives and tasks. The *structural interface*
asks how well the troublesome task flows have been placed
within rather than between subunit boundaries. Even when the
objectives and tasks are right for the organization, the struc-
turing of subunits can restrict efficient performance if many
important tasks still flow across subunit boundaries. The *job*

interface asks how well subunit managers have reduced the inefficiency of the objectives, tasks, and people under their authority. It is one thing for misdirected efforts to result from an inappropriate structure of subunits; it is another thing for misplaced efforts to be fostered by managers who have the authority to shift their members' time to the right objectives and tasks within their subunit yet fail to do so.

If the strategic interface is not conducted properly, the remaining two levels are irrelevant. In this case, the structural interface is designing the wrong objectives, tasks, and people into subunits, making managers' behavior inconsequential. There can be no meaningful discussion on the topic of efficiency if some effectiveness is not being achieved. Alternatively, if the strategic interface is conducted properly (hence, effective performance *can* be achieved) but the structural interface is not, then the job interface still cannot be accomplished efficiently. Subunits will be restricted in their efforts to perform well by the tasks they do not control. Lastly, even if both the strategic and structural interfaces are designed properly, it is still the responsibility of the subunit managers to properly allocate their members' time and efforts. However, since managers have the right objectives, tasks, and people under their authority, both effectiveness and efficiency are now possible.

In the case of DEC, a major strategic and structural realignment was undertaken in order to reverse its increasing sluggishness in the marketplace—to improve efficiency and effectiveness. Subunit boundaries were redesigned so that the critical task flows could be directly controlled by managers within each subunit. Only in this way could its new strategic shift—to become a strong, market-oriented company—be realized.

To get the Maynard (Mass.) company back on track, the 57-year-old Olsen has again moved into the company's day-to-day operations and launched a massive—and risky—corporate overhaul. Olsen's goal: a radical transformation of his engineering-oriented company into a tough, market-driven competitor. . . .
To restore DEC's fighting trim and speed up product developments, Olsen in July [1982] placed the main engineering

and manufacturing operations under one umbrella organization. Then, in January [1983], he consolidated the operations of 12 U.S. product groups into three regional management centers, leaving the product groups with only marketing duties. Each center has profit-and-loss responsibility and gives administrative support to the sales force. They also act as the direct link from the field to manufacturing, a job formerly done by the product groups at headquarters ["A New Strategy for No. 2 in Computers," 1983, pp. 66, 68].

Strategy and Structure with MAPS

It seems worthwhile to consider why so many organizations can be expected to have significant inefficiencies due to structural misalignments. In my experience, the boundaries of divisions and departments are generally regarded as being correct and fixed. For example, most industrial firms are organized by production, marketing, finance, R&D, and human resource subunits. Hospitals are organized by medical specialties. Universities are organized by the same departments that were in existence hundreds of years ago.

Is there any unique magic or special truth regarding the traditional, stereotyped subunit boundaries? It does not seem so. The design of subunits is very much man-made—it is not cast in stone, although it may be cast in outdated assumptions of how to organize task flows. It is worth repeating: Even if the traditional structures were effective many years ago, it does not follow that these same structures are correct for high performance today—such a notion is just another instance of erroneous extrapolation. With changing stakeholders, it seems rather unlikely that these classic structures are still best for capturing the important task flows within subunit boundaries. Only in a simple machine view of the world could one expect that particular subunits would be true for all time and for all situations. With a holographic view of the world, one would expect the viability of any structure to change over time.

Yet managers do try to adjust their organizational structures. In fact, one hears of reorganizations and restructuring all the time. However, these structural changes are usually quite piecemeal and superficial—a few people get moved around on the organization chart, or a few boxes get shifted to emphasize this or that function a bit more. It appears to be easier, mentally and emotionally, to add a new department, work group, or committee whenever a new problem emerges than to reexamine why the structure did not handle such a problem in the first place. However, the wholesale investigation of division and department structures for purposes of integrating, consolidating, and synthesizing a truly new structure of subunits is very unusual. Rarely do we see the sweeping kind of strategy-structure changes illustrated by DEC. Rarely does a company grow and prosper so magnificently.

A simple illustration suggests the immense complexity of analyzing the organization's structure of subunits. Consider the number of two-way flows that are possible with a given number of tasks. If an organization has 25 tasks, there are 300 unique two-way flows to consider. For 100 tasks, there are 4,950. Doubling the number of tasks to 200, which is not an unusual number of tasks for a large organization, results in 19,900 task flows! Because of the mental limitations of human beings, most people have trouble analyzing a problem with more than 10 variables. How can individuals comprehend, let alone analyze, 19,900 task flows in order to design subunit boundaries? They cannot. Without a method for overcoming these human limitations, efforts at restructuring will be simplistic, not systematic.

The strategy-structure track is aided by the MAPS Design Technology (Kilmann, 1977). The acronym *MAPS* (Multivariate Analysis, Participation, and Structure) summarizes the key ingredients of this computer-based method for restructuring organizations. Basically, MAPS collects information, in a participative way, which is needed for the most computationally complex aspects of restructuring: to search out and find all the troublesome task flows so that they can, as much as possible, be placed within new subunit boundaries. This method uses multivariate statistics and computer technology to analyze the large quantities of information required for designing a new structure.

The eight steps for the strategy-structure track are (1) making strategic choices, (2) developing objectives and task dictionaries, (3) responding to the dictionaries, (4) calculating inefficiencies, (5) diagnosing structural problems, (6) designing a new structure of subunits, (7) implementing the new structure, and (8) evaluating the new structure.

Step One: Making Strategic Choices

First the organization reaffirms, alters, or develops its mission statement. From this mission statement, it makes its strategic choices. Often this process requires performing an extensive assumptional analysis of the competing choices using a wide representation of inside and outside experts. The reader is referred to Chapter Five, in which this method of problem management was presented in detail.

Step Two: Developing Objectives and Task Dictionaries

The second step is to ensure that the strategic interface is conducted properly—which sets the stage for the proper design of the structural and job interfaces. Using a participative process, members are asked to develop an "objectives dictionary" and a "task dictionary." The objectives dictionary is a listing of all the objectives that have to be accomplished in order to realize the firm's strategic choices. The task dictionary is a listing of all the tasks that need to be performed in order to accomplish the firm's objectives. It may take a few days to a few weeks to develop these dictionaries, depending on how familiar the organization is with specifying objectives and tasks. Eventually, the two dictionaries together comprise items that are well understood by all members (no jargon or ambiguities) and include all important objectives and tasks. Often, the dictionaries go through a number of editing cycles before this point is reached. A typical firm can condense its two dictionaries to 30 to 50 objectives and 50 to 100 tasks.

Some selected examples of objectives are: Maximize net income to sales ratio; maintain favorable return on investment; continue to retain competitive cost leadership; maintain leadership position for customer service; hold and improve high-quality image; maintain an excellent working environment; improve domestic market share; penetrate international markets; increase productivity. These objectives are more specific than the organization's mission and yet are not so specific that they indicate what has to be done in terms of task performance.

Examples of tasks are designing new and modified products; building and maintaining tools and jigs; product cost and inventory accounting; budgets, forecasts, and measurements; market analysis; materials handling; requisition engineering; technology study; sales promotion; pricing; packing and shipping. These tasks, as the examples suggest, are not so detailed as to describe day-to-day activities but are more specific than the basic functions of finance, marketing, or engineering.

Step Three: Responding to the Dictionaries

Each member is asked to respond to each objective according to the following typical instruction: "Please indicate the extent to which you have the interest and ability to contribute to each of the following objectives." Next, each member is asked to respond to each task: "Please indicate the extent to which you need to participate in, or be aware of, each of the following tasks in order to accomplish your organizational objectives." All responses are given on a scale of 1 ("not at all") to 7 ("extremely so") and should not be constrained by present job assignments. Instead, members should feel free to respond according to how they can best contribute their talents to the organization.

Next, each member is asked to distribute 100 percentage points across the list of tasks according to his average annual time *actually* spent on each task. Responses might be 5 percent on task one, 20 percent on task five, 10 percent on task twenty-one, and so forth, realizing that all the percentages will add up to 100. Lastly, each member is asked to distribute percentage points across the same list of tasks according to how much of his time *should* be spent on each task in order to accomplish his organizational objectives.

Step Four: Calculating Inefficiencies

Knowing these time percentages and obtaining the annual salary for each member (confidentially from the members themselves or from the personnel department) allows one to calculate the total cost of inefficiency in the organization: the sum for all tasks and for all members of actual versus desired costs for performing each task. Knowing which tasks are currently assigned to each subunit allows one to calculate how much of the total cost of inefficiency stems from tasks that flow *outside* versus *inside* the boundary of each subunit. As a result, the total cost of inefficiency can be partitioned into the *structural* and the *job* interfaces. In a nutshell, each member's perception of how he should be spending his time on tasks in contrast with his current time expenditure—in order to accomplish organizational objectives—constitutes a potential misallocation of resources. Weighting each member's misalignment by his "value" to the organization—his annual salary—enables the inefficiencies to be represented as costs.

Consider a division of 1,000 members with an average annual salary of $20,000. This makes for a yearly payroll of $20 million. If the members indicate that the difference between their actual versus desired time spent on tasks amounts to $5 million (when weighted by each member's salary), this figure represents the total inefficiency of operations. In this case, a staggering 25 percent of the organization's human resources is being diverted to spending the wrong time on tasks. If $2 million of the total inefficiency stems from the structural interface (cross-boundary task flows) while $3 million stems from the job interface (within-boundary task flows), both the amount and the source of these inefficiencies have been determined.

It is important to appreciate why all these calculations are highly dependent on the validity and reliability of the data. Generally speaking, the more the organization is a simple machine, the more these calculations are exact over a long period of time; the more the organization is a complex hologram, the more these calculations are only rough approximations over a short time span. Since the complex hologram is the norm, the purpose of quantitative measures for restructuring organizations is twofold: to enhance conceptual understanding and to provide rough guidelines for action. The purpose is *not* to develop an elaborate accounting procedure, pretending that the numbers are exact in dollars and cents.

Step Five: Diagnosing Structural Problems

The most hoped-for result of organizational diagnosis is to uncover minimal inefficiencies without regard to their source, suggesting that the organization's structures are already in tune with its strategy. The next hoped-for result is to uncover large inefficiencies but to find that these are contained within subunit boundaries at the job interface, suggesting that only changes in job structure are needed. The least hoped-for result is to uncover large inefficiencies but to find that these occur between subunit boundaries. In this latter case, if the inefficiencies are to be corrected, a restructuring of subunits must occur *before* a restructuring of jobs.

Step Six: Designing a New Structure of Subunits

Restructuring the organization for the purpose of better containing the important task flows within subunit boundaries is necessary for the third type of diagnostic outcome noted above —in which most of the inefficiencies were sorted into the structural interface. The more a new structure can transfer these costs from the structural to the job interface, the more subunit managers will be able to redirect resources from the actual to the desired. The result should be a decrease in inefficiency and, hence, an increase in performance.

The next step is to design a new structure of subunits that contains, as much as possible, the critical task flows. It is beyond the scope of this chapter to detail the complicated multivariate statistics used to design a new structure that satisfies this criterion. First, all the task flows are identified and calculated via correlational analysis. Then subunit boundaries are formed around reciprocal and sequential task flows at each level in the hierarchy via factor analysis. The output of the MAPS computer program suggests a new structure of subunits to improve effectiveness (the right objectives and tasks) and efficiency (each subunit is provided more authority over its whole job).

The new MAPS design can be very different from the current structure of subunits. Combinations are created from tasks that previously were assigned to different departments. For example, certain R&D tasks might be combined with marketing research tasks *and* with other tasks concerning new production methods to form a new subunit. After the top managers have had a chance to examine this new arrangement, they recognize how much of their time has been spent in trying to foster communication and cooperation among these separate functions: R&D has been conducting research that has been viewed as useless by the rest of the organization; marketing has been dominated by its short-term sales objectives while putting aside market research questions; manufacturing has continued to resist any new products that require changes in the assembly process. The new MAPS subunit will enable shared objectives, group pressures, and monetary rewards to get members working together—both effectively and efficiently.

Identifying the critical task flows and then placing them in the same subunit—whereas these tasks previously were performed in different subunits—is what MAPS was designed to do. Thus, these new subunits are created out of old structural interface problems. For example, in one MAPS case, a perpetual conflict between sales and manufacturing resulted in a consolidated customer services group, enabling the firm to respond more rapidly with custom-tailored products for new customers. In another case, a long-standing "war" between engineers and technicians resulted in project groups that combined both types of experts into one team. When top managers saw these new MAPS designs, they proclaimed: "Of course that makes sense. It's obvious!" Yet, before the MAPS analysis, the overwhelming number of alternative structures was paralyzing.

Breaking down traditional subunit barriers so that the

critical task flows can be managed efficiently in a new structure of subunits represents a promising approach to improving productivity. A recent article in *Business Week,* "The Revival of Productivity" (1984, p. 100), shows the benefits of this kind of structural realignment:

But the most striking structural change in U.S. industry may be the way companies are deploying their people in the workplace. For Northrop, this means eliminating the physical barriers between engineers and production workers. At the company's new building in Hawthorne, Calif., where it makes the Tigershark fighter plane, engineers work right on the line so problems can be ironed out swiftly. "You can make changes on the plane together rather than sending memos," says Welco E. Gasich, senior vice-president for advanced projects. The result: The second Tigershark was made in 30% fewer work hours than the first. And the third plane "had zero defects on the fuselage, which is unheard of," Gasich says.

Step Seven: Implementing the New Structure

One should not expect that the new structure, when implemented, will be identical to the one suggested by the MAPS analysis. Other criteria come into play besides the containment of task flows within subunit boundaries, such as politics and vested interests. However, in order to enable the managers of the new subunits to recover the inefficiencies located within their new subunits, the new structure should be better at managing task flows than the old structure (even if it is not as good as the "optimal" structure derived from the MAPS analysis).

In all applications of MAPS—in fact, with all major reorganizations—a plan for a gradual transition is needed to guide the old structure to the new one. Since a change in group membership represents a difficult adjustment for most people, it is important that top management be sensitive to member anxieties. "Will I get along with the new people in my subunit? Will I be able to learn the new skills needed to work with people with different backgrounds and training? Will I still be an important asset to the corporation?" Recognizing these feelings and providing information and support to work them through will facilitate the transition process.

Once the new structure of subunits is in place, a partici-pative process is used to develop the more detailed job struc-tures: new job descriptions, work procedures, rules, and regula-tions. Each job should guide the occupant to spend the right amount of time on the right tasks with the right objectives in mind. Furthermore, the more the *scope* of each job is designed by the same criteria as the *boundary* of each subunit—that is, containment of a total piece of work so that responsibility equals authority—the more jobs will be designed to maximize performance and morale (Hackman and Oldham, 1980).

Step Eight: Evaluating the New Structure

During the implementation phase of the new structure and especially after the new structure is in place, the organiza-tion may be interested in evaluating the results. We can approx-imate the impact of the new structure on the efficiency side of performance if we assume the validity of all relevant calcula-tions.

Another reading of the efficiency measures can be taken after the new structure has had sufficient time to be felt. For example, one year after the new structure is implemented, it may be reasonable to expect that the new job structures and re-ward systems have taken hold. If this is indeed the case, then the inefficiencies that were transferred from the old structure (task flows between subunits) to the new structure (task flows within subunits) should have been reduced.

The Problem Management Organization

The foregoing discussion has shown how the firm's strat-egy can be aligned with its structure. Naturally, as major changes occur in the organization's external setting, or as the organization experiences significant internal growth, it may be necessary to modify its strategy and structure. However, this should not happen every year. Otherwise, the organization will spend most of its time designing rather than performing. For this reason, any company should organize its resources and structures to last at least a few years or maybe longer. However, given dynamic complexity, the strategies and structures of today will not last forever.

Since the formally documented systems are designed primarily to produce well-defined products and services, how can the organization address new problems that do not sort neatly into its everyday subunits? How can it handle the many "complex surprises" created by its stakeholders? Can the organization avoid restructuring for every new problem that emerges? What is needed is a supplementary structure. In order to define and solve those problems that cannot be anticipated or formalized, the second structure should involve members who are scattered across the everyday subunits. All the relevant expertise and information can be brought to bear on new and emerging problems. Thus, complex problems that affect many groups will be dealt with systematically rather than falling between the cracks.

Zand (1981) has suggested such a structure for organization-wide problem solving, referred to as the "collateral" structure. The members in this structure spend approximately two to ten hours per week working on new complex problems; the remainder of their time is spent back in the operational structure. Figure 15 shows the separateness of, as well as the linkages between, the operational and the collateral design. Both designs together form the Problem Management Organization (PMO).

The major reason for using parallel structures with overlapping memberships in the PMO is to increase the likelihood that creative solutions to problems will be implemented in the operational structure. The PMO fosters the ongoing cycle of sensing problems (in the operational design), defining problems and deriving solutions (in the collateral design), and implementing solutions (back in the operational design). While the operational design may place different types of people within each specialized subunit, the collateral design has even a greater mixture of experts in each of its groups. As Figure 15 shows, the members in each collateral group come from different subunits in the operational design.

Howard C. Carlson, assistant director of organizational research and development at General Motors (GM), describes how a "parallel organization"—a collateral design—functions in

Figure 15. The Problem Management Organization.

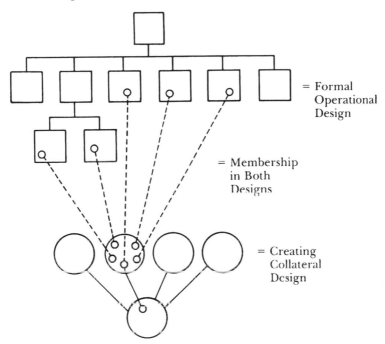

= Formal
Operational
Design

= Membership
in Both
Designs

= Creating
Collateral
Design

the Central Foundry Division of the company (Miller, 1978, p. 69):

> The parallel organization only recommends; the line organization must approve and implement or return unresolved issues to the parallel organization for further study. Keep in mind, though, that the same people who did the planning are now responsible for approving and implementing their recommendations. From such a process, that division has managed to achieve phenomenal rates of change—at all levels—in difficult areas that had resisted innovation throughout the history of the division.

Designing the Collateral Structure

Since the operational structure has been presented in the first part of this chapter, I will concentrate on the collateral side of the PMO. The eight steps for designing collateral structures are (1) formulating the mission, (2) specifying objectives, (3) specifying tasks, (4) identifying people, (5) responding to objectives and tasks, (6) designing the collateral groups, (7) implementing the collateral groups, and (8) evaluating the Problem Management Organization. Several of these steps are similar to the eight steps for designing operational structures; therefore, I will discuss these steps rather briefly by including only those aspects that are different from what was presented earlier.

Step One: Formulating the Mission

Top management must realize that a very ill-defined, far-reaching problem will be very difficult to address in the operational structure. With the recognition that some special-purpose collateral structure is needed, the mission must be formulated. Some possible missions include strategic planning; developing an organization-wide information system to aid in the decision-making process of middle managers; planning organizational changes and then guiding the implementation of these changes; evaluating organization-wide policies; anticipating and monitoring environmental changes.

Step Two: Specifying Objectives

Once the mission has been chosen, the managers are asked to consider the objectives the collateral design would be expected to achieve. Some possible objectives include: Plan for the utilization of scientific knowledge; define the major problems facing the organization over the next ten years; design an organization-wide management information system; assess R&D's role in corporate planning; evaluate the implications of human resource planning for all subunits in the organization.

Step Three: Specifying Tasks

After the objectives have been listed, the managers are asked to list the specific tasks that need to be performed in order to accomplish these objectives—that is, what work must be done, what information must be collected, what resources need to be acquired, what decisions and actions are necessary. Some possible tasks include: Conduct a market survey of consumer interest in this product; ask potential users for their opinions on the design of the management information system; monitor the pricing decisions of major competitors.

Step Four: Identifying People

This step concerns the human resource aspect of the collateral design. Specifically, given the objectives and tasks, who are the best people to staff the new design, how many are needed, what are their characteristics and areas of expertise, and where in the operational design are they now located? Only if the necessary people number less than ten or twelve is it feasible to have just one group, similar to a single committee or task force, for the collateral design. In most large organizations, the mission may break down into ten objectives, fifty tasks, and forty people. This is not an uncommon scope for a mission that is absolutely critical to the long term survival of the firm, that affects most or all subunits in the operational design, and that therefore requires a broad base of expertise from all these segments in the organization. This is precisely why a collateral design is needed.

Step Five: Responding to Objectives and Tasks

All members who will be involved in the collateral design are asked to respond to both objectives and tasks on seven-point scales. For the objectives, the typical instruction is: "Please indicate the extent to which you have the expertise and interest to work toward each of the following objectives." For the tasks, the typical instruction is: "Please indicate the extent to which you need to be involved in each of the following tasks in order to accomplish your objectives."

Step Six: Designing the Collateral Groups

The criterion of maximizing the containment of task flows within subunit boundaries is used to form the collateral groups, just as it was used in designing the operational structure. In the case in which each of the collateral groups will conduct an assumptional analysis according to its initial view of the problem, the MAPS analysis helps make each group quite different in outlook from the others. At the same time, the members in each group have indicated a shared endorsement of objectives and tasks. These two design properties foster a Lockean consensus within groups and a Hegelian dialectic between groups—just what assumptional analysis requires.

Step Seven: Implementing the Collateral Groups

Once the MAPS analysis presents a few alternative designs for the collateral groups, the members can debate and then choose a particular structure. They also may modify one of the MAPS designs to incorporate their insights and experiences. The MAPS analysis is just a tool to help sort out the large number of task flows; other criteria can be applied along the way.

Each newly formed group meets to specify its set of objectives and tasks further and perhaps to give itself a name. Attention then shifts to establishing group norms, work procedures, policies, expectations, and plans to ensure that effective performance will occur. At this point, the members realize that the collateral groups cannot be as formally organized as are their operational subunits. A collateral design deals with even more ambiguous and complex problems than does the operational structure. As a result, the collateral groups function in a loose, adaptive manner in contrast to the operational subunits, which function in a more controlled, regulated manner. Performance in the collateral design is more a matter of being effective than of being efficient.

Step Eight: Evaluating the Problem
Management Organization

The last step is evaluating how well the two designs work together. Top management also should be interested to learn whether the mission undertaken by the collateral design was accomplished. Sometimes, all that can be said is that the Hegelian approach was applied to a complex problem. Similarly, the members' level of confidence in the results may be the only immediate sign of a successful mission. At other times, bottom-line measures for evaluating results are available, as in the case of the GM parallel organization. Howard C. Carlson describes how one council (a single group in the collateral structure) was able to derive significant cost savings for the Central Foundry Division (Miller, 1978, p. 65):

The function of the parallel organization in this division is strategic planning, so it involves potentially almost every salaried management-level employee in affecting the future destiny of the division. The employee's work in the parallel organization gets him or her away from normal duties and into the damndest kinds of things. As an example, one of the councils in the parallel organization was charged with controlling the accelerating cost of administering fringe benefits. It was headed by a general superintendent of manufacturing. There were no personnel people on it. (One of the purposes of the parallel organization is to create new combinations of people and give them a chance to look at important, overall business problems in new and different ways—without taboos or unnecessary restrictions.) The council went to personnel people and others, learned about what was going on, and, as good managers do, found out how costs were allocated and so on. In one plant, they found that people had been sent home on short workweeks to effect a saving in the plant report. But in fact, they found that an apparent saving of $304,000 cost the plant $575,000, the allocated supplemental unemployment benefits (SUB pay) for those on short workweeks in the plant.

As you can see, these councils consist of line managers digging and learning for themselves, and, as a result, you have immediate change, once these managers have discovered things for themselves. As a matter of division policy now, no one is automatically sent home on short workweeks if they are eligible for SUB pay; instead, they're given gainful employment whenever possible in another area of the plant.

The pilot study showed that 60,000 additional manhours could be saved that way in that one plant. For the division as a whole, a very substantial dollar saving resulted from applying the work of just this one council in the parallel organization.

Return to the SFD Story

Since a two-year effort had resulted in a well-developed strategic plan for SFD, the strategy-structure track began where this document left off. In one of the workshops in April 1983, all thirty-eight managers spent an entire day listing the objectives and tasks that followed from their strategic choices. After an extensive editing process, the objectives and task dictionaries were formed and then responded to by the entire membership of the division. The MAPS analysis was used to search out the reciprocal and sequential task flows. Subunits at each level in the hierarchy were formed by enclosing the troublesome task flows within boundaries, as much as possible. The MAPS design was shown to the top managers, who then developed a synthesis by incorporating their ideas and insights.

In this application of the strategy-structure track, no information was collected to measure the inefficiencies of the current structure or the new structure of subunits. When the possibilities for these measures were discussed with the top managers, it became apparent that the key performance issue for SFD was effectiveness, not efficiency. Since the setting of SFD was changing all the time, the major problem was adapting to these changes. The operational structure of SFD had to be loose, flexible, and ready to shift gears at any moment. Therefore, the restructuring was intended to ensure that the strategic interface was conducted properly (having the right objectives and tasks in the division) and that the structural interface was a useful approximation to the typical task flows. The purpose of the new organizational structure was to provide a better match with SFD's new commercial strategy, but it was understood that the job structures could not be specified in much detail.

During the third management skills workshop in June 1983, the consultants helped the thirty-eight managers form a collateral design, which continued after the workshop. While SFD's everyday problems were complex enough, their long-term prospects were even more uncertain. The managers began by listing more than twenty complex problems that needed attention in a collateral design. They then formed into several temporary groups to rank the problems in order of importance. The groups came up with three categories that contained all the separate problem items: (1) survival issues, (2) people issues, and (3) technical issues. Since the number one problem, survival, was seen as completely overshadowing the other two, the managers chose to tackle this problem first.

With the mission as survival, the objective was to develop a strategic survival plan. There was simplicity in this focus, yet there was complexity in its resolution. To save time, rather than using MAPS, managers self-selected into several conclusion groups that represented different survival plans: (1) Gain self-sufficiency as an R&D group, (2) form a joint venture with one or more companies, (3) sell the business, (4) grow as a commercial division, and (5) shut down the division. Each group first met separately to develop an assumption matrix to support its "initial" conclusion. Then the groups met together to debate and then synthesize their differences.

Two of the initial conclusions, "sell the business" and "shut down the division," were first suggested as a joke, not as serious alternatives. However, several managers were willing to form groups to examine these possibilities. As a surprise to everyone, the more each group's assumptions were exposed and debated, the more plausible these alternatives became. Many managers remarked: "If we hadn't gone through this process, we would have automatically ruled out selling the division. What was first a joke turned out to be the best strategic move, under the circumstances."

The whole process, from listing the major problems facing the division to the synthesized conclusion to look for a buyer for the division, lasted about four weeks. The groups met for several hours each week, away from their regular work setting, to discuss and debate the survival problem. Afterward, they returned to their jobs in the operational structure. Movement back and forth between the collateral and operational designs was handled quite smoothly, thanks to the changes resulting from the earlier tracks. It was clear, however, that some discussion of the survival problem continued while the managers were involved with the operational design, just as some work-related discussion took place while they were involved with the collateral design. But, for the most part, the managers could distinguish between the two different designs and understand how each must supplement the other. The managers realized that if the Problem Management Organization did not allow for these two different structures, the short-term problems might be solved but the long-term problems would fall between the cracks.

Conclusion

Placing the operational structure behind the strategic choices aligns the organization's resources efficiently in the right direction. As major changes in the organization's setting develop in the future, however, another restructuring will be necessary as strategic choices are altered. With the collateral structure in place, the organization will be able to address its new problems systematically and effectively. If new problems emerge, however, new missions and new collateral structures can be created.

The ultimate test of the collateral structure occurs when the membership realizes that its operational structure has grown noticeably out of alignment with the strategy of the firm and its external setting. The mission then becomes one of redesigning the everyday structure. The Problem Management Organization continues, but the members in the collateral structures will have a different home base after the new operational structure is implemented. Without the collateral groups as a temporary home, a restructuring of the organization chart might not have taken place; the members would have been too locked into their day-to-day filters to sense their growing cross-boundary task flow problems. This again demonstrates the benefits of having a temporary structure that allows the membership to question all broader and more complex issues—those that cannot be managed within operational subunits.

Attention now turns to designing reward systems, the last of the five tracks. Here we close the circle by designing systems to motivate and reward members for efficient and effective performance. This is only possible when the culture, management skills, team efforts, and formally documented systems are all in tune with one another and with the overall mission of the organization.

CHAPTER EIGHT

The Reward System Track

Many attribute at least part of American industry's competitive decline to the short-term strategic orientation of U.S. managers, fostered by company compensation systems. It is further argued that management practices—including compensation systems—must be realigned to support long-term strategies. . . .

[However], don't expect compensation (monetary and psychological) to do all the work in implementing new strategies. Pay and reward systems need to work in concert with organization structure, management practices and systems, and corporate culture in achieving long-term economic success.

—Tomasko, 1982, pp. 8, 12

Organizations offer rewards; individuals offer performance. In the exchange of rewards for performance, a relationship is born. Organizations establish reward systems to document this relationship. While two important purposes of a reward system are to attract and retain the most able individuals as members, an important third purpose is to motivate those members to high levels of performance. Most reward systems seem to do a fairly good job of fulfilling the first two purposes, but they often are unable to motivate members to do more than what is considered satisfactory or merely acceptable.

In the world as a simple machine, attracting and retaining members is enough to ensure success, or so it seems. With such a world view, members are cogs in a wheel; as such, they are supposed to do just as they are told. A *non*performance-based reward system, which uses seniority rules or civil service codes as criteria for receiving rewards, has the simplicity and objectivity required of a simple machine. As a result, each individual is paid for routine performance, not for outstanding results.

In the world as a complex hologram, an organization cannot rely on routine performance generated under seniority or any other nonperformance-based reward system. Indeed, organizational success can be achieved only if members are motivated to use *all* their talents and energies. However, establishing a performance-based reward system, one that exchanges different rewards for different levels of performance, is a most complex problem. Such a system involves all the complexities of human nature, recognizing the critical differences between what people expect to receive and what the formal documents state. It is not a simple matter of announcing to the membership that rewards will vary according to performance.

Furthermore, a fully functioning, performance-based reward system is possible if and only if all the other four tracks have accomplished their purposes. The earlier tracks establish the right conditions for a performance-based reward system, which then allows the organization to tie compensation and other rewards directly to performance. Actually, the only time a *non*performance-based reward system should be designed is when the other four tracks cannot or will not be conducted.

As we shall see, without an organization structure that contains the troublesome task flows within subunit boundaries, it is impossible to develop objective measures of performance. If the performance ratings of members are not viewed as being at least somewhat objective, it is difficult for members to believe that the rewards they receive are based on performance. Instead, they are left to believe that rewards are based on happenstance and other nonperformance criteria.

Without effective teams, managers and members are not comfortable in openly sharing such information as the results of performance reviews and the distribution of rewards. In the absence of this information, members are left to their own imaginations in deciding whether performing well makes any difference at all. In such a situation, nobody knows for sure whether high performers receive significantly more rewards than low performers.

Without interpersonal and human relations skills, managers cannot engage in face-to-face performance reviews in an effective manner. Defensiveness-producing styles of communication prevent subordinates from hearing the performance message. Similarly, under these circumstances, managers cannot conduct numerous counseling sessions to help subordinates improve their performance, to encourage them to spend the right time on the right tasks with the right objectives in mind.

Without a supportive culture that encourages trust, members have little reason to believe in the validity of the reward system. In a holographic world in which subjective measures of performance are part and parcel of any evaluation, trust is essential in order to make the reward system work. With a dysfunctional culture, members believe, perhaps rightly so, that rewards are based on favoritism and politics.

In essence, if an organization does not establish the proper conditions for an effective reward system, it cannot use salaries, wages, bonuses, promotions, and any other forms of compensation to motivate the membership to high performance. Here the organization is wasting the motivating potential of its payroll, which may constitute as much as 25 percent to 75 percent of its total expenses. In this case, the reward system serves to attract and retain members, but it does not motivate them to excel. Naturally, individuals may strive to excel for intrinsic rewards. However, if the other tracks have not been managed properly, even the most dedicated efforts by the members will not lead to high performance for the organization. Instead, members' efforts will be blocked by all the barriers to success that are still in force: dysfunctional cultures, outdated management skills, poorly functioning work groups, unrealistic strategic choices, and misaligned structures.

The first part of this chapter outlines the theory and practice for establishing a performance-based reward system by recognizing the importance and flexibility of pay, measuring performance in both objective and subjective ways, and linking pay directly to these measures of performance. As a guide to action, a seven-step process is described for designing and implementing reward systems for a holographic world.

The second part of this chapter considers how performance results and reward decisions are communicated to each member of the organization during face-to-face meetings with a superior. Here we explore the necessity of designing two types of meetings: (1) a performance review to provide information for evaluative purposes, and (2) a counseling session to provide feedback for learning purposes. These two types of meetings ensure that members understand their performance results and will be able to improve for the next cycle. A four-step process is suggested for conducting performance reviews and counseling sessions to optimize what the organization and the individual exchange in their relationship.

Establishing a Performance-Based Reward System

Individuals have been offered numerous rewards in exchange for their membership and high performance. These rewards can be sorted into two types: intrinsic and extrinsic. *Intrinsic rewards* are those reinforcements an individual experiences from performing his assigned work. For example, if the job is interesting, exciting, and challenging, the individual experiences pleasure just by doing what the job entails. *Extrinsic rewards* are given formally by the organization rather than occurring naturally in the work setting. For example, salary, bonuses, paid vacations, fringe benefits, expense accounts, office furnishings, awards, and promotions come to the individual externally.

In the case of intrinsic rewards, all the organization can do is create conditions (e.g., particular job designs) that make it possible for the individual to experience them. In the end the individual must reward himself. Extrinsic rewards, on the other hand, differ in two important ways: they must be given to the individual or he must obtain them, and they are tangible and potentially visible to others [Porter, Lawler, and Hackman, 1975, pp. 341-342].

These two types of rewards are not as distinct as they appear. A manager has the authority to assign jobs and special projects to subordinates and, as a result, can influence intrinsic rewards. The manager can assign the member interesting, exciting, and challenging work, or he can give him boring and routine work. Likewise, doing a good job for intrinsic reasons also may result in extrinsic rewards, such as a bonus or a pay raise.

Individuals work at their jobs in order to obtain extrinsic and intrinsic rewards that satisfy their material and psychological needs. The "goodness of fit" between rewards and needs determines the level of *morale* for each individual. How well re wards are linked to results affects the level of *performance* in the organization.

Recognizing the Importance and Flexibility of Pay

Management practices in the early part of this century emphasized, almost exclusively, job security and pay as the important rewards. Managers assumed that most individuals worked primarily to survive and to satisfy basic material needs, such as food and shelter. From the 1940s through the 1960s, management practices emphasized intrinsic rewards while downplaying the impact of pay on job motivation. With growing affluence in society and a rising level of education, it was assumed that the higher psychological needs for achievement and "self-actualization" had become dominant, since basic material needs had been met. By the 1970s, the idea of motivating by pay even seemed to have negative connotations.

I believe that the impact of pay as a motivator has been

greatly overlooked in most theories of organizations. Money not only satisfies basic needs but provides purchasing power for a wide range of goods and services. It is a symbol of success and an indicator of social status. Money provides a greater choice of life-style and freedom in general. Money is very important to most people. For example, if employees' paychecks are out of line with what they believe they deserve, they become very upset. If employees feel that others are getting more pay for doing less work, they become angry. If they feel that it makes little difference how hard or how well they work in terms of the monetary rewards they receive, they become disheartened or even depressed. As employees spend more time complaining about the reward system, they have less time to do their jobs. Hence, extensive discussions about pay represent an inefficient use of time.

While pay is only one extrinsic reward, it is not only the most important one to most persons but also the most flexible for both the organization and the individual. Promotions, for example, are not always available; often, in order for someone to be promoted, an old position must be vacated or a new position must be created. Also, while fringe benefits can vary, extra vacation days and health insurance coverage have a more limited appeal. Pay, bonuses, stock options, and profit-sharing plans, however, can be offered continuously and with great variability. For example, consider how one company ("Emerson Electric: High Profits from Low Tech," 1983, p. 61) dramatically varies pay according to performance:

> Superachievers are rewarded handsomely. Division managers can increase their annual compensation up to 81% by exceeding preset goals. Managers of Emerson's In-Sink-Erator Div., for example, won 50% bonuses last year when they introduced a new kitchen hot-water dispenser and added 10 to 15 percentage points to the division's market share. Says [Chairman] Knight: "We pay for results."
>
> But those who fail are shown no mercy, as A. B. Chance Co., a sleepy electric-equipment outfit, discovered the hard way. Within two years of acquiring it, Emerson's own management team moved in, imposing new financial controls and selling four product lines. One Chance casualty observes: "The

amount of interjection depends on how your performance compares with Emerson's."

Measuring Performance Objectively and Subjectively

Pay and other forms of compensation cannot be linked to performance if performance cannot be measured in a convincing manner. An ongoing debate concerns whether an individual's contribution to the organization can be measured objectively *or* subjectively. I have found that the assessment of an individual's performance should contain *both* objective and subjective aspects.

In most cases, measures are considered objective when hard numbers based on a well-formulated system of counting are available. Objectivity is thus more apparent when discrete quantities of value added are available, such as number of units produced, dollars of sales generated, dollars of costs saved, and number of clients served. While the many rules for counting are subject to debate and adjustment, once established they do provide consistency across different raters—which is the mark of objectivity.

Although an objective measure of performance—such as earnings per share or return on investment—often is available at the organization level, it may be more difficult to construct such measures for subunits within the organization. Specialized subunits may not produce a distinguishable part of the whole, which makes it difficult to construct an objective measure of results. Each subunit's output may be of value only when it is combined with the outputs of other subunits. When several subunits are combined into a larger, more encompassing unit, it is easier to construct objective measures. However, the more performance assessment takes place away from the individual level, the more the link between performance and rewards is weakened. Members have difficulty seeing how their own efforts contribute to return on investment at the organization level.

Lawler (1981, p. 86) offers a useful framework for identifying performance units by taking into account the nature of task flows across subunit boundaries:

One way to identify performance units is to start with individuals at the bottom of the organization and work up through the hierarchy until a level is reached at which (1) performance is clearly measurable in relatively objective terms, (2) no important interdependencies which affect that individual's work fall into parallel parts of the organization, and (3) the individual controls most of the factors that influence his or her performance results. At this point, a performance-based pay system should be considered—be it at the individual, group, or even divisional level.

In the case in which significant task flows exist between subunit boundaries, however, it becomes impossible to establish an objective measure of performance other than for the whole organization. In such an instance, every subunit is so highly interrelated with other subunits that performance cannot be distinguished at the boundary; each subunit's performance is completely dependent on how other work units perform. With such a design of subunits, the design of jobs similarly prevents members from controlling an identifiable piece of the whole. It is difficult to hold each individual accountable for his results even if one can measure them.

The successful completion of the strategy-structure track sets the stage for objective measurement as close to the individual level as possible, given dynamic complexity and corresponding task flows. Specifically, the more the organization is structured to contain the troublesome task flows within subunit boundaries, the more objective performance measures can be established for various subunits. Each subunit then has a total piece of work under its own authority. With minimal task flows between subunits, the discrete outputs of each unit can easily be added together at some later time. In addition, the more each job has been designed to contain a complete piece of work that is under the direct control of the job holder, the more performance can be measured objectively at the individual level.

However, no matter how perfectly the organization is structured to contain the task flows within subunit boundaries and jobs, objective measures of performance cannot capture all the necessary contributions required of members for long-term organizational success. Only in a simple machine view of the world can one believe that objective measures present the whole picture. In a holographic view of the world, below-the-surface aspects of organizational life must be considered, assessed, and rewarded as well.

Peers in each work group, for example, can regularly have a discussion on how well each member contributes to the holographic aspects of the organization: (1) supporting an adaptive culture, (2) exposing his assumptions and challenging others' assumptions, (3) adding to the team spirit of his work group, and (4) supporting cross-boundary flows of information and tasks. Then, on various rating forms, members can rate or rank order one another's contributions in fostering these subjective aspects.

Determining the proportion of objective and subjective aspects of any performance rating (a summary index of any member's total contributions during a specified time period) is important in designing a performance-based reward system and thus will take place when the reward system is designed by the membership. The proportion may vary from job to job and certainly will vary from division to division, depending on the nature of the work to be done. In general, however, objective measures attempt to capture the desired *outcomes* while subjective measures seek to portray the *processes* expected to lead to these outcomes. In a holographic world, since performance results may not materialize for some time and are affected by uncontrollable events as well (from shifting internal and external stakeholders), short-term performance ratings should partially rely on process judgments—how well each individual contributes to those activities that are expected to lead to organizational success.

Linking Pay Directly to Measures of Performance

The major challenge for any reward system is to tie rewards directly to the objective and subjective measures of performance. This is more difficult than it appears. Designing a performance-based reward system is a complex problem if only because it is intimately related to the complexities of human nature: psyches. It is essential to understand how individuals make their performance decisions and how psychological dynamics can so easily distort the "reality" of any documented reward system. What is established on paper can be quite different from what members believe to be the current practice.

While performance at the organization level is determined by all the categories in the Barriers to Success model (Figure 1, Chapter 2), performance at the individual level is based on at least five immediate factors: (1) the motivation to work, (2) the ability to work, (3) whether the individual applies his energies and talents to the right tasks with the right objectives in mind, (4) the amount of control the individual has over the outcomes of his work, and (5) whether the cultural norms of the work group support or restrict efforts at high performance.

It seems that an individual's motivation to perform in a given job situation initially results from a rather deliberate decision process—at least until cultural forces take over. An individual first surveys the situation to see if there are any rewards available that suit his needs. If none is available, he either leaves the situation or does the minimum to remain as a member until he has a better alternative. If there are rewards that suit his needs, he then estimates the likelihood that he can do what it takes to receive those rewards. In essence, the individual considers what the job requires, whether he has the ability to do the job, and how much effort will be required to be successful. As long as he *believes* that the available rewards will be forthcoming after he achieves an expected level of performance, the individual will expend his efforts and talents in the right direction. Not believing that effort and performance lead to rewards will stifle his efforts just as if no rewards were available in the first place.

Where do such beliefs come from? The formation of beliefs about any reward system is affected more by social and cultural forces than by a simple cost/benefit analysis conducted by each individual member. Even if the formal reward system explicitly states that the distribution of rewards is based on performance, members go by their *shared* experiences, comparisons, and expectations. Consequently, there may be a large difference—a reward system gap—between what the documented system states and what the membership believes. In order for this gap to be closed, there must be accessible information that can be trusted in order for "the group" to be convinced that rewards are linked to performance.

If this information is to be trusted, positive experiences and consistent practices must be associated with the reward system. If members do not receive the rewards they feel they deserve (based on their performance), the reward system loses some of its credibility. As members share these negative experiences with one another, they develop revised, collective beliefs about the reward system. Making matters worse, it seems that just a few violations of a reward system can be very damaging, while many positive experiences may be ignored and forgotten. This is how individuals protect themselves from pain or hurt. We have to accept the psyche's tendency toward selective recall if we wish to understand the delicate nature of credibility and the way beliefs are formed.

In order for individuals to know whether high performers are rewarded more than low performers, information to judge the pay/performance connection must be accessible. Ideally, each individual should have explicit data on (1) the criteria for high performance, (2) everyone's actual performance, and (3) the actual distribution of rewards to each person.

It is surprising to find many instances in which complete secrecy is the norm and salaries and wages are considered private matters. This attitude generalizes to all information having anything to do with reward systems. However, there is much room for variation between complete secrecy and full disclosure. For example, I have found that even if individual salaries are kept secret most members desire to know the salary ranges of different job positions, the ranges of various bonuses, and the average percentages of salary increases. Also, it may be useful to make available the performance ratings of each individual, along with the actual amount of his increase in salary, or just the percentage change in his salary. How else can members know what rewards are received for a certain level of performance? However, it generally is unnecessary to show each person's total salary, since salary is determined by factors other than current performance: that is, education and training, supply and demand for different types of jobs, and previous levels of performance. But information showing how performance *this* year resulted in rewards *this* year is absolutely critical for judging whether rewards indeed are based on performance.

If such information is not provided, individuals will invent it. This becomes a very dangerous situation: The more people are kept in the dark, the more their psychological dynamics are free to distort reality, with all its consequences. For example, since most people are not 100 percent confident of their abilities and self-worth, there is a tendency to see others as performing less but being paid more. Exaggerating one's own performance helps protect one's ego, since it is hard to admit that one performed worse than one's coworkers. Deflating what one received helps perpetuate the myth that we never get what we deserve: "Everyone else except me is treated fairly." These feelings may develop from sibling rivalries, in which each child believes his brother or sister is really the favored one. Even adults seem to remember when they did not get what they wanted more than when they did.

Distortions seem to be pervasive in organizations, just as the psychodynamics that create them are widely evident in most societies. Worse yet, groups have the power to develop a social reality even more exaggerated than average individual distortions. If we understand these tendencies, we can realize how absolutely critical it is to provide some information about pay/performance connections to counter such distortions. If this sort of information is not shared openly, regardless of the intention behind the current reward system, individuals will be convinced that performance is not related to rewards.

Another advantage for having a nonsecretive reward system is that it helps keep everything and everyone honest. When information is made available, gross inequities or questionable practices become quite transparent. With an open system, managers have to be prepared to defend the reason for anyone's receiving or not receiving a particular reward. This, of course, may be why some firms do not like to establish an open reward system.

Secrecy about management pay rates seems to be an accepted practice in many organizations. However, organizations typically do not keep secret how other extrinsic rewards are administered. They do not keep promotions or who gets certain status symbols secret; in fact, they publicize these things. Why then do they keep salaries secret, and what are the effects of keeping them secret? It is usually argued that the pay of individuals is kept secret in order to increase pay satisfaction. Presumably secrecy increases satisfaction because if employees knew what other employees were earning, they would be more dissatisfied with their own pay. This may in fact be true in organizations where the pay system is chaotic and cannot be rationally defended, but it is not clear that it is better to keep pay information secret when it is being well administered. In fact, there is evidence that keeping it secret may increase dissatisfaction and make it more difficult to use it as a motivator [Porter, Lawler, and Hackman, 1975, pp. 354-355].

The culture track creates a social reality of trust and openness that tends to support the public display of pay/performance information. Similarly, the team-building track, through open discussions and candid feedback about delicate topics, prepares the members to be comfortable with such reward system information. In fact, by the time the organization has progressed to the fifth track, the sharing of pay/performance information is often a minor issue compared to the information about interpersonal styles and difficult problems that has already been shared. Moreover, in a holographic view of the world, suppressing any information of any kind is to be discouraged. The quality of any decision or action can be affected significantly by not having the necessary information—be it for an important business decision or for deciding whether to risk one's efforts for the promise of future rewards.

Designing Reward Systems

A participative process among managers and employees is recommended for developing the most effective reward system for the organization. Members from the personnel or human resource department should play a special role in this process, since their expertise typically includes pay and compensation systems. However, if these specialists are not familiar with alternative reward systems, outside experts can be called in to provide the latest views. It should be emphasized, however, that even if all the human resource experts believe that they can design the "perfect" system, I still recommend the full participative process for the organization. Even in the remote case in which these staff experts can design the same system as can the line membership, the acceptance of and commitment to the new reward system will not be present. There is quite a difference between being handed the new system as a finished product and having the opportunity to design it. This same participative philosophy was recommended in the preceding four tracks.

If any members of the organization are unionized, a special effort can be made to try to remove the constraints imposed by the collective bargaining agreement. If this is not feasible, then some part of the organization will be governed by the union contract (even if this represents a nonperformance-based reward system) while the other parts will be free to consider alternative performance-based systems. But the mere existence of union membership should not preclude the possibility of gaining union/management cooperation. This same sort of effort may have been necessary in the prior tracks when jobs were redesigned as a result of strategy-structure changes.

In addition, one must recognize that a large organization with several divisions in different businesses will not be best served by one centralized reward system. While there may need to be some shared philosophies, policies, and procedures across all subunits, each subunit may need to have a somewhat different system to fit with its unique setting, strategy, structures, and culture. But the centralized policies for a reward system should be designed in an integrated manner with the decentralized systems established in each major division in order to achieve some form of equity and to aid in human resources planning.

Paulson (1982, p. 27) describes how reward systems must be aligned with the nature of the business, unit by unit:

Some of the most effective incentive systems, designed around the concept of multiyear planning to achieve both financial and business objectives, clearly allow for differences among business units, their respective managers, and different performance periods. Thus, incentives for the aggressive manager of a high-growth business should encourage building for the long term, while the manager of a mature business should be rewarded primarily for maximizing and sustaining near-term performance.

The following seven steps enable the membership to design a performance-based reward system for the whole organization, as well as for unique variations across divisions: (1) forming a collateral design, (2) reviewing the types of reward systems, (3) forming groups around alternative reward systems, (4) performing assumptional analysis, (5) designing the detailed reward system, (6) implementing the new reward system, and (7) evaluating the new reward system. For convenience sake, I will often refer to *reward system* in the singular to refer both to the centralized system of a company and to the variations in reward systems across its divisions.

Step One: Forming a Collateral Design

The design of the reward system is a most complex problem. Not only does this documented system affect everyone in the organization, but it is rooted in some very basic assumptions regarding what motivates people. Naturally, there are some simple aspects to the reward system, such as selecting a health insurance company and establishing an appropriate contract. However, the reward system involves the distribution of a large proportion of the organization's resources with the potential for creating a political conflict. Consequently, wide-scale member involvement is needed as much for generating ownership and equity as it is for providing diverse information and expertise to solve the more complex aspects of the problem. As such, a collateral structure should be used to design the reward system, involving perhaps thirty to fifty representatives throughout the operational structure.

Step Two: Reviewing the Types of Reward Systems

In many organizations, I have been surprised to learn that members know very little of the fundamental purposes of re-

ward systems. Therefore, it is important that all members in the
collateral structure review the whole topic of reward systems,
including all alternative possibilities. Members from personnel
or human resources can be asked to share their knowledge of
the topic, or outside experts can be brought in to explain different reward systems in different types of organizations. This
generally raises the members' level of awareness of the great
variety of reward systems that can be established.

Step Three: Forming Groups Around
Alternative Reward Systems

After they have gained a deeper understanding of this
subject, the members divide up into small groups to generate
ideas about different kinds of reward systems. These systems include some of the following distinctions: piece rate versus hourly rate, hourly rate versus salary, individual versus group incentives, individual versus company-wide incentives, profit sharing
versus employee stock ownership, executive bonus versus stock
options, and fixed versus flexible (cafeteria-style) benefits.
When the groups come together, the members pick three to five
of the most varied packages. (It will be recalled that the Hegelian dialectic for complex problems chooses to debate the extreme differences and initially ignores the middle-of-the-road
alternatives.) While the final synthesis will consider combinations and integrations of these varied packages, for now it is the
extremes that will be examined. Specifically, the most diverse
alternative reward packages become the "initial conclusions"
that will be subjected to a probing debate. The thirty to fifty
representatives form three to five conclusion groups (C-groups).

Step Four: Performing Assumptional Analysis

This step follows the previously outlined methods of assumptional analysis first covered in Chapter Five. Briefly, each
C-group meets in a separate room. First, all the relevant internal
and external stakeholders are listed—for example, prospective
employees, competitors, unions, and government agencies that

affect personnel practices. Then, the members in each C-group construct all the assumptions for each stakeholder that would have to be true in order to argue most strongly for their reward system. Finally, each C-group plots its assumptions onto the assumption matrix, taking special note of the assumptions that are placed in the critical region. Any assumption in this region is most important to the group's conclusion *and* there is considerable uncertainty regarding the truth of the assumption.

The several C-groups meet in the community room to share their assumption matrices. Once it begins, the debate is a study in contradictory yet plausible assumptions about human nature and performance and about how to tie the two together. Each debate becomes a clinical experience as individuals reveal their deepest beliefs about why people work. Some individuals are astounded at the assumptions that other groups make to support their reward systems. For example, a group that supports a cafeteria-style benefits plan has to assume that people will make responsible choices about health care benefits and will not take all their compensation in the form of cash. Another group, arguing for a fixed compensation package, has to assume that all individuals have the same needs and cannot make these choices for their own good.

When the debates are concluded, a number of unresolved issues still remain. These issues represent the core arguments that continue to divide the C-groups. These issues may pertain to different assumptions concerning human nature as well as to other aspects of a reward system. Some fundamental questions to be resolved might include:

1. At what level (division, department, group, or individual) can performance be measured objectively?
2. What constitutes objective measurement?
3. What subjective measures will be acceptable?
4. Will corporate headquarters allow reward systems that are different from the standard mold?
5. What will be the consequences of decentralizing the design and administration of reward systems for each division in the organization?

6. Will the reward system serve to attract or scare away new members?
7. Will the organization correct any inequities that exist before information on pay and performance is made public?
8. Do managers have the skills necessary to conduct effective performance reviews?
9. Will the members be rewarded for continuing with the change program and making it successful?
10. Will the members be rewarded for their contributions in both the collateral and the operational structures?

The resolution of these important issues can be explored now that they have been surfaced. Thus, information can be collected to help move any assumptions toward the certainty region of the matrix. This will enable the designing of the new reward system to proceed with much more conviction. For example, in the case of item (4), representatives from corporate headquarters can be asked to comment on this issue and to establish a policy if one does not now exist.

The next step is forming several synthesis groups (S-groups) from representatives of each of the C-groups. The function of the S-groups is to resolve these different issues, develop a synthesized assumption matrix, and then derive the "final" conclusion from this matrix. This final conclusion represents the best possible reward system that can be designed, one that is most consistent with all available knowledge in the manner of the Hegelian dialectic.

This participative process for designing reward systems reveals some interesting patterns: (1) In most cases, each different business unit derives a unique reward system on the basis of the nature of the work to be done. The importance of this is obvious after the fact but is always ignored by the mandated, standardized reward system of old. (2) A cafeteria-style benefits plan is often an outgrowth of the process. Here, the members learn through their open debates that individual needs for different fringe benefits vary considerably. (3) One of the most creative aspects of any synthesis is the recognition that any valid measure of performance must contain subjective elements. Often, the members have complained about this subjectivity in the past, but now they understand why culture, team efforts, and cooperation cannot be assessed with "hard" measures. (4) Perhaps the most important outcome of the whole process is for all to accept the difficulty of linking pay to performance but to realize that this link must be formed if organizational success is to be achieved.

Step Five: Designing the Detailed Reward System

Once the basic parameters and attributes of the derived reward system have been established, the next step is to formulate the various systems in detail. Representatives from the different collateral groups can meet with members of the personnel department and other experts to compile all the necessary specifics. An important part of this process is to establish the objective measures of performance to be used for each work unit. Also to be considered is how these hard measures can be combined with subjective ratings of the intangible contributions each member makes to his work group and to the whole organization. In deriving both of these performance measures, it always is necessary to include criteria required by federal, state, and local laws.

As a part of the overall reward system, certain guidelines can be suggested concerning how performance reviews—the one-on-one meetings between a manager and each of his subordinates in which performance ratings and rewards are shared—should be conducted. It is also important to consider how the counseling sessions should be conducted so that members can receive useful feedback to improve their performance. During these meetings, each manager and subordinate must agree on the relative priorities of tasks and objectives; as discussed in Chapter Seven, this is the only way that the inefficiencies in performance can be corrected once the structural barriers to success have been removed. These sessions also should consider how skills can be improved so that effort *and* talent are applied in the right direction.

Step Six: Implementing the New Reward System

The detailed reward system should be shared with the rest of the organization. Several open forums should be provided so that all members have an opportunity to hear and discuss all aspects of the proposed reward system. The process by which the system was developed should be shared as well so that all members can understand the assumptions that drive the new system.

During these meetings, issues might be raised that were not recognized in the collateral structure; while the process used was a very comprehensive one, it still was conducted by a small percentage of the whole organization. Besides, it is always possible that, by focusing so extensively on differences, some very simple commonalities were overlooked. This is the time to test out the new reward system, being especially open to—and not defensive about—whatever comments are given. The comments will help fine tune the system and gain a broader base of support and commitment. As a result of all the inputs from the membership, the collateral groups modify the reward system and conduct its implementation.

Step Seven: Evaluating the New Reward System

Does the newly designed and implemented reward system accomplish the three purposes of attracting, retaining, and motivating employees? Various surveys and opinion polls can be used to answer this question. Evaluating more objective measures, such as absenteeism, turnover, and performance changes, might be helpful as well, provided that we keep in mind the dynamic nature of organizations: Besides the reward system, all sorts of other changes are occurring.

Furthermore, it is important to realize that the characteristics of the reward system will need to be altered as the composition of the work force changes. Specifically, as employees get older and as they progress through the stages of life, their need for fringe benefits can vary quite a bit. Health and life insurance policies and pension plans tend to be valued more in later years, whereas individuals who are single or newly married without children prefer most of their total compensation in wages and salaries. The reward system should remain flexible in adjusting to these shifting needs and preferences.

A cafeteria-style package of compensation is becoming more popular as organizations recognize differences in individual needs. An excellent example of designing and implementing a flexible benefits program is shown by the American Can Company (Gibson, Ivancevich, and Donnelly, 1982, pp. 488-489):

American Can Company now has nearly 9,000 employees who design their own personal benefits package. The company provides a core of nonoptional benefits and then employees can select from a group of options on the basis of flexible "credits" that are allocated to each participant in the plan. Employees enrolled in the program are also able to buy additional benefits through payroll deductions.

American Can keeps a close watch on how employees spend their money. Management at first feared that they would find employees making foolish choices. However, the profile of how benefits are selected is really fairly predictable. Young single employees take more time off. So do married women, who usually want the same number of vacation days as their husbands. Those with young families tend to choose more medical and life insurance coverage. Older employees are more concerned with savings, first for their children's education and later, as their children leave home, for their retirement.

Benefit options can be changed once a year. In September, every employee receives a form stating his or her existing program and the credits earned. Employees may then choose to remain with the same options or elect completely different options.

What if the nature of the work changes, which creates new task flow problems across subunit boundaries? It may then become more difficult to measure performance objectively. The reward system should be monitored periodically to make sure that the measures for performance that were first designed are still accurate and valid over time. If not, either new measures should be considered or performance should be assessed for more encompassing work units—such as departments and divisions. Naturally, if restructuring helps reduce the task flows between subunits, then objective measures of performance for smaller, more specialized work units can be developed.

As long as the new reward system requires openness with respect to performance ratings and "who got what," the reward system will be evaluated by everyone. Also, as suggested earlier, this openness motivates managers to make reward decisions that they can justify and defend. Only with secrecy and poorly designed reward systems do imaginations run wild and are managers free to use whatever criteria they please in rewarding or not rewarding the members.

Performance Reviews and Counseling Sessions

Any organization that attempts to tie rewards to performance must have some means of letting members know their performance ratings and what rewards they will receive. Only intrinsic rewards are experienced without any formal mechanism or procedure. Furthermore, since a performance review involves a face-to-face meeting between the manager and each of his subordinates, sometimes these meetings are used simultaneously as counseling sessions. The manager suggests which behaviors and attitudes need improvement. Plans to monitor the learning process may be considered as well.

I have found it important to distinguish the evaluative component (during which performance ratings, salary information, and promotion decisions are communicated) from the learning component (when feedback is given on how the person might improve his performance). While these two components most often are discussed together in the same annual meeting, they really need to be handled in separate meetings and to be separated in time as well. It seems that being reviewed for one's performance raises questions and anxieties about one's self-worth in general, especially since our society labels people according to the work they do.

Performance appraisal systems are often used to accomplish two conflicting objectives: determining the rewards an individual will receive and providing counseling and feedback for purposes of improvement and development. These goals call for different discussion emphases and can have different effects on the employee. When the performance evaluation is used in determining the rewards an individual will receive, employees have a reason for defending their performance and presenting themselves in the best possible light. Under such circumstances, they are likely to give invalid data about themselves in order to look good. As such, the performance appraisal serves neither purpose well [Allenbaugh, 1983, pp. 22-23].

In order for individuals to learn and to improve their performance, they have to be receptive to hearing what might be ineffective about their behavior or attitudes. Thus, to be helpful for learning and improving, feedback should be (1) asked for, (2) specific, (3) descriptive, (4) sincere, and (5) balanced. If the individual who will be getting the feedback initiates the request, he is more likely to be in a state of readiness than if the superior decides when it is time to be "helpful." Feedback that focuses on very specific behaviors in a descriptive way tells the recipient exactly what is causing the problem without adding any evaluative overtones of goodness or badness about the individual in general. If the person providing the feedback is sincere, then worrying about the possible threat of ulterior motives will not distract the recipient from hearing the message. If the individual is told about those behaviors that should be encouraged as well as those that should be discouraged, the discussion will not become one-sided and, hence, the recipient will not become defensive.

At ROLM Corporation, a computer manufacturer based in Santa Clara, California, providing effective feedback is referred to as *leveling*. Stagnaro (1982, pp. 16, 17) summarizes the approach, which clearly recognizes the sensitive nature of a person's ego:

Leveling is honesty with employees about their performance, function, goals, good points and bad, where they are going, what they can expect, and what they should do to improve their capabilities. It means making sure employees are in tune with their abilities, strengths, and weaknesses. It means giving employees support, improving their performance . . .

Leveling is speaking the truth. But the truth must be made palatable. It must be leavened, flavored, made acceptable to the person. Truth in leveling is important, but it cannot be presented in such a manner as to destroy a person's ego and feelings. The broadside approach is not effective. The person takes umbrage, rightfully, and in all probability doesn't hear the real meaning of the message. The manager closes the communications channel, which is exactly the opposite of what leveling seeks to achieve.

In contrast, information that conveys the results of a performance appraisal is typically (1) not asked for, (2) general, (3) evaluative, (4) impersonal, and (5) one-sided. In this case, the individual's performance is reviewed when the organization or his boss decides that it is time for such an assessment, usually once a year. The appraisal is very general, focusing on a summary score rather than providing any detailed information on how the score was derived. The appraisal also is evaluative, since the information is added to the employee's file and used to determine salary increases, bonuses, job assignments, and promotions. These decisions *should* be based on a valid appraisal of each member's performance. However, since an appraisal comes from the organization through the role of a superior, it tends to be more impersonal than sincere and, therefore, it does not foster learning. Also, since information for evaluative purposes tends to focus on negatives, as in "management by exception," subordinates often feel that their performance is never quite good enough.

As a result, feedback for learning should not be given or discussed during the performance review. Under these circumstances, the individual is likely to respond defensively—to protect his ego. Defensiveness is revealed in denying the results of the appraisal, blaming other individuals or circumstances for what happened, or even blaming the manager for not providing more direction and resources. While any of these excuses might be valid, such defensiveness does not allow one to calmly assess one's own behavior or other factors in the situation. Examination of the various causes of the performance results should take place during the counseling sessions.

By cycling between periodic performance reviews and frequent counseling sessions, managers can provide each subordinate with the best setting first to find out the assessment and then to learn how to improve. The process of scheduling and conducting these two different meetings takes place in four steps: (1) establishing expectations for evaluation and learning, (2) scheduling performance reviews, (3) scheduling counseling sessions, and (4) cycling between evaluation and learning. While these steps may vary depending on the particular reward system that was designed by the membership, they do cover the essential issues.

Step One: Establishing Expectations for
Evaluation and Learning

When reward systems are designed in a thorough manner with wide representation in a collateral structure, the performance review and counseling sessions generally are conducted separately. Each subunit manager meets with his immediate work group to discuss how the two types of meetings can be designed to best meet the needs of the organization and its members. It is desirable to establish in advance just what will be expected in both meetings so that everyone will know how to prepare for them. As mentioned earlier, the performance review, and to a lesser extent the counseling session, arouse some anxiety and defensiveness. These feelings and reactions can be alleviated by having an open discussion. When the culture, management skills, and team-building tracks have had their full impact, sharing expectations and developing agreements occur quite naturally. However, I cannot overemphasize the importance of having discussions about evaluation rather than keeping these feelings buried, which tends to make the anxiety much worse.

The particular expectations and agreements established could be as follows:

1. The manager will meet with each member on a monthly basis to review objectives, tasks, and problems.
2. Each member will provide a self-assessment of his work before any formal review takes place.
3. Each member can arrange a counseling session with his boss whenever he needs more input.
4. If the manager feels that a subordinate needs help, the manager should suggest that they sit down and discuss "how things are going," but it is up to the member to decide when this meeting should take place.
5. Any member, upon request, can see the information that is entered into his file.
6. Any member can request an appeals process, without any negative consequences, if he disagrees with the results of his performance review.

Perhaps the most important agreement to establish is how initial understandings can be adjusted as the situation changes. In a holographic world, new events necessitate that jobs and objectives be changed. It would be unfair to hold a member accountable for an objective that becomes outdated or irrelevant. Instead, a procedure should be in place that allows for flexibility—not as an excuse for failing to attain a realistic objective but as an acknowledgement of dynamic complexity. An adaptive management-by-objectives philosophy is the key.

Step Two: Scheduling Performance Reviews

The timing of the performance review depends on the particular cycle of work in each subunit. While it often is convenient for an organization to establish the tradition of having only one review at the same time each year, this may not be desirable if divisions, departments, and work groups have different types of jobs with different completion cycles. Essentially, there is no magic to the once-a-year review, even though this seems to be the most popular choice. In a dynamic and changing work setting, it might be useful to review performance more frequently. If several performance cycles take place within one year, holding only annual reviews means that opportunities are missed to adjust performance from one cycle to the next. However, holding reviews too frequently will hamper the learning process by allowing evaluative information to overwhelm the feedback that is best for improving performance.

Some guidelines can be offered for the length of time that should be allowed between performance reviews. In general, the higher one's position in the organizational hierarchy, the more time is needed between performance reviews; the lower one's position, the less time is needed, all else being equal. Specifically, top managers need more time to alter the performance of the whole organization than supervisors at the shop level need to make short-term changes in work group performance. Interestingly, if top managers were given a very short time frame, such as six months or a year, this might encourage short-term results; strategic changes, restructuring, investment plans, and R&D studies probably would be sacrificed in order to maximize annual profitability. If the period between performance reviews for top managers were longer, such as three to five years, they would then have the time to optimize long-term performance.

Nurtured by stockholders and security analysts, the emphasis on short-term performance at the expense of long-run results and productivity has become endemic to American business culture. The horizons of the average American manager seem to be several years nearer than the horizons of most of his or her counterparts in other countries. While managers in other countries, particularly in countries with whom we compete for markets, have been seeking to optimize productivity and competitiveness over the long-run, American managers have been increasingly preoccupied with immediate results [Shetty, 1982, p. 39].

Step Three: Scheduling Counseling Sessions

The manager and the members of each subunit usually agree to frequent one-on-one meetings to review work, clarify expectations, provide suggestions for improvement, and give encouragement. These sessions focus on behaviors, attitudes, cul-

tural norms, and interpersonal obstacles. Often these problems
have been identified during the previous performance review,
and an attempt is made to provide a constant stream of support
and information so that individuals can improve their performance—in terms of both efficiency (the proper allocation of
time on tasks) and effectiveness (completing the tasks correctly).

Allenbaugh (1983, pp. 23, 24) describes the method of
coaching (as a supplement to performance reviews), which is
similar to what I refer to as counseling:

Coaching is defined as an ongoing, face-to-face process
of influencing behavior by which the manager and employee
collaborate to assist in achieving: increased job knowledge; improved skills in carrying out job responsibilities; higher level of
job satisfaction; a stronger, more positive working relationship;
and opportunities for personal and professional growth. . . .

As a collaborative process that emphasizes the employee's
strengths, coaching tends to overcome most of the objections of
the performance appraisal process. Because of ongoing feedback, employees know where they stand with their supervisor
and are generally more receptive to interactions of a develop-
mental nature. Furthermore, as coaching is not necessarily
linked with rewards, employees tend to be more open and honest in self appraisal and managers tend to be more comfortable
in exploring performance factors. . . .

As an ongoing, participative process, coaching assures
that the manager and the employee agree on performance goals,
on how performance is to be measured, and on appraising performance against those goals. Thus, coaching focuses on collaborative measures to attain objectives and results. . . .

Virtually every contact with the employee provides an
opportunity for coaching.

Incidentally, the assumption is often made that if the
counseling sessions are left up to the subordinates, they will not
take place. I have found, however, that when the first step of
this process is carried out as intended (establishing expectations
for these meetings), individuals will schedule counseling sessions. Further, they will be encouraged to do this if the meetings turn out to be helpful in improving their performance and,

consequently, providing them with more pay and other rewards. Certainly, the manager can recommend to a particular member that a counseling session be scheduled, leaving it up to the member to take the next step. However, if the member does not take that step, I would not expect much to develop from a manager-initiated meeting at this time: The employee would be too defensive.

In a case in which one or more members cannot get into the learning mode regardless of the way the whole reward system is designed, another approach can be used. If these individuals have significant behavior and performance problems, the "troublemaker" tact can be considered. As discussed in Chapter Six, the steps for managing troublemakers can be modified so that the manager can initiate a more confronting approach. The purpose is to get any disruptive, self-serving behavior under control. Other members should not be harmed by the troublemakers—by their unwillingness to learn or to work with others. However, by the time this last track is being implemented, the troublemakers not the healthy objectors—should be in check, whether they be high-level managers or shop floor employees.

Step Four: Cycling Between Evaluation and Learning

Switching back and forth between formal evaluation meetings and informal counseling sessions takes some experience. Nevertheless, after a while members can easily distinguish which type of meeting is taking place and which hat the manager is wearing. The importance of having evaluation and learning take place in two separate meetings becomes quite apparent as members come to recognize the different purposes of these two types of encounters.

After several performance cycles have occurred, a pattern evolves for these two types of meetings. The performance meetings take place regularly every quarter, six months, year, or three years, depending on the agreement. The counseling sessions take place much more frequently, between the performance reviews. In some cases, the counseling sessions occur almost every week and at least once a month. Even though the counseling sessions are meant to be initiated by the members, a regular pattern develops in most cases. In a sense, the counseling sessions become institutionalized, even though they are intended to be more spontaneous. As long as the emerging pattern does not turn these sessions into a formal performance review, with its corresponding defensiveness, there is nothing wrong with having regularly scheduled sessions in which feedback can be given in a helpful way.

I might mention that this cycle of evaluation and learning is in marked contrast to what usually takes place before the reward system track is implemented. In my experience, most organizations generally offer very little in the way of counseling for members unless some grave problem has developed. Formal performance reviews are held by dictate only and offered as infrequently as possible. In fact, managers often complain that they do not have enough time to conduct more than one annual performance review per subordinate and that they certainly do not have the time to conduct frequent counseling sessions—even one per month. They say that they have other, more important things to do. Who, then, will guide their employees to spend the right time on tasks with the right objectives in mind? Who will help employees learn new skills to improve performance? To assume that individuals "know where they stand" and that they "know what is required to succeed" is to view the world as a simple machine. Alternatively, time spent correcting behavior and expectations now will probably save a lot of disappointment later when miscommunications and misunderstandings take their toll—perhaps when it is too late to save an important project.

Honeywell is working to combine performance appraisal (reviews and counseling) with a performance-based reward system in an integrated manner. Not only does this company seem to recognize the importance of paying for results, but it seems to appreciate why the reward system is needed to sustain all other efforts at organizational change (Kanarick and Dotlich, 1984, pp. 14–19).

At Honeywell, we're utilizing all our human resource subsystems—communications, training, development, selection, compensation, and appraisal—to *sustain* organizational change. These subsystems are the carriers of organizational values—the ways in which people are trained, appraised, and rewarded says everything about a corporation's culture. Hence, it is vital that these activities are integrated and that all of them reinforce the desired change.

We are currently examining our performance appraisal system to ensure that we are measuring—and rewarding—the type of management style we wish to endorse. More specifically, at corporate headquarters we are attempting to introduce a performance appraisal system that evaluates people with respect to the Honeywell Principles. In short, we think a company should put its money where its mouth is.

For one of its divisions, Honeywell has utilized an extensive collateral structure to design a profit-sharing, performance-based reward system, but only *after* sufficient progress had been made with the earlier tracks.

The pilot gainsharing program being conducted in our Seattle-based Marine Systems Operations seems to be a logical extension of our participative culture. If people are participating in goal setting and productivity initiatives, it seems reasonable that they should participate in the financial benefits that result. That is what gainsharing is all about.

Gainsharing is not just an incentive program, it is an outgrowth of our way of working. About 50 employees were involved in designing the system, with corporate and outside compensation consultants available to them. Thus, the gainsharing program was not only designed for but by employees. This is another example of our intention of providing employees with the means to motivate themselves, rather than top management pushing down a program to motivate them [Boyle, 1983, pp. 23-24].

Return to the SFD Story

Since the change program with SFD was put on hold just before the reward system track was to begin, I cannot report on the unique way this track was designed and implemented. However, I can suggest what might have been done and what is still left to do. This plan, of course, will be modified during the actual design of the reward system, especially when the new owner comes on the scene.

It will be recalled that significant problems with the current reward system had been reported. The diagnostic interviews had revealed the following perceptions: For some groups, there was no merit system, and thus rewards were not tied to performance; rewards were based on being liked and being in the right clique. Performance appraisal was seen as personal appraisal. Regardless of how hard or how well one worked, there were few rewards to go around. Suggestions were not rewarded; rather, it was best to keep new ideas to oneself. Counseling sessions were almost nonexistent, especially since the trust between members and their managers had eroded. In addition, many felt that it was questionable whether the current reward system mandated by corporate Westinghouse could be modified to suit the unique needs and circumstances of the division.

In developing their strategic survival plan, SFD managers became well acquainted with problem management, assumptional analysis, and collateral structures. Thus, it would be natural for SFD members to tackle the reward system problem with this same kind of approach. In this case, however, a much broader base of membership for the collateral design would be needed. Not only would a greater variety of members from all levels in the hierarchy be included, but experts from outside and inside SFD would be needed to review both the policies at the new corporate headquarters and reward systems in general.

A special problem arises whenever a new reward system is designed where one already exists. The new owner, in this case, may have his own corporate-wide system, which each division is expected to use. The first task, then, is to learn what the established reward system entails. A second task is to learn how much freedom a particular division has in adjusting the mandated reward system to its own needs and preferences. A third task is to see if any constraints can be removed if the formal reward system does not allow much leeway for modification. I always emphasize to the members that just because a policy exists does not mean that it cannot be questioned and changed. Members should not assume that documents are fixed for all time; often, they seem to be fixed only because they have not been tested.

The selected members in the collateral design will go through all the steps for designing a performance-based reward system, given the freedom they have or the freedom they take from corporate headquarters. After the reward system has been reviewed by all members and modified accordingly, it will be up to each work unit to design and conduct performance reviews and counseling sessions, following whatever guidelines were agreed upon by the whole membership.

Conclusion

When the entire reward system track is operational, members receive extrinsic rewards for performing well in their new organization in a new way according to a new culture. Coupled with the intrinsic rewards they experience automatically since the earlier tracks have been implemented, a salient reward package is available to everyone. If the organization has made use of all available expertise and information in each track, at this point it will be managing its most important problems to the best of its ability: All the controllable variables are being managed as well as possible, and all the uncontrollable variables are being monitored as much as possible.

Now the organization can solve complex problems whether they be technical and business related or human and organization related. Continuing cycles of planned change can be conducted on any of the five tracks as new problems unfold. This is what managing dynamic complexity is all about.

CHAPTER NINE

Commitment
to Organizational
Success

Top managers are the villains who get blamed for
steering organizations into crises, and they are the heroes
who get the credit for rescuing organizations from crises.
Such blaming and crediting are partly ritualistic, but also
partly earned. Top managers do in fact guide organizations
into crises and intensify crises; they also halt crises by dis-
closing opportunities, arousing courage, and stirring up
enthusiasm.

The top managers who instigate dramatic turn-
arounds deserve admiration, for they have accomplished
very difficult tasks of emotional and conceptual leadership. Even greater heroes, however, are the top managers
who keep their organizations from blundering into trouble
in the first place.
—Nystrom and Starbuck, 1984, pp. 64-65

The five tracks provide the theory and practice necessary to revitalize our organizations. Now top managers must do the rest:
commit the time, energy, and resources to identify all the barriers to success and transform them into channels for success.

Will top managers take the responsibility for change? Will top managers commit beyond the quick fix?

Commitment to act—to put oneself on the line, to risk failure and humiliation—is a very difficult proposition. Most individuals are uncomfortable with the idea of fully committing to anything, whether it be another person, an idea, or an integrated solution to a complex problem. Moreover, choosing to commit is not just an individual matter. Cultural forces affect an individual's willingness to act, especially since objective reality is shaped by a group's social reality. Furthermore, everyone makes implicit assumptions about what—and how—things can be changed in their organization. These assumptions can be grossly inaccurate if they were formed in a pre-holographic time and before integrated methods for planned change were even available. One is not likely to commit to an action that is assumed to be futile. Thus, in order to understand the dynamics of commitment, we must again rely on the holographic diamond. If we can peel away some of the cultural, assumptional, and especially the intrapsychic barriers to change, perhaps we can challenge chief executive officers to take the chance for long-term success.

The realization of the American dream rests on the promise of commitment. If top managers do not act on this promise, the five tracks and all other efforts at providing integrated programs will be wasted. Chief executives will continue to search for the Holy Grail, whether it be a magical machine to solve their business problems or a quick fix for their organizational problems. Continuing with such misplaced efforts eventually will decrease our productivity as a nation, threaten our standard of living and political freedom, and erode our position of world leadership. The alternative is to address explicitly the fundamental problem facing our society today: failure to place long-term, total commitment behind an integrated program of planned change.

This chapter shows how CEOs can commit the time, energy, and resources to doing what needs to be done. First, I will examine the roots of individual responsibility to see why most people are afraid to commit to any action that could hurt others. Second, I will consider the ideal composition and purpose of the CEO's inner circle—a small group of leaders and friends who can supply multiple perspectives to address complex problems and, in addition, provide the emotional support to overcome the fear of sole responsibility. The inner circle enables the CEO to commit to action in a holographic world. Third, I will emphasize how responsible action must be directed toward the right solution—integrated programs of planned change, not more quick fixes.

Taking Responsibility for Actions and Outcomes

It is important to realize that all persons have neurotic tendencies to some degree. Only when we make the naive assumption that people are entirely rational and objective do we continue to be startled by irrational and confusing behavior. Why do top managers sit on their thrones while their organizations become increasingly out of touch with today's world? Why do top managers resist change and work so hard at convincing themselves that what worked in the past will also work in the future? It is time to accept the neurotic tendencies in all of us in the human psyche—if we wish to learn how to mobilize commitment to organizational success.

We all have certain mildly dysfunctional neurotic traits. These might involve shyness, depression, irrational fears, suspicion, and so on. Everyone shows some of these characteristics sometimes. Indeed, "normality" entails many quite different neurotic traits. But occasionally people will exhibit a good number of characteristics that all appear to manifest a common neurotic style. They display these characteristics very frequently, so that their behavior becomes quite rigid and inappropriate. These individuals usually do not appear to be sick, they do not exhibit bizarre behavior, and they do not have to be treated by a psychiatrist in order to function well in day-to-day life. *But their inflexible behavior does limit their effectiveness as top managers.* It consistently distorts their perceptions of people and events and strongly influences their goals, their modes of decision making, and even their preferred social setting [Kets de Vries and Miller, 1984, p. 19]. [Emphasis added.]

Perhaps one of an individual's greatest fears is that he will be held responsible for some outcome, particularly an outcome that can hurt other people. This fear seems to derive from the egocentricity of children: At an early age, children believe that they are the center of the universe, that all life revolves around them, and that if something goes wrong it is their fault. Even events and outcomes beyond their control are seen as stemming from their innocent actions or their idle thoughts. Children feel that they are responsible for everything.

As a child develops into an adult, he learns to distinguish cause from effect and to separate what he did (and consequently is responsible for) from what was done by others, caused by nature, or induced by other forces. Through common experience and formal training, the adult learns physics, geometry, biology, chemistry, and psychology—the cause-and-effect sciences that explain everyday experiences. What we cannot explain we assign to superstition, chance, and religion.

Most people, however, do not make the full transition from egocentric child who believes in magic to renaissance adult who knows all science. Instead, most people worry about the consequences of doing something wrong, unintentionally causing harm to other people, or being punished for having caused an undesirable outcome. Some people are so afraid of being held responsible that they do not act. Other people are willing to act as long as they can blame someone else for the results. Naturally, if the results are positive, many people would enjoy taking the credit. The paralyzing fear, however, is that they will be held accountable for something negative. This fear can be so strong that some people do not risk reaching for the positives because someday they might have to accept the blame for the negatives. Consequently, people often remove themselves from outcome-producing situations in order to take the burden of being responsible off their shoulders.

Individuals appreciate being part of a group because this diffuses their responsibility for action. Each member can blame the others for what happened rather than having to take the blame himself. Some of the horrible crimes that have been committed by large crowds, such as mass lynchings and gang rapes, stem from the almost complete diffusion of responsibility among a loose collection of individuals. As the size of the group increases, everyone's accountability becomes a smaller portion of the whole. If thousands of individuals are involved, each individual's equal share of responsibility is only one thousandth of the total.

Accepting responsibility for one's behavior is at the root of most definitions of mental health, not just adulthood. Various coping styles for dealing with life are termed *neurotic* if they allow individuals to avoid responsibility in one way or another, thereby preventing functional, adaptive behavior from occurring. For the present, one such coping style is especially relevant to corporate life: obsessive-compulsive neurosis.

We define obsessive-compulsive neurosis as a faulty practice in living and value system evolved over a lifetime in which the individual abdicates a responsible role to others, yet chooses to be a power of influence and control over them by manufacturing character traits that are devised to perpetuate the conception that the obsessional is the perfect, uniquely ideal, noble person who is above question. The entire process is fraught with conflict since the individual attempts to maintain the image of competence, respectability, and admiration, the responsibility for which he is not willing completely to assume. . . . Therefore, the obsessive-compulsive could be viewed as an individual who "fears" a loss of control—not because he cannot stand disorder per se, but rather because he is most anxious to avoid a situation where he may be responsible to or answerable to a person, situation, or force outside himself [Gelfman, 1970, pp. 37, 39].

One of the classic ways for an obsessive-compulsive to avoid responsibility is to be a "perfectionist." Such an individual is always striving for perfection as a way to control his surroundings. If only everything could be perfect, then everything would be in its proper place: orderly, predictable, and exact. However, the goal of perfection is deceitful. Perfection is impossible to obtain. The following insights are derived from clinical analyses of patients who have deeply succumbed to the perfectionistic syndrome.

Those who must live with him are forced to deal with his deceitfulness and inauthenticity, which may make their lives difficult and at times unbearable. The patient seems to live in this manner because as long as he can strive for that which is impossible, he does not have to attain, nor can he be expected to attain, that which is possible. Such a position, of course, is the epitome of irresponsibility, although it is not usually seen as such by the outside world or by the patient himself. In this sense, much of the obsessive's perfectionism becomes a charade. . . .

He strives for "perfectionism" to attain his goal of admiration and worship, not for the normal satisfaction of accomplishment. Many times, in fact, he does succeed in reaching a state of extreme competence in this manner, but may never be satisfied because the admiration and worship which he feels are his due are never completely forthcoming. For that reason, he sets on a compulsive course of further accomplishment. The patient may actually wish to get out of this "rat race," sit on his throne of self-importance, and rest on his laurels. That is his fantasied objective. In this position, through the waving of his magic wand, he would be in absolute control and answerable to no one [Gelfman, 1970, pp. 42, 43-44].

We can see the impact of these psychic tendencies on the functioning of our organizations. This portrait of the obsessive-compulsive neurotic fits many successful executives. Getting to the top clearly requires extreme dedication, persistence, attention to detail, and precision—the classic traits of the obsessive-compulsive. Even if various top managers did take on risky missions on their way up the hierarchy, they generally had many peers around them to diffuse responsibility. When one gets to the top, however, it becomes more difficult to distribute responsibility onto others as a way of moving forward. Instead, as Harry Truman once said regarding responsibility in the Oval Office: "The buck stops here!" So also stops orderliness and tight control on all that transpires. Can today's CEOs sit on their organizational thrones in total control of dynamic complexity, external stakeholders, and human nature?

It is worthwhile to examine the fit between the obsessive-compulsive's approach to life and the image of the world as a simple machine. In essence, if the organization and the world conformed to the properties of the simple machine, then perfection would be possible. This is why the obsessive-compulsive is resistant to seeing the world as an open system. The latter view makes perfection a less attainable goal. Worse yet, to see the world as a complex hologram is to expose the perfectionist charade of the obsessive-compulsive once and for all. Trying to create perfect and detailed order in a world that is constantly changing, both above and below the surface of experience, is not just impossible—it is ludicrous.

Many of today's CEOs rose to the top in yesterday's world; thus, the obsessive-compulsive traits that made them so successful are precisely what prevents them from assuming full responsibility in today's world. Not only are these executives uncomfortable with responsibility when there are fewer persons to blame for failure, but the nature of the world requires executives to be comfortable with imperfection, disorder, uncertainty, and complexity. How are executives likely to deal with the anxiety that now confronts them? They will demand guarantees before they take even one step forward into the uncharted world of dynamic complexity. They will insist on quick-fix solutions to today's complex problems. Anything that smacks of uncertainty, such as an integrated program for organizational change, is not likely to be accepted. Instead, the CEO will continue to do what made him successful before, even when a completely different approach to organizational success is needed.

Kets de Vries and Miller (1984, pp. 28-29) provide a rich description of the obsessive-compulsive organization as nurtured, if not created, by the psychic tendencies of obsessive-compulsive executives.

The compulsive firm is wed to ritual. Every last detail of operation is planned out in advance and carried on in a routinized and preprogrammed fashion. Thoroughness, completeness, and conformity to standard and established procedures are emphasized. These are central tendencies manifested by the organization structure, decision-making processes, and strategies of the compulsive firms. . . . There is an emphasis on formal controls and information systems to ensure that the organizational machine is operating properly.

The organization is exceedingly hierarchical. Much status

is accorded individuals simply because of their position. This may be because the leader personally has many compulsive characteristics, generally manifested by a strong concern with control. The compulsive person is always worried about the next move and how he is going to make it. . . . Consequently, compulsive executives try to reduce uncertainty at all costs and to attain a clearly specified objective in a determined manner. Surprises must be avoided.

Kets de Vries and Miller (1984, pp. 34, 35, 36) also show how a related syndrome—depressive neurosis—underlies some of the passivity and inactivity observed in many troubled firms, much like the avoidance of responsibility:

Inactivity, lack of confidence, extreme conservatism, and a bureaucratically motivated insularity characterize the depressive organization. . . . Most depressive firms are found in stable environments—the only setting in which they can survive for any length of time. . . . The organization operates like a machine; its gears and energy are formal procedures, routines, and prescribed methods. In fact, the depressive organization shows great similarities to the Weberian bureaucracy. . . .
The firm is not guided by any real leader and does not show evidence of making major decisions. Control and coordination are really exercised by formalized programs and policies rather than by managerial initiatives. Suggestions for change are resisted; inhibition of action seems to prevail. It is almost as if the top executive group shared a feeling of impotence and incapacity. It is thought that there is no way to change the course of·events in the organization. Managers just do not feel they have what it takes to revitalize their firm.

Sharing Responsibility with the Inner Circle

Since CEOs, like everyone else, have neurotic tendencies that limit their inclination to be proactive in a holographic world, we must find a way to encourage them to act despite these intrapsychic barriers. It appears that a support group is absolutely essential to convince the individual's psyche that he can take action under such difficult circumstances—that it is all right for him to risk billions of dollars and the welfare of thousands of people. Consider Roush's (1983, p. 55) description of the support group—the inner circle—to help top managers wade through difficult problems and, of course, decide whether or not to commit to new directions and approaches:

> Every organization has a top management group which is considered to be the "inner circle" of leadership in the organization. In reality, there usually are two inner circles in any organization: the circle comprising those who *think* they are and who are even perceived by others to be in the inner circle, and those who *really* are members of the inner circle. The latter refers to those officers whom the chief executive officer thinks of as his or her primary advisors, helpers, and confidants. These two circles are often different.
>
> Being in the real inner circle in an organization has its privileges and its responsibilities. The privileges usually include high pay, greater status, and the intangible benefit of being in the know. Of the responsibilities, one of the most important is loyalty.

The inner circle serves two fundamental purposes. The first is to provide diversity of information and expertise to help manage dynamic complexity. The second is to provide emotional support for taking responsibility for action under conditions of extreme uncertainty, imperfection, and complexity.

The worst case is for the CEO to have an inner circle with a very narrow range of expertise and information. Most often, in fact, I find that the inner circle is purposely composed of top managers who see the world just as the CEO sees it. Not surprisingly, this group comes to easy agreement on any decision or action. If the CEO spends most of his time with his similarly minded colleagues instead of interacting with many others in the organization, he will be shielded from what goes on outside this boundary of misrepresentation. In addition, if the CEO views loyalty as blind acceptance of his ideas, the inner circle will provide strong support for solving the wrong problem in the wrong way. This situation illustrates *dysfunctional loyalty.*

The best case is for the CEO to have an inner circle with a diverse mix of talent and information so that any complex problem will be seen from multiple, conflicting perspectives— applying the Hegelian dialectic. At the same time, it is most use-

ful for the CEO to interact frequently with those outside the
inner circle and to do so with an open mind. In this way, the
CEO is always informed of new problems *and* new perspectives.
However, once any decision or plan for action is derived, the
inner circle should provide a strong base of emotional support
for the CEO, despite the risks and imperfections of the situation. This illustrates *adaptive loyalty*.

Vancil and Green (1984, p. 73) offer a comparative
analysis of IBM's corporate management committee and GE's
corporate policy board regarding the role each plays in supporting its CEO. They summarize their findings as follows:

The primary objective of top management committees is
that they are flexible, personal tools for enhancing leadership
effectiveness. . . .
The benefits of such committees clearly outweigh their
costs or they would not be so pervasive. Critics sometimes claim
that committees are an inefficient use of executive time and a
device for diffusing or ducking responsibility for tough decisions. Our conclusions argue just the reverse. These committees,
fostering shared objectives and the commitment to achieve
them, are the glue that helps to hold a corporation together.

How do groups insulate their CEOs from the potential
guilt and agony of making a wrong decision and inflicting
"pain" on so many individuals? The power of the group is partially derived from its ability to distort the reality of any situation—to create a social reality in place of an objective reality.
As discussed during the culture track, groups can convince individuals to misperceive all sorts of objective phenomena in exchange for group membership. Thus, if the inner circle says that
the decision is absolutely right, the CEO is able to move forward believing that the positive outcomes of the decision are
more certain than they really are. The purpose is not to deceive
anyone, per se, but to provide a strong psychic foundation to
share responsibility so that action will be taken. So long as multiple perspectives and open debates are first used to derive a
high-quality decision, the inner circle should continue to define
social reality to support the whole implementation process. In
the case of efforts to revitalize the organization, such certainty

of view and intensity of commitment are essential to move forward in a holographic world. Only in the world as a simple machine can one believe that such emotional support is irrelevant while the cost/benefit methods of economics and finance are all that count.

To get commitment and support for a course of action may require that it appear essential—not as one of a number of possibilities. By the time a decision is announced, it may need to be presented as the *only* choice, even if there are many people aware of how much debate went into it or how many other options looked just as good. The announcers—the champions of the idea—have to look unwaveringly convinced of the rightness of their choice to get other people to accept the change. Unambivalent and unequivocal communication—once a variety of alternatives have been explored—provides security [Kanter, 1983, p. 20].

Mobilizing commitment by sharing responsibility, while counter to the old American notion of the "rugged individualist," is necessary for today's interconnected world. Yankelovich (1981, pp. 250, 261, 262) powerfully describes the much-needed shift to a broader base of social and organizational commitment. It is on these foundations of collective commitment that the healing of America surely rests:

There are scraps and shreds of evidence that American culture is now evolving toward a new *ethic of commitment*. The word "commitment" shifts the axis away from the self (either self-denial or self-fulfillment) toward connectedness with the world. The commitment may be to people, institutions, objects, beliefs, ideas, places, nature, projects, experiences, adventures, and callings. . . .
A replacement strategy will be based on these premises: that genuine self-fulfillment requires commitments that endure over long periods of time, and that the expressive and sacred domains can be attained only through a web of shared meanings that transcend the self conceived as an isolated physical object. . . . At least until the end of the 1980s we should expect intense social conflict, economic stress, and confusion in signals as we confront the damage done by our neglect of fundamental values in the transition to a new American outlook on life.
We have to face the rot in our institutions and infrastruc-

ture—the inability of our schools to teach; slovenliness in standards of efficiency and precision; the decay of our railroads, bridges, harbors, and roads; the aging of our industrial plants; the litigiousness of an over-lawyered society; the decline of our political parties; the bland arrogance of the news media; the living-in-the-past of our labor unions; the irrelevance of our colleges; the short-term myopia of our industrial leaders; and the seeming inability of government to do anything efficiently and well. *These and other symptoms of a troubled society nag at us like a neurotic boss who is aware of his own power and prerogatives but has forgotten how to do his job.* [Emphasis added.]

Beyond the Quick Fix

All members in every organization have heard the message: The world is characterized by dynamic complexity. Toffler's (1970) *Future Shock* has been with us for more than a decade. Why do organizations still act as if the world is a simple machine? Why do managers speak of complexity yet act out of simplicity? What does it take to finally come to grips with a holographic world?

Recently I described the three world views of a simple machine, open system, and complex hologram to a diverse group of forty middle and top managers representing some of the largest industrial corporations in the world. I asked them to sort their organizations into the three categories according to which metaphor best illustrates how their organizations are designed and managed. More than 75 percent of this group indicated that their companies are being run as a simple machine! Then, I asked them to develop a comprehensive list of all their major organizational problems. Next, I asked them to sort these problems into the same three categories: simple machine, open system, and complex hologram. After an extended discussion, not one individual could think of one major problem that fit the category of simple machine! All problems were sorted into the complex hologram. This diverse group of managers came to the conclusion that most of their organizations are designed and managed for simple problems while none of the problems they actually face are of this variety. No wonder problems do not get resolved. The American system is designed for yesterday.

When managers are asked what can be done to transform

their organizations from simple machines to complex holograms, they are perplexed. Some assume that it cannot be done. Others are still waiting for the right quick fix to come along. Most are not aware of any alternatives to the quick fix. Nobody even knows what to call "it" other than a *non*quick fix. Certainly, one important step in the right direction is to question the long-held assumptions about planned change: Can our organizations be revitalized? Are methods now available that can tackle such a complex arrangement of strategy, structure, rewards, culture, assumptions, psyches, and skills? This book answers "yes"—if managers will *unlearn* their old ways and be willing to adopt a new way of managing the holographic world around them.

One of the reasons CEOs are willing to spend so much time and money on one quick fix after another is that they know in their hearts that the quick fix will not change much of anything. The quick fix is the best way to avoid responsibility: It diverts the organization's energy while absolutely maintaining the status quo. Although no one will benefit from the quick fix, the important thing is that no one will get hurt either! The quick fix is relatively safe—and therefore perfect—from the point of view of any obsessive-compulsive executive.

The time has come to fight against the lure of the next quick fix. We must make sure that we do not fall prey to its trap—one more time. The danger of the quick fix is slowly being recognized, but the necessary defenses to ward off the temptation are not yet firmly ingrained in the ways CEOs think and CEOs act. For example, a very popular quick fix today is "quality circles"—the new promise of greater productivity and worker satisfaction. In the past few years, many companies in the United States have taken the plunge and learned the hard way that quality circles are not enough to manage "the problem"— the whole web of holographic forces that envelops today's organizations.

In a recent *Fortune* article, "The Trouble with Managing Japanese-Style," Main (1984, pp. 50, 56) underscores the difficulty of implementing change in a machine-like manner. While gains can be realized if the method is applied continually and if supporting adjustments are made in other aspects of the organization, it is not the simple remedy that was promised:

Many American companies are discovering that, unlike a new piece of machinery, quality circles cannot simply be acquired, installed, and left to run on their own. This lesson was brought home repeatedly to managers and workers at General Motors' Chevrolet plant in Adrian, Michigan, southwest of Detroit, where they're now trying to make quality circles work for the third time. . . . It's just a lot harder than many fix-it-quick, fix-it-once Americans thought it would be.

Hinrichs (1983, pp. 40-41) puts the quality circle in its proper place as he convincingly argues for integrated approaches:

Now, American managers in desperation are rediscovering participation. It's ironic, though, that they're going to Japan to do so. And it's also unfortunate that they're putting it into place with an oriental cast rather than ensuring that it fits with American systems. Once again, it's the quick fix, the bandwagon mentality. Predictably, many American quality control circle programs being introduced today with such ballyhoo, will soon quietly fold their tents and steal away.

It seems that American managers still haven't learned that, if they're really serious about changing their organizations and enhancing productivity, they can't be simplistic. They can't willy-nilly grab the latest gimmick, and they must devote some serious thought and effort to sustaining any gains.

What's essential is a systematic assessment of just what is needed (where and what are the problems, what changes are possible, what support systems are required, and so forth). They must look at their total organizational system (management; work and the way it's organized; design of the organization; workers, technology and the potential for investment in new facilities). They will probably have to focus on multiple change efforts rather than counting on the quick fix from something like quality circles. And they'll have to continually monitor and provide tender loving care to nurture any innovations and new systems.

The five tracks to organizational success are at hand. The need for a holographic approach to planned change is clear. It is time to move beyond the quick fix. *Will* CEOs commit their organizations to success?

Bibliography

Allen, R. F. "The Ik in the Office." *Organizational Dynamics,* Winter 1980, pp. 26-41.

Allen, R. F., and Dyer, F. "A Tool for Tapping the Organizational Unconscious." *Personnel Journal,* March 1980, pp. 192-198.

Allen, R. F., and Kraft, C. *The Organizational Unconscious: How to Create the Corporate Culture You Want and Need.* Englewood Cliffs, N.J.: Prentice-Hall, 1982.

Allenbaugh, G. E. "Coaching: A Management Tool for a More Effective Work Performance." *Management Review,* May 1983, pp. 21-26.

Argyris, C. *Intervention Theory and Method: A Behavioral Science View.* Reading, Mass.: Addison-Wesley, 1970.

Asch, S. E. "Opinions and Social Pressure." *Scientific American,* Nov. 1955, pp. 31-34.

Beer, M. *Organization Change and Development.* Santa Monica, Calif.: Goodyear, 1980.

Benét, S. V. *John Brown's Body*. New York: Holt, Rinehart and Winston, 1927.

Bennis, W. G. *Changing Organizations*. New York: McGraw-Hill, 1966.

Bennis, W. G., Benne, K. D., and Chin, R. *The Planning of Change*. (3rd ed.) New York: Holt, Rinehart and Winston, 1976.

Blake, R. R., Mouton, J. S., and Sloma, R. L. "The Union-Management Intergroup Laboratory: Strategy for Resolving Intergroup Conflict." *Journal of Applied Behavioral Science*, 1965, *1* (1), 25-57.

Bolman, L. G., and Deal, T. E. *Modern Approaches to Understanding and Managing Organizations*. San Francisco: Jossey-Bass, 1984.

Bowen, D. D., and Kilmann, R. H. "Developing a Comparative Measure of the Learning Climate in Professional Schools." *Journal of Applied Psychology*, 1975, *60* (1), 71-79.

Boyle, R. J. "Designing the Energetic Organization: How a Honeywell Unit Stimulated Change and Innovation." *Management Review*, Aug. 1983, pp. 20-25.

Bramson, R. M. *Coping with Difficult People*. New York: Ballantine, 1981.

Burck, C. G. "Will Success Spoil General Motors?" *Fortune*, Aug. 22, 1983, pp. 94-104.

Capra, F. "The Turning Point: A New Vision of Reality." *The Futurist*, Dec. 1982, pp. 19-24.

"Changing Phone Habits." *Business Week*, Sept. 5, 1983, pp. 68-76.

Churchman, C. W. *The Design of Inquiring Systems*. New York: Basic Books, 1971.

Colvin, G. "The Astonishing Growth of DEC." *Fortune*, May 3, 1982, pp. 91-96.

"Conversation with Edson W. Spencer and Foster A. Boyle." *Organizational Dynamics*, Spring 1983, pp. 30-45.

"Conversation with Roy L. Ash." *Organizational Dynamics*, Autumn 1979, pp. 48-67.

"Corporate Culture: The Hard-To-Change Values that Spell Success or Failure." *Business Week*, Oct. 27, 1980, pp. 148-160.

"Culture Shock Is Shaking the Bell System." *Business Week,* Sept. 26, 1983, pp. 112-116.

Davis, S. M., and Lawrence, P. R. *Matrix.* Reading, Mass.: Addison-Wesley, 1977.

Day, G. "Gaining Insights Through Strategic Analysis." *The Journal of Business Strategy,* 1983, *4* (1), 51-58.

de Board, R. *The Psychoanalysis of Organizations.* London: Tavistock, 1978.

Deal, T. E., and Kennedy, A. A. *Corporate Cultures: The Rites and Rituals of Corporate Life.* Reading, Mass.: Addison-Wesley, 1982.

Dessler, G. *Personnel Management.* Reston, Va.: Reston Publishing, 1978.

"Detroit's Merry-Go-Round." *Business Week,* Sept. 12, 1983, pp. 72-81.

Diamond, M. A., and Allcorn, S. "Psychological Barriers to Personal Responsibility." *Organizational Dynamics,* Spring 1984, pp. 66-77.

Dollard, J., and Miller, N. E. *Personality and Psychotherapy: An Analysis in Terms of Learning, Thinking, and Culture.* New York: McGraw-Hill, 1950.

Downs, A. *Inside Bureaucracy.* Boston: Little, Brown, 1967.

Dyer, W. G. *Team Building: Issues and Alternatives.* Reading, Mass.: Addison-Wesley, 1977.

"Emerson Electric: High Profits from Low Tech." *Business Week,* April 4, 1983, pp. 58-62.

Emshoff, J. R., Mitroff, I. I., and Kilmann, R. H. "The Role of Idealization in Long Range Planning: An Essay on the Logical and Social-Emotional Aspects of Planning." *Technological Forecasting and Social Change,* 1978, *11* (4), 335-348.

Ewing, D. W. "How to Negotiate with Employee Objectors." *Harvard Business Review,* Jan.-Feb. 1983, pp. 103-110.

Fenichel, O. *The Psychoanalytic Theory of Neurosis.* New York: Norton, 1972.

"Following a Tough Act at Commodore." *Business Week,* Jan. 30, 1984, pp. 29-30.

French, W. L., and Bell, C. H. *Organization Development: Behavioral Science Interventions for Organization Improvement.* Englewood Cliffs, N.J.: Prentice-Hall, 1978.

"The Future Catches Up with a Strategic Planner." *Business Week,* June 27, 1983, p. 62.

Galbraith, J. *Designing Complex Organizations.* Reading, Mass.: Addison-Wesley, 1973.

Gelfman, M. "The Role of Irresponsibility in Obsessive-Compulsive Neurosis." *Contemporary Psychoanalysis,* 1970, 7 (1), 36-47.

Gibson, J. L., Ivancevich, J. M., and Donnelly, J. H., Jr. *Organizations: Behavior, Structure, Processes.* (4th ed.) Dallas: Business Publications, 1982.

Hackman, J. R., and Oldham, G. R. *Work Redesign.* Reading, Mass.: Addison-Wesley, 1980.

Hax, A. C., and Majluf, N. S. "Organization Design: A Case Study on Matching Strategy and Structure." *The Journal of Business Strategy,* 1983, 4 (2), 72-86.

Hayes, R. H., and Abernathy, W. J. "Managing Our Way to Economic Decline." *Harvard Business Review,* July-Aug. 1980, pp. 67-77.

Hector, G. "Atari's New Game Plan." *Fortune,* Aug. 8, 1983, pp. 46-52.

Hinrichs, J. R. "Avoid the 'Quick Fix' Approach to Productivity Problems." *Personnel Administrator,* July 1983, pp. 39-43.

"How One Bell Baby Struggled to Its Feet." *Business Week,* Sept. 26, 1983, pp. 116-118.

Huse, E. F. *Organization Development and Change.* (2nd ed.) St. Paul, Minn.: West, 1980.

Kanarick, A. F., and Dotlich, D. L. "Honeywell's Agenda for Organizational Change." *New Management,* 1984, 2 (1), 14-19.

Kanter, R. M. "Change Masters and the Intricate Architecture of Corporate Culture Change." *Management Review,* Oct. 1983, pp. 18-28.

Kaplan, J. M., and Kaplan, E. E. "Organizational Restructuring: How Managers Can Actively Assist in Shaping a Firm's New Architecture." *Management Review,* Jan. 1984, pp. 15-21.

Katz, D., and Kahn, R. L. *The Social Psychology of Organizations.* New York: Wiley, 1966.

Kets de Vries, M. F. R., and Miller, D. *The Neurotic Organization: Diagnosing and Changing Counterproductive Styles of Management.* San Francisco: Jossey-Bass, 1984.

Kiechel, W., III. "Corporate Strategists." *Fortune,* Dec. 27, 1982, pp. 34-39.

Kilmann, R. H. "The Effect of Interpersonal Values on Laboratory Training: An Empirical Investigation." *Human Relations,* 1974a, *27* (3), 247-265.

Kilmann, R. H. "An Organic-Adaptive Organization: The MAPS Method." *Personnel,* 1974b, *51* (3), 35-47.

Kilmann, R. H. "Participative Management in the College Classroom." *Journal of Applied Psychology,* 1974c, *59* (3), 337-338.

Kilmann, R. H. "Designing and Developing a 'Real' Organization in the Classroom." *Academy of Management Journal,* 1975a, *18* (1), 143-148.

Kilmann, R. H. "A Scaled-Projective Measure of Interpersonal Values." *Journal of Personality Assessment,* 1975b, *39* (1), 34-40.

Kilmann, R. H. *Social Systems Design: Normative Theory and the MAPS Design Technology.* New York: Elsevier North-Holland, 1977.

Kilmann, R. H. "On Integrating Knowledge Utilization with Knowledge Development: The Philosophy Behind the MAPS Design Technology." *Academy of Management Review,* 1979a, *4* (3), 417-426.

Kilmann, R. H. "Problem Management: A Behavioral Science Approach." In G. Zaltman (Ed.), *Management Principles for Nonprofit Agencies and Organizations.* New York: American Management Associations, 1979b.

Kilmann, R. H. "Improving Productivity Through Organization Design: Developing Conceptual and Methodological Linkages." *Proceedings of the Southern Management Association,* Nov. 1980, pp. 123-125.

Kilmann, R. H. "Organization Design for Knowledge Utilization." *Knowledge: Creation, Diffusion, Utilization,* 1981a, *3* (2), 211-231.

Kilmann, R. H. "Toward a Unique/Useful Concept of Values

for Interpersonal Behavior: A Critical Review of the Literature on Value." *Psychological Reports,* 1981b, *48* (3), 939-959.

Kilmann, R. H. "The Use of Problem-Defining Groups for Better OD Diagnosis: Alternatives and Consequences." *Proceedings of the Eastern Academy of Management,* May 1981c, pp. 203-207.

Kilmann, R. H. "Designing Collateral Organizations." *Human Systems Management,* 1982a, *3* (2), 66-76.

Kilmann, R. H. "Getting Control of the Corporate Culture." *Managing,* 1982b, *3,* 11-17.

Kilmann, R. H. "The Costs of Organization Structure: Dispelling the Myths of Independent Divisions and Organization-Wide Decision Making." *Accounting, Organizations, and Society,* 1983a, *8* (4), 341-357.

Kilmann, R. H. "A Dialectical Approach to Formulating and Testing Social Science Theories: Assumptional Analysis." *Human Relations,* 1983b, *36* (1), 1-22.

Kilmann, R. H. "A Typology of Organization Typologies: Toward Parsimony and Integration in the Organizational Sciences." *Human Relations,* 1983c, *36* (6), 523-548.

Kilmann, R. H. "Understanding Matrix Organization: Keeping the Dialectic Alive and Well." In D. D. Warrick (Ed.), *Current Developments in Organization Development.* Glenview, Ill.: Scott, Foresman, 1984.

Kilmann, R. H., Benecki, T. J., and Shkop, Y. M. "Integrating the Benefits of Different Efforts at Management Consulting: The Case of Human Resources, Organization Development, and Organization Design." In G. J. Gore and R. G. Wright (Eds.), *The Academic/Consultant Connection.* Dubuque, Iowa: Kendall/Hunt, 1979.

Kilmann, R. H., and Ghymn, K. "The MAPS Design Technology: Designing Strategic Intelligence Systems for Multinational Corporations." *Columbia Journal of World Business,* 1976, *11* (2), 35-47.

Kilmann, R. H., and Herden, R. P. "Towards a Systemic Methodology for Evaluating the Impact of Interventions on Organizational Effectiveness." *Academy of Management Review,* 1976, *1* (3), 87-98.

Kilmann, R. H., and McKelvey, B. "The MAPS Route to Better Organization Design." *California Management Review,* 1975, *17* (3), 23-31.

Kilmann, R. H., and the MAPS Group. "MAPS as a Design Technology to Effectively Mobilize Resources for Social and Organization Problem Solving." In R. H. Kilmann, L. R. Pondy, and D. P. Slevin (Eds.), *The Management of Organization Design.* Vol. 1: *Strategies and Implementation.* New York: Elsevier North-Holland, 1976.

Kilmann, R. H., and Mitroff, I. I. "Qualitative Versus Quantitative Analysis for Management Science: Different Forms for Different Psychological Types." *Interfaces,* 1976, *6* (2), 17-28.

Kilmann, R. H., and Mitroff, I. I. "Problem Defining and the Consulting/Intervention Process." *California Management Review,* 1979, *21* (3), 26-33.

Kilmann, R. H., Mitroff, I. I., and Lyles, M. A. "Designing an Effective Problem Solving Organization with the MAPS Design Technology." *Journal of Management,* 1976, *2* (2), 1-10.

Kilmann, R. H., Pondy, L. R., and Slevin, D. P. (Eds.). *The Management of Organization Design.* Vol. 1: *Strategies and Implementation.* New York: Elsevier North-Holland, 1976a.

Kilmann, R. H., Pondy, L. R., and Slevin, D. P. (Eds.). *The Management of Organization Design.* Vol. 2: *Research and Methodology.* New York: Elsevier North-Holland, 1976b.

Kilmann, R. H., and Sanzgiri, J. M. "Confronting the Problem of Sexism in Organizations: Structural-Humanistic Versus Legal-Coercive Efforts at Change." *Proceedings of the Academy of Management,* Aug. 1976, pp. 296-300.

Kilmann, R. H., and Saxton, M. J. *The Kilmann-Saxton Culture-Gap Survey.* Pittsburgh, Pa.: Organizational Design Consultants, 1983.

Kilmann, R. H., and Seltzer, J. "An Experimental Test of Organization Design Theory and the MAPS Design Technology: Homogeneous Versus Heterogeneous Composition of Organizational Subsystems." *Proceedings of the Eastern Academy of Management,* May 1976, pp. 93-97.

Kilmann, R. H., and Seltzer, J. "Laboratory Simulations with the MAPS Design Technology: The Effect of Subsystem Composition on Organizational Effectiveness." *Proceedings of the Southern Management Association,* Nov. 1978, pp. 139-141.

Kilmann, R. H., Slevin, D. P., and Thomas, K. W. "The Problem of Producing Useful Knowledge." In R. H. Kilmann and others (Eds.), *Producing Useful Knowledge for Organizations.* New York: Praeger, 1983.

Kilmann, R. H., and Taylor, V. "A Contingency Approach to Laboratory Learning: Psychological Types Versus Experiential Norms." *Human Relations,* 1974, *27* (9), 891-909.

Kilmann, R. H., and Thomas, K. W. "Four Perspectives on Conflict Management: An Attributional Framework for Organizing Descriptive and Normative Theory." *Academy of Management Review,* 1978, *3* (1), 59-68.

Kilmann, R. H., and others (Eds.). *Producing Useful Knowledge for Organizations.* New York: Praeger, 1983.

Kilmann, R. H., and Associates. *Gaining Control of the Corporate Culture.* San Francisco: Jossey-Bass, 1985.

King, W. R., Kilmann, R. H., and Sochats, K. "Designing Scientific Journals: Issues and Survey Results." *Management Science,* 1978, *24* (1), 774-784.

Lamb, R. "Is the Attack on Strategy Valid?" *The Journal of Business Strategy,* 1983, *3* (4), 68-69.

Langley, M. "AT&T Marketing Men Find Their Star Fails to Ascend as Expected." *The Wall Street Journal,* February 13, 1984, p. 1.

Lave, C. A., and March, J. G. *An Introduction To Models in the Social Sciences.* New York: Harper & Row, 1975.

Lawler, E. E., III. *Pay and Organizational Effectiveness: A Psychological View.* New York: McGraw-Hill, 1971.

Lawler, E. E., III. *Pay and Organization Development.* Reading, Mass.: Addison-Wesley, 1981.

Lawrence, P. R., and Lorsch, J. W. *Organization and Environment.* Boston: Division of Research, Graduate School of Business Administration, Harvard University, 1967.

Lee, C. "Raiders of the Corporate Culture." *Training,* Feb. 1984, pp. 26-32.

Levinson, H. *Organizational Diagnosis.* Cambridge, Mass.: Harvard University Press, 1972.

Lewicki, R. "Organizational Seduction: Building Commitment to Organizations." *Organizational Dynamics,* Autumn 1981, pp. 5-21.

Lewin, K. *Field Theory in Social Science.* New York: Harper & Row, 1951.

Littlejohn, R. F. "Team Management: A How-to Approach to Improved Productivity, Higher Morale, and Longer-Lasting Job Satisfaction." *Management Review,* Jan. 1982, pp. 23-28.

Lombardo, M. M., and McCall, M. M., Jr. "The Intolerable Boss." *Psychology Today,* Jan. 1984, pp. 44-48.

McKelvey, B., and Kilmann, R. H. "Organization Design: A Participative Multivariate Approach." *Administrative Science Quarterly,* 1975, *20* (1), 24-36.

Mackenzie, K. D. *Organizational Structures.* Arlington Heights, Ill.: AHM Publishing, 1978.

Main, J. "The Executive Yearn to Learn." *Fortune,* May 3, 1982, pp. 234-245.

Main, J. "The Trouble with Managing Japanese-Style." *Fortune,* April 2, 1984, pp. 50-56.

Marchione, A. R., and English, J. "Managing the Unpredictable —A Rational Plan for Coping with Change." *Management Review,* Feb. 1982, pp. 52-57.

Mason, R. O., and Mitroff, I. I. *Challenging Strategic Planning Assumptions: Theory, Cases, and Techniques.* New York: Wiley, 1981.

Mathis, R. L., and Jackson, J. H. *Personnel: Contemporary Perspectives and Applications.* (2nd ed.) St. Paul, Minn.: West, 1979.

Mayer, R. J. "Don't Be Hoodwinked by the Panacean Conspiracy." *Management Review,* June 1983, pp. 23-25.

Mendel, W. M. "Responsibility in Health, Illness, and Treatment." *Archives of General Psychiatry,* 1968, *10* (18), 697-705.

"Merrill Lynch's Big Dilemma." *Business Week.* January 16, 1984, pp. 60-67.

Meyer, H. H., Kay, E., and French, J. R. P., Jr. "Split Roles in Performance Appraisal." *Harvard Business Review,* Jan.-Feb. 1965, pp. 123-129.

Miller, E. "The Parallel Organization Structure at General Motors . . . An Interview with Howard C. Carlson." *Personnel,* Sept.-Oct. 1978, *55* (5), 64-69.

Mitroff, I. I. *Stakeholders of the Organizational Mind: Toward a New View of Organizational Policy Making.* San Francisco: Jossey-Bass, 1983.

Mitroff, I. I., Barabba, V. P., and Kilmann, R. H. "The Application of Behavioral and Philosophical Technologies to Strategic Planning: A Case Study with a Large Federal Agency." *Management Science,* 1977, *24* (1), 44-58.

Mitroff, I. I., Emshoff, J. R., and Kilmann, R. H. "Assumptional Analysis: A Methodology for Strategic Problem Solving." *Management Science,* 1979, *25* (6), 583-593.

Mitroff, I. I., and Kilmann, R. H. "On Evaluating Scientific Research: The Contributions of the Psychology of Science." *Technological Forecasting and Social Change,* 1975a, *8* (4), 163-174.

Mitroff, I. I., and Kilmann, R. H. "Stories Managers Tell: A New Tool for Organizational Problem Solving." *Management Review,* 1975b, *64* (7), 18-28.

Mitroff, I. I., and Kilmann, R. H. "Systemic Knowledge: An Integrated Program of Research on Science." *Theory and Society,* 1977a, *4* (1), 103-129.

Mitroff, I. I., and Kilmann, R. H. "Teaching Managers to Do Policy Analysis: The Case of Corporate Bribery." *California Management Review,* 1977b, *20* (1), 47-54.

Mitroff, I. I., and Kilmann, R. H. "On Integrating Behavioral and Philosophical Systems: Toward a Unified Theory of Problem Solving." In R. A. Jones (Ed.), *Research in Sociology of Knowledge, Sciences, and Art.* Vol. 1. Greenwich, Conn.: JAI, 1978a.

Mitroff, I. I., and Kilmann, R. H. *Methodological Approaches to Social Science: Integrating Divergent Concepts and Theories.* San Francisco: Jossey-Bass, 1978b.

Mitroff, I. I., and Kilmann, R. H. "The Four-Fold Way of

Knowing: The Varieties of Social Science Experience." *Theory and Society*, 1981, *10* (2), 227-248.

Mitroff, I. I., and Kilmann, R. H. "Intellectual Resistance to Useful Knowledge: An Archetypal Social Analysis." In R. H. Kilmann and others (Eds.), *Producing Useful Knowledge for Organizations*. New York: Praeger, 1983.

Mitroff, I. I., and Kilmann, R. H. *Corporate Tragedies: Product Tampering, Sabotage, and Other Catastrophes*. New York: Praeger, 1984a.

Mitroff, I. I., and Kilmann, R. H. "Corporate Tragedies: Teaching Companies to Cope with Evil." *New Management*, 1984b, *1* (4), 48-53.

Mitroff, I. I., Kilmann, R. H., and Barabba, V. P. "Avoiding the Design of Management Misinformation Systems: A Strategic Approach." In G. Zaltman (Ed.), *Management Principles for Nonprofit Agencies and Organizations*. New York: American Management Associations, 1979.

Moch, M., and Seashore, S. E. "How Norms Affect Behaviors in and of Corporations." In C. P. Nystrom and W. H. Starbuck (Eds.), *Handbook of Organizational Design*. London: Oxford University Press, 1981.

Naisbitt, J. *Megatrends: Ten New Directions Transforming Our Lives*. New York: Warner Books, 1984.

"A New Strategy for No. 2 in Computers." *Business Week*, May 2, 1983, pp. 66-71.

Nystrom, P. C., and Starbuck, W. M. "To Avoid Organizational Crises, Unlearn." *Organizational Dynamics*, Spring 1984, pp. 53-65.

O'Toole, J. *Making America Work: Productivity and Responsibility*. New York: Continuum, 1981.

O'Toole, J. "Declining Innovation: The Failure of Success, A Summary Report of the Seventh Twenty-Year Forecast Project." Los Angeles: Center for Futures Research, Graduate School of Business, University of Southern California, Los Angeles, 1983.

Ouchi, W. *Theory Z: How American Business Can Meet the Japanese Challenge*. Reading, Mass.: Addison-Wesley, 1981.

Pascale, R., and Athos, A. *The Art of Japanese Management.* New York: Simon & Schuster, 1981.

Paulson, R. D. "The Chief Executive as Change Agent." *Management Review,* Feb. 1982, pp. 25-28, 41-42.

Peace, W. H. "Successful Change of Organizational Culture: A General Manager's Perspective." Paper presented at conference on "Managing Organizational Change Through People." University of Pittsburgh, Nov. 1983.

Peter, L. J., and Hull, R. *The Peter Principle.* New York: Morrow, 1969.

Peters, T. J., and Waterman, R. H., Jr. *In Search of Excellence: Lessons from America's Best-Run Companies.* New York: Harper & Row, 1982.

Pollack, A. "$4.9 Billion Loss Posted at AT&T." *The New York Times,* Jan. 27, 1984, p. 25.

Popper, K. R. *The Logic of Scientific Discovery.* London: Hutchinson, 1959.

Porter, L. W., and Lawler, E. E., III. *Managerial Attitudes and Performance.* Homewood, Ill.: Irwin-Dorsey, 1968.

Porter, L. W., Lawler, E. E., III, and Hackman, J. R. *Behavior in Organizations.* New York: McGraw-Hill, 1975.

Renner, W. B. "The New Corporate Culture." *Alcoa's Public Relations and Advertising Department,* 1981, pp. 1-4.

"The Revival of Productivity." *Business Week,* February 13, 1984, pp. 92-100.

Rose, F. "The Mass Production of Engineers." *Esquire,* May 1983, pp. 76-84.

Rosen, E., Fox, R. E., and Gregory, I. *Abnormal Psychology.* (2nd ed.) Philadelphia: Saunders, 1972.

Roush, J. A. "Loyalty in the Inner Circle." *Business Horizons,* Sept.-Oct. 1983, pp. 55-56.

Salmans, S. "New Vogue: Company Culture." *The New York Times,* January 7, 1983, pp. D1, D27.

Sanderson, M. "Managing the Right Project." *Advanced Management Journal,* Winter 1982, pp. 59-62.

Sashkin, M. "Participative Management Is an Ethical Imperative." *Organizational Dynamics,* Spring 1984, pp. 5-22.

Schein, E. H. *Process Consultation: Its Role in Organization Development.* Reading, Mass.: Addison-Wesley, 1969.

Schwartz, H., and Davis, S. M. "Matching Corporate Culture and Business Strategy." *Organizational Dynamics,* Summer 1981, pp. 30-48.

Seashore, S. E. *Group Cohesiveness in the Industrial Work Group.* Ann Arbor, Mich.: Institute for Social Research, 1954.

Serpa, R. "Why Many Organizations—Despite Good Intentions—Often Fail to Give Employees Fair and Useful Performance Reviews." *Management Review,* 1984, *73* (7), 41–45.

Shetty, Y. K. "Management's Role in Declining Productivity." *California Management Review,* 1982, *25* (1), 33–47.

Sieber, J. E., and others. "Warranted Uncertainty and Students' Knowledge and Use of Drugs." *Contemporary Educational Psychology,* 1978, *3,* 28-39.

Sieber, J. E., and others. "A New Era for Management." *Business Week,* April 25, 1983, pp. 50-84.

Slater, P. *Earthwalk.* New York: Anchor/Doubleday, 1974.

Stagnaro, F. "The Benefits of Leveling with Employees: ROLM's Experience." *Management Review,* July 1982, pp. 16-20.

"Texas Instruments Cleans up Its Act." *Business Week,* September 19, 1983, pp. 56-64.

Thompson, J. D. *Organizations in Action.* New York: McGraw-Hill, 1967.

Tichy, N. M. *Managing Strategic Change: Technical, Political, and Cultural Dynamics.* New York: Wiley, 1983.

Toffler, A. *Future Shock.* New York: Bantam, 1970.

Toffler, A. *The Third Wave.* New York: Morrow, 1980.

Tomasko, R. M. "Managing Compensation Strategically: Focusing Company Reward Systems to Help Achieve Business Objectives." *Management Review,* October 1982, pp. 8–12.

Tunstall, W. B. "Cultural Transition at AT&T." *Sloan Management Review,* Fall 1983, pp. 15-26.

Uttal, B. "Texas Instruments Regroups." *Fortune,* August 9, 1982, pp. 40-45.

Vancil, R. F., and Green, C. H. "How CEOs Use Top Management Committees." *Harvard Business Review,* Jan.-Feb. 1984, pp. 65-73.

Wallach, E. J. "Individuals and Organizations: The Cultural Match." *Training and Development Journal,* February 1983, pp. 29-36.

Walton, R. E. *Interpersonal Peacemaking: Confrontations and Third Party Consultation.* Reading, Mass.: Addison-Wesley, 1969.

Weinshall, T. D. "Help for Chief Executives: The Outside Consultant." *California Management Review,* 1982, *24* (4), 47–58.

Yankelovich, D. *New Rules: Searching for Self-Fulfillment in a World Turned Upside Down.* New York: Random House, 1981.

Zand, D. E. *Information, Organization, and Power.* New York: McGraw-Hill, 1981.

Index

291

Breinigsville, PA USA
10 May 2010
237703BV00001B/15/A